A Salute to Patriotism

Books by
Jean Peckham Kavale

A Salute to Patriotism:
The Life and Work of Major General
Howard L. Peckham

Faith and Philosophy:
A Study of Their Interrelationship

From the Potomac to the Seine:
The Personal Story of an Army Family

A Salute to Patriotism

The Life and Work of
Major General Howard L. Peckham

★ ★

JEAN PECKHAM KAVALE

ISBN: 978-0-9665855-5-1

Printed in the United States of America
Second Printing with Re-sized Photographs

SECOND EDITION

Published by:
Cypress Publishing
Manteca, CA 95336
cypresstree123@hotmail.com

10 9 8 7 6 5 4 3 2

Contents

Contents

Preface

Duty, honor, country: Those three hallowed words reverently dictate what you ought to be, what you can be, what you will be.

—DOUGLAS MACARTHUR

WHEN MY FATHER, Howard Louis Peckham, was a boy, he often imagined himself dressed in a gray cadet uniform, marching in cadence on a vast parade ground. Because he was an excellent student, especially in arithmetic, Howard could easily picture himself attending mathematics classes taught by a knowledgeable instructor.

Howard Peckham was born on May 29, 1897, in Norwich, a lovely harbor city located in the southeastern part of Connecticut, adjacent to the confluence of the Yantic, Thames, and Shetucket Rivers. It was an ideal fishing area, a fact that Howard and his younger brother, Oliver, took advantage of as much as possible. After an afternoon of successful fishing, they would eagerly bring their catch home, where their mother, the former Frances Lila Beckwith, would clean it and prepare it for dinner. Frances was an outstanding cook, so she used just the right amount of parsley, salt, pepper, and other spices to sprinkle on top of the fish before popping it into the oven.

Howard also seemed to enjoy doing chores for his dad, Frank Everett Peckham, who ran a flourishing truck farming business. Dad would fill to the brim large straw baskets of tomatoes, corn, lettuce, celery, and other vegetables—as well as flowers such as colorful zinnias and marigolds—that he had helped to plant and pick. Frank would then sell this delectable and fragrant produce to local markets.

Dad wasn't interested in truck farming as a profession for himself, however. He also didn't want to spend all his life in one location. Instead, he felt attracted to the more adventurous and less-settled life of a U.S. Army man. After graduating from the Norwich Free Academy, he received an appointment to the United States Military Academy at West Point, thus fulfilling his dream of an army career. That career would take him all over the world, but his binding loyalty and love for the ideals of his alma mater, from which he received a bachelor's degree in November 1918, continued. (It was at West Point, decades later, that General Douglas MacArthur spoke the famous words that appear at the beginning of this Preface.)

Upon his retirement from the U.S. Army forty years later, he eagerly volunteered for alumni tasks. He served as president of his class for three years and was also a member of the prestigious West Point Board of Trustees. Whenever he spoke at Board meetings, Howard Peckham's appearance commanded attention. His height was five feet ten inches, but he gave the impression of being much taller, largely because of the military bearing he had acquired at the Academy. Dad's straight posture, sturdy frame, broad shoulders, penetratingly blue eyes, and sharp features made him look like a prototype for a professional soldier.

My father never tired of driving through the winding, bucolic hills that surround West Point to attend a school reunion or an informal gathering of alumni at a football game, even when he chose to travel to the state of New York from as far away as Washington, DC.

I wasn't able to join him on those particular trips, but I do recall the many other times when I was his passenger. "I enjoy driving a car," he would say, although it didn't always appear that way to other people. I can still see the way he would grasp the steering wheel tightly with both hands, his back straight and unbent as he stared intensely and carefully at the road ahead. He certainly didn't look casual while driving a car.

Because my father dutifully answered his country's call, my parents moved often during his military career. This pattern continued after he retired in 1956, I suppose because moving from place to place had become such a familiar way of life for them.

Finally they settled down in Washington, DC, the historic city on the Potomac that my mother, the former Marion MacFarlane Shaw, considered to be her real home. Both of my parents loved people and had many friends everywhere they lived, usually army families whom they had met somewhere else. Socializing with old and dear friends was especially evident in Washington, DC, their last home. They had many good times there. Sadly, the good times ended in 1963 when my mother, who had been in failing health for several months, died of a cerebral hemorrhage. Nine years later, after four months of grueling treatment at Washington's famed Walter Reed Army Hospital, my father succumbed to the effects of leukemia and joined my mother at Arlington National Cemetery.

I will never forget the summer day a few years after my mother's death when my father and I visited her gravesite. While we were walking down one of the many pathways, he pointed out the names of a few of his friends, whose names were neatly carved in the granite stones.

These men were members of his generation and, like him, had served in the army during World War II. A few were his West Point classmates, joined by wives who either predeceased them or died after they did. The men had always seen my father as a leader. When they were cadets, he was selected as first captain of his class, the highest rank in the cadet chain of command. This title gave him the privilege of speaking to the administration on their behalf and directing their training.

There was a matter-of-fact tone in my father's voice as he spoke their names—nothing forlorn. He was well aware of his own mortality and knew that one day, maybe not too far in the future, he would be laid to rest on those same hallowed grounds. Although Dad was a realist in regard to his inevitable demise, he was also optimistic. Ever since his boyhood years, he maintained a strong religious faith and the belief in an afterlife. He was entirelyconvinced that he would one day see his deceased family members and good friends again.

In the chapters that follow, Howard Peckham's life and work are described, with an emphasis on his Quartermaster Corps service during and after World War II. I have always felt that the difficult and often heart-wrenching efforts of the United States Army's Quartermaster Corps haven't been publicized enough.

The book also briefly describes the careers of several other members of his band of compatriots, those senior officers who were his friends and who performed admirable service to their country. A few of those men are not well known to the general public. With this book, readers will get to know them. At the same time, they will learn new facts about the better-known members of that group, such as George S. Patton Jr. and Omar N. Bradley. My father and his army compatriots would see each other at several different places over the years and during changing circumstances. They would meet during catastrophic wartimes that shook America like ponderous earthquakes—World War II, Korea, and Vietnam.

During those dark days, my father and his army friends resembled ships that pass each other in the bleak nighttime of world conflict. All of those wars affected them in one way or another, especially those men who came through World War II unscathed but who lost their sons in the fighting in Korea or Vietnam. When the storm clouds of war finally drifted away, and tranquility again temporarily hovered over our land, the men resembled travelers who greet each other during the bright daylight of peace. Those are the days they especially treasured.

Dedication: Ever since the end of the Vietnam War, which is the last major conflict discussed in *A Salute to Patriotism,* the drumbeat of United States Army history has continued to move steadily forward, and other soldiers have answered the call to duty and country in faraway, dangerous lands. As I complete my writing of this book, American young people are stationed in Iraq and Afghanistan, helping to keep us free. *A Salute to Patriotism* is dedicated to them.

ONE OF THE OLD BUILDINGS ON THE CAMPUS OF NORWICH FREE ACADEMY

NORWICH HARBOR: CIRCA 1909

WEST POINT CLASS OF 1918 AT TROPHY POINT

Chapter 1

The Peckhams and the Cornings

Liberty, when it begins to take root, is a plant of rapid growth.

—GEORGE WASHINGTON

FRANK EVERETT PECKHAM owned some of the largest flower and vegetable gardens in Norwich, a lovely city located on a harbor in southeastern Connecticut. His children—my dad Howard, born in 1897; Oliver, born in 1899; Mildred, born in 1905; and Mary, born in 1910, often worked in the greenhouses on their property. Aunt Mary wrote me about their tasks years later:

> We had four greenhouses on our land. One was used for storage of needed supplies. Another was used for growing lettuce (curly, Boston). In another one, wire was strung up for cucumber vines to grow on. The third had dirt-filled flats, into which we children dug small holes. One of our jobs was to set out tiny plants in the holes.

The children also helped to sell produce at a roadside stand near the entrance to the property, where a large brightly painted sign described the unique quality of their wares:

"VEGETABLES WITH CHARACTER"

Frank drove most of the produce by truck to local markets. On the preceding evenings, the whole family would assemble at their various workstations to tie the carrots and beets together in bunches. Afterwards they would hose down all the vegetables, including the lettuce and cucumbers, and stack them carefully in Granddad's truck. As a result of these diligent preparations, the vegetables were set to go to market before the truck left early the next morning.

Whenever Frank's business was especially good, the family celebrated by going on short trips in and around New England. In the summertime, their favorite destination was Ocean Beach in New London, Connecticut, on Long Island Sound. "We packed our bathing suits and caps in a bag, and lunch was put up in a shoebox," Aunt Mary wrote in her letter to me about their preparations for the trip. "Then we rode from Norwich to New London on the open trolley car. What a refreshing ride it was on a hot summer day!" After their happy day by the sea, they boarded the open trolley again for the long ride home.

Another trip they made was particularly exciting for my dad, who was a good arithmetic student at his historic school, Norwich Free Academy. Aunt Mary described the trip in a letter to me:

> When your dad was a little boy, my parents took him and his brother on a cruise up the Hudson River. When they passed by the United States Military Academy at West Point, your dad said, "Papa, that's where I want to go to school some day."

As much as he enjoyed visiting other states, such as New York and New Hampshire, my father's roots in Connecticut were as deep as the Atlantic Ocean. His paternal grandmother, the former Ann Matilda Corning, was born in Preston, Connecticut. Preston was also the birthplace of my father's dad, Frank Everett Peckham.

According to family records, our Cornings have traced their roots to Saundby Parish, Nottinghamshire, England, to the late fifteenth century. The first Corning to settle in America was Ensign Samuel (sometimes spelled Samuell) Corning, who was born in 1616 in Norfolk, England. After arriving in Massachusetts, he first lived in Salem but didn't stay there long. He and his wife Elizabeth chose to settle down in the smaller town of Beverly, approximately four miles north of Salem, because of its better opportunities.

It turned out to be an auspicious move. In 1641, Samuel became a freeman, a title that conferred franchise and provided him with other privileges in the community. He also established himself as a trusted citizen of Beverly by serving as a selectman, a responsible job given to a town officer who, because of his capabilities, had been chosen to manage certain public affairs.

Samuel was a Puritan in his religious beliefs. This was not a problem in Massachusetts, as it had been in England. There, as he learned through his own experience, the domineering Church of England harassed Puritans because of their belief that people should use the Bible as a guide in social, financial, and even— much to the horror of British authorities—political issues.

Puritans believed that when the Bible reigns as supreme authority in the foregoing matters, religion stays simple, pure, and unscathed. Undoubtedly his tenacious hold on Puritan beliefs was the precipitating factor that brought Samuel to the New World, where he was sure to find religious freedom. And find freedom he did. Historical records indicate that he was one of the founders of First Church in Beverly, where he and his family enjoyed worshiping freely and in peace. As evidence that he was a hard worker, another trait of the Puritans, he himself built the church's meeting house. Because he wanted to keep his mind on God, Samuel had no use for ornate rituals or vestments, thus ensuring that the meeting house's interior was kept spartan.

He carried his religious beliefs into his home by living a simple lifestyle, although it is known that Samuel had some real estate holdings within the community. It is also known that he was fairly well off financially in his later years (which he interpreted as a blessing from God).

Samuel's great-grandson Nehemiah, born in 1717, was the first of my family's Cornings to settle in Connecticut. He was married twice, first to Mary Pride and then to Freelove Bliss, the mother of Uriah Corning. It's unknown whether Uriah, born in 1758, followed a traditional Puritan lifestyle of hard work, but it is certain that he heeded the call to arms after Congress voted to accept the Declaration of Independence in 1776.

Uriah's ancestors had found religious freedom but he, like other Colonists, yearned for political and economic freedom. He sensed that the appropriate time for breaking the heavy chains of domination by the British Empire—and the time for liberty—was looming on the horizon like a huge bonfire. And when the time came to fight the Redcoats, Uriah eagerly participated.

Benjamin Corning, Uriah's uncle, faced unexpected tragedy too soon for him to live in a free America or even to participate in the war for very long. According to records of the Daughters of the American Revolution (DAR), after he joined the Continental Army the British captured him and placed him with thousands of other captured Continental soldiers on one of the British prison ships.

His ship, the infamous *HMS Jersey*, was moored in New York Harbor, and its crowded, unsanitary conditions were notoriously horrible. Because they had little food and no medical provisions, many of these unfortunate prisoners of war died on the ship. That's what happened to Private Benjamin Corning, who died in 1783, the year in which the British surrendered at Yorktown. The *Jersey* was abandoned not long thereafter.

Uriah had much better luck than Benjamin in fighting the Redcoats and surviving the war. He served the Colonies in several capacities, according to data that I obtained from the Veterans Administration (Certificate 3543 issued December 26, 1832). His first assignment was as a private in Colonel Samuel Sheldon's regiment, in which he served in the Battle of Long Island—the first major conflict of the Revolution—and the Battle of York Island (which is also called the Battle of the Orchard).

Following these conflicts, Uriah became a mariner for five months on board the *Confederacy*, a Continental frigate whose main job was to protect convoys. It was under the command of Captain Seth Harding. The primary task of personnel on board was to discreetly raid British merchant ships. It was dangerous work, but Uriah came through unscathed.

After he completed a couple of other assignments, which included his being present at the burning of New London and the massacre at Fort Griswold by the British, Uriah received an honorable discharge (signed by George Washington himself). He then returned to Preston, where he and his wife, the former Elizabeth Willett, raised their family. Along with other former Colonists, they cheered heartily in 1789 when George Washington was sworn in as America's first President.

In 1868 a significant event occurred for the Cornings. That's when a descendant of the first Corning in America, whom I described earlier, became entwined in the Peckham family tree. It was in that year that Ann Matilda Corning, granddaughter of Uriah and Elizabeth, married James Riley Peckham of Norwich, Connecticut. As a result, two clans with deep roots in New England were forever united. Ann Matilda was the mother of my grandfather, Frank E. Peckham, and thus Dad's grandmother (and my great-grandmother).

Like the Cornings, Granddad's ancestors from the Peckham side of his family also served in the War of Independence. DAR records show that John Peckham of Rhode Island served with Colonel Archibald Crary's regiment in 1776, but he was not permitted to see action in battle because of his advanced age. His wife was the former Deborah Sweet.

Their son, William Sweet Peckham, who was married to the former Hannah Clark, took part in a daring raid. "Barton's Raid," as it was called, became an esteemed episode in the history of the state of Rhode Island. DAR records note William's participation in that 1777 event:

> William Sweet Peckham served six years during the American Revolution and was one of the members of the raid [which was composed of approximately 40 men] which crossed Narragansett Bay with [Lieutenant Colonel William] Barton and captured [British General Richard] Prescott.

Documents on file with the Rhode Island Historical Society describe the raid in more detail:

> On a moonless night in July, the forty or so Continentals boarded five whale boats and silently rowed from Warwick Neck to Aquidneck Island, their destination. After coming ashore, they quietly crept inward to the home in which General Prescott was known to be staying. Upon reaching the house, they overpowered the general's sentries, then broke down the door into the general's bedroom and took the astonished man captive. When the politicians who made up the Continental Congress heard about this feat, they were duly impressed. They expressed appreciation to Barton and his men and then presented the colonel with an elaborate engraved sword.

Granddad Peckham was immensely proud of the valiant Revolutionary War soldiers on both sides of his family. He expressed his own patriotism by enlisting in the Connecticut National Guard, with which he served during World War I. He never failed to display the American flag in front of his home on patriotic holidays.

In addition to their patriotism, the Peckhams had firm religious convictions. Granddad believed that thirteenth century Archbishop of Canterbury, John Peckham, was an ancestor of ours, but he couldn't obtain the documents to prove it. The Archbishop appears to have had a keen insight into the origins of his surname, however. According to Stephen Farnum Peckham, author of *Quotes from the Peckham Family Genealogy*, these words appear in Archbishop Peckham's own writings:

> In a dim and unremembered past—and from which no record remains—an Anglo-Saxon reared his dwelling on the crest of a hill on the North Downs, in southwest Kent, and called it 'Peac House,' for which the English equivalent is 'Peak House,' or 'House on the Peak.'

The Archbishop lived in the thirteenth century, long before the Reformation and the subsequent founding of the Church of England, and was a devout Roman Catholic. He was a member of the Franciscans, a Catholic order known for its humility and simplicity. Nevertheless, and probably a bit ironically, after his death he was buried in a prominent and ornate crypt at the large and often-visited Canterbury Cathedral, near London. His burial was far from simple.

In addition to knowing the origin of his surname, the Archbishop undoubtedly had considerable knowledge of the noted Peckhams who preceded him. Some of those people are interestingly described in Farnum Peckham's *Quotes from the Peckham Family Genealogy*:

> Under the Roman kings, Robert de Peckham [the de came as a result of the Norman Conquest] was Chaplain to Henry 1. Hugo de Peckham was constable of Turnbridge Castle. His sons, Peter and John de Peckham, went on the 3rd Crusade, and came home with Richard Coeur de Leon [Lion Hearted] from the Siege of Acre, in 1191. It was there that the two brothers won their Coat of Arms by their valor and bravery. The families of the two brothers have bourne Arms since that date. Peter de Peckham is regarded to have been the ancestor of the Denham Peckhams, while John de Peckham is considered the ancestor of the Yaldham Peckham branch [my family's branch].

The first of our Yaldham Peckham ancestors to set foot on American soil—another John Peckham—was born in the Parish of Boxgrove in England. In 1634 he was appointed Chaplain to the Earl of Hertford, a prestigious assignment.

Nevertheless, instead of feeling more love for the English Church, he became increasingly disenchanted with it. The Church had grown much too powerful and domineering, he believed. He therefore renounced Anglicanism and sailed for America in 1634, the same year he had been appointed Chaplain. He was now a Baptist.

Like so many other English seekers of religious liberty, John lived first in Massachusetts, where there existed an ironic twist in the fate of the Puritans, who had fled earlier from England. In their homeland the Puritans had been persecuted by the English Church, but in Massachusetts they gained a firm upper hand and were persecuting the Baptists. Because of this attitude of the Puritans, John Peckham hadn't yet found the religious freedom he had sought by making the long journey to the New World.

John's luck changed sometime in 1636. That's when he became the friend of a kind and respected Baptist minister, Reverend John Clarke, who had sailed from England's shore to Massachusetts with his sister Mary. Upon getting to know them, John Peckham became a compatriot of Reverend Clarke's in the cause of religious liberty—and he fell in love with Mary, the Reverend's charming sister.

John Peckham and Mary Clarke were married in 1638, the same year that Roger Williams, who was the founder of the first Baptist church in Rhode Island and a close friend of Reverend Clarke's, invited the newlyweds to settle in Rhode Island. The move turned out well for them. In 1644, John became one of the founders of First Baptist Church of Newport. Four years later, he was privileged to become one of only ten male members in full communion with that church. God had finally blessed John with his true religious calling.

He and Mary were blessed with five children, but her health worsened as time went on, and she subsequently died ten years after their marriage. According to family records, John Peckham, who lived until the age of eighty-five, had two more marriages and many more offspring. It's little wonder that the surname "Peckham" is so common in Rhode Island.

Ann Matilda Corning, my grandfather's mother, exemplified the good traits of both sides of her family. She devoutly practiced the Baptist faith of the Peckham clan into which she had married, but she also abided by the Puritan work ethics of her Corning ancestors. Family records proclaim that when she was a teenager, she worked as a typesetter in Hartford for the *Evening Press*. This was during the struggle between the North and South when labor was scarce. In 1865, the year of President Lincoln's assassination, she worked all night long to set up type for a story of the assassination.

Ann Matilda carried this talent for industriousness with her throughout her life. For example, she often arose before dawn to pull weeds from her flower garden and perform other household tasks. "Land sakes, folks would think I was lazy if I stayed abed," she often declared.

Like his mother Ann Matilda, Granddad was a Baptist. His wife, the former Frances Lila Beckwith, was a member of that faith as well. Granddad's serious romance with Frances, however, was not his first, as was common knowledge among his kin. His first love was a beautiful girl from the Island of Majorca who, my father once told me, "temporarily stole his heart away." He had met her during one of his travels to faraway places. When their long-distance romance faded and eventually ended, he turned his attentions to Frances Lila, a local girl who had probably been waiting patiently for him a long time. A strong-faced woman with bright, determined eyes, she was the prototype of a stalwart Connecticut Yankee. She and Granddad were married in 1894, and their marriage was happy, by all accounts.

Frances Lila was noted for her thorough housekeeping and excellent cooking, so no doubt they lived in a tidy house and ate very well. In fact, my Aunt Mary, when she was a resident of Newport, Rhode Island, wrote an article in 1989 for *The Newport Daily News* in which she extolled her mother's delectable Fourth of July dinners:

> Mother put fresh salmon into a cheesecloth bag for steaming. In the meantime, she made a cream sauce, with hard-boiled cut-up eggs in it. Small new potatoes were peeled for boiling. Peas were cooked with salt pork, which gave them that extra good Yankee flavor. When the potatoes were done, melted butter was poured over them and chopped parsley sprinkled on them. When all was ready, our family sat down to eat a delicious meal—tiny white

potatoes, goodly servings of salmon covered with the cream and egg sauce, and a soup plate filled with fresh peas, a bit of salt pork, and some of the tasty liquid from the cooking. How my mouth waters as I remember one of the traditional and delicious meals prepared by my wonderful Yankee cook—my mother.

A couple of Frances's other specialties were parsnip stew and turkey with oyster stuffing, but she got help from her husband when it came to preparing clams, and he thoroughly enjoyed the task. In regard to culinary skills Granddad was no slouch, at least as far as clambakes were concerned. He even acquired the title of "bakemaster" and put on clambakes annually for the United Commercial Travelers of eastern Connecticut, as well as for appreciative family and friends. These events often took place at Poquetanock Cove, which was near Preston and named after the Indian tribe that at one time inhabited that area of the state.

Frances was also known to be a kind, but strict, mother who made sure that her children attended church on Sundays. My father, his brother Oliver (called Ollie), and his sisters Mary and Mildred were brought up in the Central Baptist Church in Norwich, where they always wore their Sunday-best clothes. For my father, this consisted of knickers, long black socks, a clean pressed shirt, a fancy bow tie, and polished brown-leather shoes.

Often after the conclusion of church services, Frank, Frances, and their four children would stroll down to Ann Matilda's house. They didn't have far to go. As Ann often said, "My house is just down the road apiece from my son's house, and it has shade trees aplenty in the front yard." They all lived on Corning Road, which was named for their Revolutionary War ancestors.

These Sunday visits were imprinted in the memories of all the grandchildren, but they especially impressed Dad's younger sister, Aunt Mary. She reverently recalls them in a reminiscence she wrote:

> A Sunday afternoon treat was a visit to Grandma's parlor, which was permeated with the sweet scent of the potpourri she

regularly made by crushing dried rose leaves and placing them in jars. Family portraits hung on the walls, and a large family Bible was on the table. With a feeling of awe, I would walk through the room to the front entry, where I was allowed to play the gramophone. How mysteriously melodious it sounded to my childish ears when hymns such as "Rock of Ages" and "Nearer My God to Thee" came forth.

Granddad's religious faith, nurtured during his childhood, sustained him when he faced the loss of his son Ollie, who died at the age of twenty-nine after succumbing to a respiratory illness.

Howard was also devastated by this tragic loss, since he and Ollie were always quite close to each other. The two brothers had often fished together at ponds between Westerly and Norwich, such as Long Pond, Factory Hill Pond, and Lantern Hill Pond, where the perch and pickerel were usually plentiful.

Only two years after Ollie breathed his last painful breath, another tragedy struck the family: the death of Frances, who died of what was believed to be a broken heart. She was not as strong as she looked, at least not emotionally. Her first child, Jamie—the brother my father never had a chance to meet—had died in infancy, and she never completely got over that loss. And now Ollie had been taken away.

For a long time to come, the deaths of Frances and Ollie enveloped the remaining members of the family in a melancholic shroud. Nevertheless, like the forward-flowing Shetucket River, their lives eventually flowed onwards.

A few years after losing his wife, Granddad started courting a vivacious widow, Watie Ann Whiting. She and her husband had been longtime friends of Granddad and Frances, so they knew each other well. After Watie Ann and Granddad were married, and after an inevitable period of adjustment, she was welcomed into the lives of my father and his two sisters the way Connecticut welcomes spring flowers.

Dad maintained fond memories of Grandmother Whiting, as everyone referred to her, a stout, good-natured lady who always made us grandchildren feel welcome. She didn't know as many recipes as Frances (who died when I was two), such as the turkey with oyster stuffing for which Frances was famous. Grandma Whiting's specialty was freshly baked cookies. She kept two big cookie jars on the kitchen counter, and I knew she would keep refilling them as long as we children were there. Upon our arrival in Connecticut for a visit, the wonderful odor of vanilla, molasses, and ginger would surround us as soon as we stepped inside the front door, a sure sign that Grandma had been baking cookies for us children.

During those summertime visits, my grandparents' two-story, sprawling farmhouse in eastern Connecticut would be surrounded by scarlet zinnias and bright orange marigolds, among which butterflies danced like tiny ballerinas. The family had moved from Dad's childhood home soon before I was born, so it wasn't the same house in which he had grown up. This one was set on smaller acreage than his boyhood home, but Granddad continued to produce vegetables and flowers for local markets.

The Peckham clan got together traditionally on the Fourth of July. No matter where we lived in the United States, my father made it a point to get into the car and drive my mother, brother, and me to his father's house for the July Fourth holiday (which also happened to be Granddad's birthday).

My father appreciated being back in his home state, and my brother and I looked forward to playing games with our cousins: Kent and Diane Lawrence, the children of Aunt Mary and her husband Dick, a navy dentist; and Gage and Carol Durling, the son and daughter of Aunt Mildred and her husband Ed, a civilian dentist whose practice was in Belmont, Massachusetts.

All four cousins were younger than Howie and I. Although his hair darkened somewhat by the time he was a teenager, Kent's hair in his childhood was as golden as the corn in Granddad's vegetable garden. A graduate of Annapolis, he had a navy career, like his dad, except that Kent's career encompassed many months of submarine training in New London and subsequent submarine duty. Gage, a cute-faced but mentally retarded little boy, died in childhood. I have kept in touch over the years with Diane and Carol.

At dawn on July Fourth, Granddad—always an early riser—would raise the beautiful American flag in front of his house. Before noon, large folding tables would be set up under tall maple trees in the backyard, where we would eat our picnic lunch. Our plates would be loaded with green salad, baked beans, "cawn on the cob," as Granddad would say, and delicious molasses cookies that Grandma Whiting had baked. In the afternoon, we children would set off a few firecrackers. Also, we never failed to play with the farm menagerie, which one summer included a huge sow and her tiny, newborn piglets.

I had an animal encounter of another sort that was not fun at all, however; in fact, it was really frightening. Mounted on a wall in Granddad's sitting room was a stuffed moose's head, which he had acquired on a hunting trip. He was proud of it, but to me its wide antlers and protruding face were large and scary. One night I dreamed that a mooing sound came out of its mouth. When I awoke from that portentous dream and heard Granddad's cow mooing impatiently in the backyard, I was greatly relieved. Since then, I've been glad my father stayed with the sport of fishing and never took up hunting!

Whenever darkness began to creep over the farm, my brother, my cousins, and I would light our sparklers and Roman candles and then send them off into the sky, as if they were rockets headed towards Mars. Later, in the cozy sitting room on the first floor, Granddad sometimes told us fascinating stories about his youth, his blue eyes shining like stars. "I enjoyed boxing as a young man," he once told us. "In one of my bouts, I knocked out a former champion from England." We were very impressed.

As I mentioned previously, Granddad Peckham also enjoyed traveling in his younger days. He usually paid for the trips by working his way. For example, he worked on the night boat from New London to New York City. "The city pubs were a welcome sight when I got off the boat in the morning," he said. "They served beer, rye bread, pickles, and cheese, all for five cents."

Once he worked on a freighter that sailed to Caracas, Venezuela. He had enjoyed these travels because they enabled him to gain insight into what his life's work should be. He concluded that he wanted to be "out in nature with the good earth," as he described it, helping things grow and then reaping the rewards of his labor.

After reaching late middle age, he relegated most of the farm chores to hired helpers and slowed down his outdoor activities a bit, especially the physically taxing chore of moving a big plow through the cornfield. I watched him do this more than once. I saw a determined-looking man with arms as strong as steel, forcefully guiding his plow through packed brown soil. On sunny days, he often wore a big straw hat.

---

23 of 4th mo'th 1667:--

"Wee whose name are vnder written the brethren & sisters belonging to Basse Riuer doe present our desires to the rest of the Church at Salem that with their consent wee and our children may be a church of our selues. W'ch wee also present unto Mr HAILES desiring him to joine with us and to be our Pastor with the approbation of the rest of the Church:

Roger CONANT	Sarah CONANT
Thomas LOTHROPP	Bethiah LOTHROPP
William DIXSY	Anna DIXSY
Richard DODG	Mary DODGE Senr
Samuell CORNING	Elizabeth DODGE
Henry HERRICK	Elizabeth CORNING

PORTION OF THE DOCUMENT ESTABLISHING REGISTER OF FOUNDERS OF FIRST CHURCH IN BASS RIVER (LATER NAMED BEVERLY) WHEREIN SAMUELL AND ELIZABETH CORNING ARE LISTED (*PARTIAL LIST OF FOUNDERS*)

Granddad stayed reasonably well during his later years, until he reached the age of ninety-one. By that time, he was more than ready to "meet my Lord," as he often said. He died four years later after his left leg became badly infected and had to be amputated, causing him to go into shock.

Howard Peckham and his father had always enjoyed a close relationship, for which Howard would be forever grateful. Often during his army career, nostalgic thoughts about his father and former life in Connecticut would enter Dad's mind, like rays of sun lending brightness to a shade-covered landscape. This was especially true when he was a young lieutenant and served in a faraway American colony—the exotic and tropical Philippine Islands.

First, though, he needed to complete his education. After graduating from Norwich Free Academy, a school with high scholastic standards (even requiring prospective students to pass entrance examinations), he received an appointment to West Point. His boyhood daydream about having a career in the U.S. Army was about to become a reality.

THE HOUSE IN WHICH BRITISH GENERAL PRESCOTT WAS CAPTURED: R.I., 1777

HMS JERSEY, THE BRITISH PRISON SHIP ON WHICH BENJAMIN CORNING DIED: N.Y., 1783

FRANCES PECKHAM WITH SONS HOWARD *(LEFT)* AND OLIVER, 1900

HOWARD *(FRONT ROW FAR LEFT)* AND OLIVER *(SECOND ROW FAR RIGHT)* AT A
NEIGHBORHOOD GATHERING: NORWICH, CIRCA 1905

HOWARD'S STEPMOTHER WATIE WHITING PECKHAM

HOWARD'S PARENTS FRANK AND FRANCES PECKHAM IN THEIR LATER YEARS

Chapter 2

Army Engineers in the Great Depression

People grow through experience if they meet life honestly and courageously. This is how character is built.

—ELEANOR ROOSEVELT

ON BATTLEFIELDS THROUGHOUT EUROPE, the thunderous sound of artillery weaponry finally ended. Replacing it, in addition to a ghostly silence, was the awareness that the Germany of Kaiser Wilhelm II had thankfully been defeated. An armistice that was signed on the eleventh of November 1918 assured that Germany's defeat was official.

To many people in the United States and abroad, the "war to end all wars," which shook the world for four long years, had been senseless. So many young Europeans, representing several different countries, had lost their lives in battle. Thousands of American soldiers had died, too, after obeying the directives of President Woodrow Wilson and crossing the Atlantic to help save the citizens of Europe.

The West Pointers who graduated in November of 1918 celebrated the end of World War I with clapping, cheering, and joyful celebrations. Because the war was still raging while they were at West Point, two classes graduated that year—first in June and again in November.

Howard Peckham was one of those newly commissioned second lieutenants who graduated in November 1918. He had appreciated his studies (especially mathematics) and had enjoyed the drills, parades, and other aspects of cadet life. Unlike some of his city-bred classmates, arising at dawn every day had been no problem for him, since he had done that throughout his childhood on his dad's farm.

Howard corresponded as much as possible with his parents, and his letters were generally enthusiastic. While he was growing up, he had regularly attended services with them at Central Baptist Church in Norwich, so they approved highly when he wrote of his consistent church attendance at West Point on Sundays and membership in the cadet choir.

They were also pleased when he wrote that he firmly believed in the West Point code of honor: "A cadet does not lie, cheat, or steal—nor tolerate those who do." Along with the firmly entrenched religious convictions he had held since boyhood, Howard suspected that the code of honor would serve as his moral guideline for the rest of his life, as it did.

Although the war was over by the time Howard's years at West Point ended, his studies did not end. He and other high-achieving second lieutenants, who had graduated into the Corps of Engineers, reported soon after graduation to the U. S. Army Engineer School in Virginia, which had a curriculum known to be rigorous and demanding. Even though he had been awarded a bachelor's degree from West Point, he looked forward to continuing his studies. Also, he revered military engineering and knew that military engineers had played a vital role in overseeing the construction of buildings, fortifications, canals (including the Panama Canal), and other structures that had made America great. He was overjoyed about becoming part of that history.

In addition to his classes in basic construction, classes in battlefield engineering were an important part of his course of study. During the summer of 1919, he and his engineering school classmates visited Europe to inspect the battlefields in France and Germany. They focused primarily on the engineering aspects of battlefields, which involved learning to build bridges, construct airfields, transport troops across rivers, lay roads, and destroy enemy fortifications in a combat-style environment. They were aware that these and other engineering tasks could be better learned on the actual battlefields of World War I than in classrooms.

Like most of the young men in his group, Howard Peckham had never before traveled outside the United States, so he was glad for the opportunity to come face-to-face with the culture of the Old World. He recalled years later that he and the other officers were, for the most part, welcomed politely in postwar Europe. French people fondly remembered the Americans, many of whom were very young and had cheeks as fresh as apples on Brittany's trees, who had come to help them during the war.

At Bellicourt in northern France, the group saw the location of an offensive that had taken place in September 1918. Here troops from the United States had charged through Germany's Hindenburg Line, which subsequently crumbled like a wall of clay. The Germans had constructed that rather intricate defense system—composed of barbed wire, wide trenches, long tunnels, concrete bunkers, and machine gun pads—thinking it would be impenetrable. They were greatly mistaken. Even though the offensive had been highly successful, American casualties had been so heavy at Bellicourt that a cloud of sadness hung over Howard's group as they slowly walked along the dusty roads surrounding it.

After graduating from the engineering school in June 1920 and receiving his promotion to first lieutenant, Howard was ordered to report to the Missouri School of Mines, located in the small town of Rolla. The school, which emphasized the study of mining engineering and metallurgy, was later incorporated into the University of Missouri system. Here he served as an instructor in military science and tactics in the Reserved Officers' Training Corps (ROTC) department. At the completion of his two-year assignment, he enjoyed a similar position at the nearby University of Kansas.

These Midwest assignments were not only very pleasant interludes—they bolstered my father's leadership image among his superior officers. They now saw him as a very professional officer who was also an excellent instructor. These assessments would serve him well in the future.

In February 1923 Howard boarded a transport vessel and made the long journey across the Pacific Ocean to the Philippine Islands, his next station. The Philippines, made up of seven thousand islands of various sizes and shapes, had been a colony of the United States since 1900. (For three hundred years prior to that date, it had been a colony of Spain.) A strong American military presence was evident throughout this humid land of mangoes, papayas, and milky coconuts.

Several West Point graduates who became well-known generals during World War II served in the Philippine Islands earlier in their careers—including Jonathan M. Wainwright, Dwight D. Eisenhower, and Douglas MacArthur. They and other officers learned that it wasn't an easy country in which to navigate. Like the Spanish before them, Americans in the colonial days inherited an archipelago of dense jungles and deep ravines. Residents of the various islands depended on small boats, which often moved very slowly through murky water, to communicate with each other. This was especially true in the early years of American colonialism.

When Howard's ship sailed gently into Manila Bay, located off the big island of Luzon, he paced slowly along the deck to get a better look at the city as its sprawling Spanish-style buildings became more and more visible. He also observed the hilly terrain far away to his left, where his first assignment would be—the Bataan Peninsula. It looked dark and mysterious as he glanced at it through a haze-covered sky.

In the weeks to follow, he spent sweltering days in the tropical sun working with other U.S. Army engineers on a topographical survey of Bataan. The hot climate and exotic wildlife were quite different from the mild spring weather and domesticated animals of Norwich. "When I was a lieutenant in the

Philippines," he told me once, "I used to watch lizards dash across the ceiling as I lay in bed at the end of a hard day."

Sometimes while he was resting, he could hear American soldiers singing in the distance, quite often an old song that pokes fun at the challenges of weather and wildlife in the Philippines. Here are a couple of the verses:

> Oh, the monkeys have no tails in Zamboanga,
> Oh, the monkeys have no tails,
> They were bitten off by whales,
> Oh, the monkeys have no tails in Zamboanga.
>
> Oh, the caribou have no hair in Mindanao,
> Oh, the caribou have no hair,
> Holy smoke, but they are bare,
> Oh, the caribou have no hair in Mindanao.

Upon completion of the topographical survey in June 1923, my father was ordered to command Company A, 14th Engineers, at Fort William McKinley, a few miles southeast of Manila. He now lived only a short distance from the city, so he learned to know it quite well.

In those years Manila was busy and bustling, and all kinds of vehicles inched their way through crowded, narrow streets. Pith-helmeted policemen stood under the welcome shade of umbrellas as they bravely directed automobiles, horse-drawn carriages, and bicycles through heavy traffic. Women in colorful long dresses, escorted by gentlemen in white tropical suits, chatted with each other in a mixture of Spanish and English. Many buildings facing those streets sported big signs above their entry doors, indicating that a dentist, a shoe store, or some other business occupied the premises.

Dad was fascinated by the noise and commotion of the city. For relaxation, he enjoyed spending occasional evenings in the attractive Army and Navy Club, located near Manila Bay, where he could socialize with other American officers.

In December he was assigned as aide-de-camp to Major General Omar Bundy, commander of the Philippine Division and an honorable veteran of the Spanish-American War, Philippine Insurrection, and World War I. The Division, established only a year earlier, was composed mostly of Filipino enlisted men led by officers of the U.S. Army. Then and also in the future, an American general commanded the division.

Howard Peckham's appointment as General Bundy's aide ultimately had a big effect on his career and on his personal life, as described later in this chapter. For this assignment, he was transferred to the cool, pine-tree-laden area of Camp John Hay at Baguio, in the mountains of northern Luzon. The locale provided a welcome relief from the humidity of Manila. When time permitted, he played golf on the beautiful eighteen-hole course at the camp.

In July 1924 my father returned with General Bundy to Fort Hayes, Ohio, where he continued to be the general's aide. At this post, named after a man from Ohio who served as President of the United States, General Bundy commanded the V Corps Area. While acting as aide to the general, my father grew fond of the wonderful Bundy family and joined them during some delightful social occasions. Serving as commander of the V Corps was General Bundy's last assignment before retiring in 1925, and he now lies at rest in Arlington Cemetery with his wife, Addie Harden Bundy. She had always treated Dad, a young bachelor living far away from his family, with kind hospitality, which he would always appreciate.

Howard Peckham would become even closer to another family. That story began when he became acquainted with Marion Shaw, the lovely stepdaughter of then-Colonel Frederick B. Shaw and his wife Mary Bell, who lived with their five children in pleasant quarters at Fort Hayes. For my father, it was almost a case of love at first sight.

One clear, sunny day while he was playing golf on the post's course, another golfer introduced them to each other. He was immediately drawn to her large brown eyes and shiny brown tresses, as well as her demure persona. A bang that swept across the left side of her forehead added to that persona. His outgoing sisters Mildred and Mary were blue-eyed and blond, like him. He enjoyed a close relationship with them, but this girl was someone different—and very intriguing.

Marion Shaw, my mother-to-be, was first enticed by Howard Peckham's military bearing and his air of self-confidence and poise. "The expression on his face was very serious," she once told me. She said that upon first meeting him, she wondered if he had any sense of humor at all. Before too long, that perception would change. When he began courting her, she noticed there was a sparkle about him whenever he laughed at a joke. He would lean his head way back, revealing an upper jaw filled with straight white teeth.

Their dates often consisted of attending parties at the post's officers' club, where they learned about each other's love of poetry, singing, dancing, and listening to music. Howard Peckham had a fine singing voice, as did Marion Shaw. She had been educated at the Washington Seminary in Atlanta, Georgia, and the New England Conservatory of Music. In addition to being a fine singer, she was an outstanding pianist.

Marion was glad that Howard Peckham enjoyed playing golf, but she was especially impressed that he, like most aides, exhibited correct protocol and impeccable manners when dealing with superior officers and their wives. This quality particularly stood out whenever he dined with her and her family at their home or at the Officers' Club. Then-Colonel Shaw approved of Howard from the start, as did his wife Bell, even though Marion's early life was quite different from Howard's.

She was born in the rugged gold-rush town of Dawson, in the Yukon Territory. Her grandfather, Judge Joseph Davis of Helena, Montana, had traveled there in search of gold and to pursue other financial ventures. Living with him in Canada—just a temporary locale for them—were his wife, Flora, and his four children.

Joseph's elder daughter, my grandmother-to-be Mary Bell (called "Bell" by her family), soon caught the eye of a Canadian man of Scottish descent, whose name was Robert MacFarlane. The attraction was mutual. Consequently, she and Robert were married in 1900. The marriage ended up being very short and having a sad and sudden end, however. Only two years after my mother's birth in 1902, Robert died of what was believed to be an overdose of medication.

My mother was proud of the surname with which she was born and the heritage it represented. For the rest of her life, she maintained a fondness for Scotland, the land of highlands and heather. In fact a poem titled *Jean*, written by her favorite poet Robert Burns, influenced her choice of a name for me.

Bell was grief stricken for a long time, but in 1908 she met and then married Frederick Shaw, a career army officer she had met while on a visit to the Philippines. He was stationed there at the time. In addition to raising my mother, Frederick Shaw raised the four children born from his marriage to Bell.

Mother's half-sister, Barbara, was eight years younger than she. Both ended up marrying West Point graduates who pursued military careers; otherwise, they were as different from each other as summer and winter. Mother often had to watch her weight, whereas Barbara usually stayed as thin as a reed, with little effort. Sometimes their personalities clashed.

On the other hand, Mother got along well with her three half-brothers, and they thought the world of her. The oldest, Fred (Frederick B. Shaw, Jr.), was born in 1913, when my mother was already eleven years old. Bob (Robert) was born in 1916, and Dan (Daniel) in 1919. All three graduated from the University of Michigan prior to World War II and were commissioned into the U.S. Army.

Fred (nicknamed "Buzz" by the family) graduated in 1934 and rose to the rank of lieutenant colonel during World War II. After the war, he worked as a business executive and lived comfortably in the Chicago suburbs with his wife, the former Althea Doyle, and beautiful daughter, Valerie.

Bob, who graduated in 1938, was the only brother to choose an army career. Like his father, he retired as a brigadier general.

Dan, the youngest, graduated in 1940; like his brothers, he attained the rank of lieutenant colonel during World War II. Unlike them, however, his postwar story did not end happily. One day a few years after the war, a mole on his back that had never caused any trouble started to bleed and was diagnosed as cancerous. Treatments he received, including amputation of his right arm to strip the lymph nodes, were unsuccessful.

The last time my parents and I saw my Uncle Dan was at Sloan-Kettering Hospital in New York City, where he had gone for experimental care. When we were leaving, he cheerfully waved goodbye to us with his remaining hand and arm, but he passed away not long afterwards. I have never forgotten the bright smile and admirable courage he exhibited that day. He died at the age of thirty-seven, leaving behind his pregnant wife, Holly, and two small children.

Unlike her half-sister and three half-brothers, my mother didn't attend a university, which she may have later regretted. She loved to read, though, and our two large mahogany bookcases were filled with *The Harvard Classics,* the works of Shakespeare, a collection of Robert Frost poems, and other good books my parents enjoyed reading. My father agreed with Henry Ward Beecher's conclusion that "a house without books is like a room without windows."

As I have already mentioned, Mother was musically inclined from an early age onward, so her education was in the field of music. Her mother, an excellent pianist, had brought a grand piano with her when she moved into Frederick Shaw's home after their wedding, and it went with them everywhere they lived thereafter. A born taskmaster, Bell made sure that her elder daughter practiced regularly. In the spring of 1925, she helped my mother prepare for her upcoming wedding. These preparations required so much time and attention that my mother's piano playing and musical interests were temporarily put aside.

On Tuesday, June 16, 1925, my parents were married in the small chapel at Fort Hayes. The ceremony was conducted by John O. Lindquist, the post chaplain, in accordance with the rites of the

Episcopal Church as contained in the *Book of Common Prayer*. Members of the Shaw and Peckham families were guests, along with several of my parents' friends.

Together with her narrow, gold wedding band, my mother wore her engagement ring, which was a small gold replica of my father's West Point class ring. Hers had a diamond in the center, however, whereas Dad's had a shiny black onyx. Both of them wore their rings throughout the rest of their lives.

Soon after they were married, the newlyweds drove to Connecticut for a visit with the Peckham clan. For my mother, the visit was like a trip to a foreign country. She wasn't used to spending time in a rural atmosphere and hearing long, serious conversations about vegetables. The strong New England accents ("pahk the cah") seemed strange to her, also. Nevertheless, over the years she came to appreciate the Peckham family's traditions, rootedness, and love of nature.

Occasionally during their marriage, Howard Peckham's New England boyhood evidenced itself in comments he would make, such as "These apples want to be eaten" or "These dishes want to be washed." My mother and I would tease him playfully about his personification of inanimate objects. "Oh, I didn't hear them speak," we would say, or "Did they tell you that's what they want?" He took the kidding in stride and laughed at himself, as he usually did whenever a joke was on him.

In September 1925, after bidding farewell to my mother's parents and siblings, as well as her family's lumbering but affable dog Goofy, the newlyweds moved away from Fort Hayes. They had received the superb news that Dad had been selected to attend the highly reputable Infantry School at Fort Benning, Georgia.

My father had no intention of transferring to the Infantry, but he firmly believed that an officer's education should be well rounded and geared towards learning as much as possible about other army branches, not just one's own. He looked forward to attending the school, whose students were a tightly knit group known for their camaraderie and professionalism. My father liked that aspect of the school and its graduates, but he was not interested in leaving the Corps of Engineers at that time.

After his graduation in May 1926, he completed a three-month engineering assignment at Fort Humphreys. Located in Fairfax County, Virginia, the fort was hot and dusty in the summer, but my mother, a new army wife trying to be a "good trooper," put up with the temporary facilities and the camp-like, barren environment. It is now called Fort Belvoir and is blessed with green lawns, beautiful trees, and permanent buildings made of brick and mortar.

Fortunately for my mother, my father's next assignment was superbly located. Starting in September 1926 and for the next four years, he was an engineering instructor at West Point. He was glad to be back at his alma mater, and he loved to teach. "I enjoy being in front of a classroom again," he wrote to his family in nearby Connecticut. In a clear and firm voice he imparted engineering facts and procedures to young cadets.

When he wasn't teaching, he and my mother enjoyed the friendly campus atmosphere and active social life. They would meet other young couples at various recreational facilities, or the couples would dine in each other's homes. Whenever relatives came on a visit, my parents took them to local tourist spots, such as the Academy museum, where Indian relics, displays of military uniforms, and presentation swords of famous generals were on display, along with other interesting exhibits. `Friends and family members particularly enjoyed watching the cadets march on the parade ground, a wide stretch of grassy land referred to as "The Plain."

My parents' favorite pastime, though, was taking walks alone and eating picnic lunches in scenic locations. While sitting on top of a grassy hill, they would munch on Swiss cheese sandwiches and look down at the tranquil waters of the Hudson River, which flowed calmly in the distance. They could see green forests lining the river, which, from a distance, looked like nubby carpets. It was on an outing such as this that Marion gave Howard the good news that they were to become parents.

Near the end of her pregnancy, she visited her parents Bell and Frederick Shaw, who had moved to Washington, DC. Thus my brother Howie was born on September 5, 1927, at Walter Reed Army Hospital, set amidst verdant acreage near the Maryland suburbs. Later, my mother often joked that her son's birth on Labor Day was "very appropriate." She was glad his grandparents lived nearby and could drop by the hospital for visits. After she regained her strength, she brought Howie home to West Point, where she and my father resumed a tranquil life.

As my father would soon learn, events were far from tranquil in far-away Asia. In September of 1931, Japan invaded Manchuria. News of the invasion spread like wildfire throughout West Point's academic buildings, although the faculty and students were well aware that Japan had maintained a foothold in China for some years while searching for new territory.

I arrived on December 8 of that year, but by that time my parents and brother had moved from West Point to Cleveland, Ohio. Pictures taken during the Christmas season show me wearing a red silk ribbon around my unmistakably bald head. Here my father served as an assistant to the Great Lakes division engineer, a job requiring extensive surveys of the Great Lakes to ensure that flood control was adequate or to respond to other potential problems. Mother in the meantime happily took care of her two young children.

In January 1933, Franklin Delano Roosevelt was inaugurated President, another cheerful event—at least for Americans who yearned for a change from the gloomy persona of Herbert Hoover and who hoped for positive changes in the economy. January also ushered in some unexpected news from Europe, however. That's when it was learned that Adolf Hitler had become Chancellor of Germany, an appointment that would have a big impact on the future of our family and other army families.

Although newsreels showed him to be a charismatic man with excellent oratory skills, Dad and other officers suspected that Adolf Hitler was dangerous and unstable. This assessment turned out to be tragically correct, as later history would prove. It wouldn't be too long before newsreels would show Germans shouting *"Heil Hitler, Deutschland über Alles!"*

An unfortunate series of events had brought Hitler to power. In the years following World War I, defeated Germany was burdened with war reparations. The United States, meanwhile, was enjoying a period of euphoric financial speculation, although that period turned out to be short lived. An underlying weakness hovered like an obscure shadow underneath America's seemingly robust economy. Because of its too-rapid growth, the economy began heading downward.

After the stock market crashed in 1929, unemployment went up, factories closed, farmers reluctantly abandoned their farms, and thousands of people lost their homes. The Great Depression affected the entire industrialized world. Nations indebted to the United States, such as Germany, were hit the hardest. Hitler took advantage of his country's unrest and unemployment by vowing to restore prosperity and was thus able to push his way to the job of chancellor.

President Roosevelt's primary concern at that time was not the rise of Hitler but alleviating Depression-related hardships in the United States. In his inaugural address, he told nervous Americans that their biggest enemy was fear. In the following historic and unforgettable words, he reminded his audience about America's strong history and made some suggestions:

> This great nation will endure as it has endured; will survive and will prosper. So first of all, let me assert my firm belief that the only thing we have to fear is fear itself. . . .
>
> Our greatest primary task is to put people to work. This is no unsolvable problem if we face it wisely and courageously. It can be accomplished in part by direct recruiting by the government itself, treating the task as we would treat the emergency of a war, but at the same time, through this employment, accomplishing greatly needed projects to stimulate and reorganize the use of our natural resources.

To Howard Peckham, the President's suggestions were not only practical, they strongly related to the good work of members of the U.S. Army Corps of Engineers who oversaw hundreds of skilled, but potentially unemployed, workers.

In the fall of 1933, almost at midpoint of the Depression, Dad received orders to report to the palm-dotted island of Puerto Rico, our next home. After gliding through the azure waters of the Caribbean, our ship arrived at a dock in San Juan, the oldest city under the flag of the United States. In Puerto Rico my father was a military assistant in charge of harbor work, road and bridge construction, and malaria swamp reclamation. Needless to say, everyone in my family received vaccinations against tropical diseases. I bawled loudly, I was told years later, at the sight of each needle that stung my arm like a thin metal wasp.

Nevertheless, we all adjusted well to Puerto Rico. We had beautiful quarters on the army post located at the edge of the bustling city of San Juan, the country's capital. Surrounding our nice residential area was a high protective wall, but at night we clearly heard the waves crashing against rocky cliffs that dropped steeply into the surf. My parents admired the beauty of this friendly island, particularly the verdant area in which we lived.

Our forays into neighboring San Juan proper were quite an adventure, especially for Howie and me. We particularly enjoyed running around the walls that surround the city, poking our fingers through the lacy metal gates and jumping up and down on the many stone steps. We played hide and seek in the empty sentry boxes that had been built by the Spanish to guard the city. During our shopping expeditions into the city with my parents, townspeople gathered in groups to smile at us as our family of four made its way along the sidewalks. "Please buy this," some would plead as they urged my mother to buy whatever it was they were selling, usually a handmade craft item. "It's so nice, Madam," they would eagerly announce whenever my mother appeared hesitant.

Like so many places in the thirties, the poverty brought by the Depression had struck the island like a blustery hurricane. In addition to buying the wares of street sellers, my parents made regular monetary, food, and clothing donations to families who were the victims of unemployment and poverty. Coincidentally, President Roosevelt's renowned New Deal, the name he gave his program to put people back to work and reform the economy, picked up speed in Puerto Rico the year we arrived. The president's wife, Eleanor, even took an interest in the island's plight and visited there during the Depression.

Germany also suffered from unemployment, but even bigger problems were growing in that country. Early in August 1934, my father learned that Germany's President Paul von Hindenburg had died on the second day of that month. This sudden vacancy allowed Adolf Hitler to assume duties of both chancellor and president, which were merged into one position, head of state. Gloom swept through my father's mind when he recalled his inspections of the European battlefields after World War I. He viewed Hitler's increased strength as an ominous sign for the future of Europe.

As far as my father's own career was concerned, things got much better for him in November 1934, when he was promoted to captain. U.S. Army promotions were very slow in those pre-war days, and he had been a lieutenant for sixteen long years. He was more than ready to wear the silver bars of a captain.

Throughout the bleak Depression, Puerto Ricans who found employment with U.S. Army families such as ours were among the lucky ones. Their service was also beneficial to us. I roamed around the house spouting Spanish phrases taught by Jenny, my Puerto Rican nanny, who became like part of the family.

She was quite fond of us. I recall how forlorn Jenny looked on the day our ship pulled away from the dock at San Juan Harbor in 1935, after our two-year stay. The El Morro fortress sat like a vigilant sentinel on the rocky promontory above the harbor, providing a scenic backdrop for the dramatic event. When I vigorously waved goodbye as she stood mournfully on the shore, Jenny waved back. She intermittently used her thin, brown fingers to wipe away the tears that had fallen on her cheeks, like a

Puerto Rican farmer's wife wiping away raindrops from a stalk of sugar cane.

Our next home—Camp Roosevelt, Florida—wasn't far from Puerto Rico, comparatively speaking. Located near the mid-state town of Ocala, it was surrounded by farms and grazing land, as well as by large trees from which gray Spanish moss hung like Christmas-tree tinsel.

When explorer Juan Ponce de León arrived on Florida's coast in the sixteenth century, he thought he had discovered a large and beautiful island. After reporting his discovery, he urged more of his countrymen to follow him, which many did. Unfortunately, illness and attacks by hostile Indians hampered the attempts of Spanish settlers who tried to colonize the region. In the middle of the nineteenth century, after it had triumphed over many trials and tribulations, Florida became a state.

Even though Ponce de León never did locate the mythical fountain of youth in Florida, for which he had searched in vain, and was wrong in thinking he had discovered an island, we found many similarities to our previous home. As was the case in Puerto Rico, the Spanish influence was evident everywhere, particularly in St. Augustine on the northeast coast. During our visit to that old historic city, my brother and I again explored empty sentry boxes and walked along walls built by the Spaniards for protection, as we had done in San Juan. Attacks by the British had been a major concern to St. Augustine's early residents.

Near Camp Roosevelt, helmeted army engineers spent hot, humid days developing plans and supervising workers on a proposed barge canal that would cross Florida from the Atlantic Ocean to the Gulf of Mexico. Usually at the end of a long day spent out in the sun, my father's cotton shirts would be soaked with sweat. Construction of a water route was first proposed by sixteenth-century Philip II of Spain, but it wasn't until the days of the Great Depression that such an idea seemed acceptable and economically feasible. It would put unemployed people to work, and, equally important, President Roosevelt approved funding for the project.

It was on this job that my father first served under Brehon B. Somervell, the engineer officer in command of the canal project, who at that time was a lieutenant colonel. (He would eventually rise to the rank of four-star general.) My father respected Brehon Somervell's engineering brilliance, and he seemed able to put up with his superior officer's sometimes-difficult temperament.

The Somervell family lived in the Camp's residential area, as did we. To my brother, living in our woodsy neighborhood was like spending time at a summer camp or vacation resort. Tall, slim trees surrounded our wood-frame house and screened front porch. I liked to play in the grassy areas that bordered the house, which were kept short but were otherwise left in their wild, natural state.

It seemed particularly wild out there the day a colorful coral snake moved through the grass near me. I didn't know the creature was poisonous, so when it came slithering through our yard I called to my mother to "come see the pretty snake." To Mother this was a crisis to be taken care of quickly. She dashed into the house and returned brandishing a long-handled, sharp-edged hoe. While I stood safely far away she struck the potentially deadly creature several times and killed it. From that day onward, at least until we moved from Ocala at the end of 1935, I kept my eyes open for snakes—often from a secure, lofty height atop a neighborhood pony, on which Howie and I often rode.

Slithering across Africa that year was a reptilian force of another kind. In 1935, Fascist Italian dictator Benito Mussolini sent his troops into Ethiopia and conquered it. Horrified by this brazen action, the League of Nations imposed economic sanctions on Italy. This had the unfortunate effect of creating sympathy between Fascism and Nazism, since Germany had left the League in 1933. In Italy non-Fascists and even anti-Fascists began to support Mussolini, whom they assessed as a strong leader. In 1936, Italy annexed Ethiopia and, even more daunting, the powerful Rome-Berlin Axis was created.

Like many other career army officers, Howard Peckham was apprehensive about America's possible involvement in the war and our military's lack of preparedness. He kept abreast of these unsettling developments, but at that time he was still directly involved with the canal project.

The project faced a doomed future, however. In spite of diligent planning by army engineers, it was canceled in 1936, primarily for environmental reasons. Brehon Somervell was greatly disappointed about this turn of events, because he thought its construction would be a good use of funds that were allocated to the Works Progress Administration (WPA), an agency President Franklin Roosevelt created as part of his New Deal. It would put people to work.

In addition to providing employment, there were other reasons to support the completion of a canal. Several local politicians had predicted it would enhance transportation and commerce, thereby bringing economic prosperity to their state. Nevertheless, the dreams of those politicians did not come true, either in their lifetime or in the years thereafter. A continuous waterway across Florida has never been completed.

Howard Peckham's next engineering assignment was in a decidedly more urbane location, quite different from the tropical atmospheres of Puerto Rico and Florida. From 1936 through 1939, he worked as the director of operations and deputy administrator of the WPA in New York City. His boss was again Brehon Somervell, who had appreciated Howard's potential in Florida as a capable director and had undoubtedly put in a request for his transfer to New York.

A major goal of the WPA was to provide work for victims of the Depression, especially laborers. Army engineers, such as my father, drew plans for and oversaw the construction of roads, public buildings, bridges, and other projects. Overall, it was a very successful program. One of the most important WPA projects was the creation of North Beach Airport, which was later renamed La Guardia. Army engineers supervised construction of the airport, a project that employed hundreds of workers.

World War II, meanwhile, was inching its way towards America like a slow-moving asp. During 1937, Germany's Third

Reich was building up its muscles by intensifying the training of troops. During a visit to Germany that year from his home in Italy, Mussolini became swayed by Hitler's flattery and Germany's increasing power; he returned to his homeland convinced that he should become a partner of a "new, powerful Germany." Thus his bond with Hitler was sealed and strengthened.

In Asia, Japan invaded China, and the city of Nanking was brutalized in an especially cruel way. For three months beginning in December 1937, the invaders tortured and killed hundreds of thousands of civilians. At my Bronxville elementary school I heard about these atrocities, which I later discussed with Dad. I was reassured by his statement that President Roosevelt would probably force the Japanese to leave China. They did eventually leave, of course, but not for many more years.

In spite of our relatively comfortable life, the U.S. Army wasn't immune to the sufferings of the Depression. All military personnel, wherever stationed, were given a ten percent pay cut. Budget cutting affected both the size of the armed forces and the availability of equipment. Nonetheless many army families had an advantage over their civilian counterparts—the head of the household at least had a job and a regular salary.

As the war progressed, army engineers such as Dad were kept informed by their superior officers of major developments in Asia and Europe. In March of 1938, they learned that Germany had invaded Austria, thus rendering that small country Hitler's first victim. Next on Hitler's list of lands to conquer, they learned, was inland Czechoslovakia.

Under the terms of the Munich Pact, signed that September by Hitler, Mussolini, Prime Minister Neville Chamberlain, and Premier Edouard Daladier, Czechoslovakia was forced to cede to Germany a portion of its land known as the Sudetenland, near the German border. Hitler had stubbornly reasoned that because German-speaking people inhabited the Sudetenland, it rightly belonged to his Third Reich, even though those people were Czech citizens. Seeking a diplomatic solution and hoping to avoid war, the British and French gave in to Adolf Hitler's demands, and the Sudetenland became his possession. As time would tell, the signers had made a tragic mistake.

MY MOTHER AND HER MOTHER MARY BELL MACFARLANE: CIRCA 1904

War news like this was frequently a topic of conversation among our neighbors in Bronxville. Except for civilian friends such as businessman John Lee and his wife Theone, my parents socialized with other army families. Edmond L. Leavey and his wife Ruth were among that group. Edmond, who graduated from West Point in 1917, was the WPA's chief engineer. Years later he retired as a major general and was named President of the International Telephone and Telegraph Corporation.

While we were living in the attractive suburban community of Bronxville, Dad developed stomach ulcers, and his medicine cabinet was always filled with packages of Tums. He believed the stress of his daily commute to New York City was partly to blame, but he also wondered whether a contributing factor might be Brehon Somervell's hard-driving personality. "Later in my career, life was a lot easier than when I was a captain working under Brehon," he once remarked. His experience was not unique, according to Forrest C. Pogue in his book *George C. Marshall: Organizer of Victory*: "A hard driver and a man of quick temper, Somervell easily made enemies inside and outside the Army." Fortunately for my dad, they were on good terms, and efficiency reports that Dad received from him were always complimentary.

MY MOTHER'S STEPFATHER FREDERICK B. SHAW (WHEN HE WAS A CAPTAIN)

During the years that my father was stationed in New York, our family spent part of each summer in Maine, in a wood-frame house at Isle of Springs, near Boothbay Harbor. We rented the same two-story home each time. Dad offset some of his job tensions there, and our whole family enjoyed halcyon days in a calm environment. These summer vacations were marvelous. The sweet aroma of pine needles filled both the air we breathed and the souvenir pillows we bought at local quaint shops. We always bought extra small pillows to take back to New York as gifts.

ARMY AND NAVY CLUB: MANILA, THE PHILIPPINES, 1924 (BUILT IN 1912)

Our favorite pastime, though, was walking down tree-shaded paths, small metal buckets in hand, to collect ripe blueberries. Mother would then bake delicious muffins from them, which disappeared from our plates as quickly as raindrops vanished into Maine's ocean waters. Visitors such as the Edmond Leaveys and members of our family also savored the blueberries.

Aunts Mary and Mildred and their husbands would drive to visit us from their New England homes each summer, bringing with them their children—Kent, Diane, Gage, and Carol. After they arrived at Isle of Springs, we would eat a big picnic lunch on the beach, and then my cousins and I would climb the flat rocks near the shore. Uncle Dick, a navy captain, felt at home in any kind of boat, so he led us on some pleasurable maritime excursions when not away on sea duty. After we children were strapped into bulky life preservers, we would go for a ride off the island's coast in a motorboat. We were glad to have Uncle Dick with us whenever we careened precariously in choppy water.

LT. HOWARD PECKHAM WITH BRIDE-TO-BE MARION SHAW AND HER FAMILY'S DOG,
GOOFY: FORT HAYES, 1925

In mid-summer 1939, during our last vacation on the island, colossal rain clouds hovered over our yard one day. This was nothing, however, compared to the dark clouds of war that were getting bigger and bigger in Europe and Asia.

(LEFT) SENTRY BOXES AT EL MORRO: PUERTO RICO
(RIGHT) JEAN AND HOWIE AT CAMP ROOSEVELT: FLORIDA, 1934

**(LEFT) AUNT MARY AND UNCLE DICK WITH THEIR SON KENT
(RIGHT) UNCLE ED, GAGE, AUNT MILDRED, AND CAROL: CONNECTICUT, 1935**

On March 15 of that year, Germany's unopposed troops occupied Czechoslovakia, which had become much weaker after its concession to Germany of the Sudetenland the previous year. Japan, which throughout the thirties had steadily made gains in overtaking parts of China, was now strengthening its mandated islands in the Pacific. In view of these and other ominous events, the U.S. Army determined that it needed more officers who were highly technically trained and who were well prepared for war.

**(LEFT) JEAN IN BRONXVILLE (RIGHT) FUTURE MAJOR GENERALS LEAVEY AND PECKHAM
DIGGING FOR CLAMS: MAINE, 1936**

Chapter 3

Clouds Over Leavenworth
and Benning

*While the storm clouds gather far across the sea, let us swear
allegiance to a land that's free.*

— IRVING BERLIN

IN THE SUMMER OF 1939, Howard Peckham was elated to learn that
he had been chosen to attend the prestigious Command and
General Staff School (now called *College*), a graduate school for
future military leaders. The U.S, Army's need for highly trained
officers had precedence over my father's job with the WPA, but
that job would not have lasted much longer, anyway. After Pearl
Harbor, when unemployment ceased to be a problem, President
Roosevelt terminated the WPA and several other New Deal
programs. Even though they had been successful, there was no
longer a need for them.

Located at Fort Leavenworth, Kansas, high above the west
bank of the Missouri River, the college was established in 1881
after the American Civil War had shown the need for more highly
educated officers. It was, and continues to be, "a top school" in the
U.S. Army's educational system. Among the more famous alumni
of Dad's generation were Generals Dwight D. Eisenhower, George
S. Patton, Jr., and Omar N. Bradley, and it was an honor to be
chosen to attend classes there. The demanding curriculum of the
school, which emphasized tactical decisions, problem solving, and

logistics, served its graduates well professionally, as did classes relating to staff functions. Brehon Somervell could be tough to work for, but my father knew his former boss was fair and ethical and that he had given his endorsement for my father's admission to the college.

I was only a gangly seven, going on eight, in August 1939, so I wasn't concerned about Dad's future military career. I was more interested in closely watching the husky moving men who loaded our furniture into large crates. I wanted to make sure they didn't pack away all my favorite board games, since I planned to bring some of them with me on the trip. After they left, I loaded these possessions and a few other small items into our car. At the same time, I began to wonder what sights we would see along the way to our destination. Most of all, I was curious about what life would be like in far-away Kansas.

While preparing for our trip, Mother retold stories she had heard about her grandfather, Judge Joseph Davis, who had traveled westward at the end of the Civil War. The story of his journey is interestingly told in the book titled *Progressive Men of the State of Montana*, published by A. W. Bowen & Company circa 1902. The book also describes his life after he settled down in Helena, where he worked in the mining industry and married Flora Marsh, another pioneer.

So as my great-grandparents Joseph Davis and Flora Marsh Davis had done many years earlier, we headed west towards the middle of the United States.

The fears of travelers on the portion of the Santa Fe Trail that winds through Kansas were allayed when a U.S. Army officer, Colonel Henry Leavenworth, arrived in 1827 from Jefferson Barracks, Missouri, bringing with him officers and soldiers of his regiment. Colonel Leavenworth established a base from which to protect settlers, traders, surveyors, and other travelers on the rugged, dangerous trail. In the early days of the Santa Fe Trail, travelers feared the perils they might face—such as attacks by hostile Indians, severe hunger, serious injury, and painful wild-animal bites. All of these events had happened, at some time, to an unfortunate traveler on that busy trail. The base eventually comprised thousands of acres and became known as Fort Leavenworth. It is the oldest army post west of the Missouri River that has existed continually since its establishment. On our trip in August 1939 we didn't have the same worries as early travelers to that state.

I recall how endless the tiring drive seemed from Bronxville, however, and how intense the heat was on the day we finally arrived at our red-brick officers' quarters at Fort Leavenworth. Waves of burning air appeared to be drifting upwards from the sidewalks.

The moving men wiped perspiration off their faces with handkerchiefs as they placed our furniture and other possessions in the living room, especially when they moved the Chickering spinet up the sidewalk and into the house. The piano was soon put to use. After we got settled, I started taking piano lessons from a teacher recommended to my parents by a woman in our neighborhood.

I also became familiar with horses. Fort Leavenworth was a "horsy" post then, and riding classes for children were popular. I remember that at the end of each lesson, our class of about twenty children would form a long horizontal line atop our horses. We would then dismount and reward our horses with a lump of sugar.

In those days, foxhunts were popular at Leavenworth. Fancy riding gear, worn to the elaborate breakfasts that followed the hunts, was *de rigueur* among the younger officers and their wives. I recall watching them as they rode around in horse-drawn carriages and waved at spectators who smiled admiringly as they waved back at them. America's involvement in World War II, which loomed ominously ahead, ended this type of frivolity.

We found out that the winters are even more severe than the summers on the Kansas plains—the dry cold air bit like pepper and went right through my clothes. My father was the only one in the family who didn't seem to mind the frosty weather, and I thought he looked handsome and comfortable in the heavy blue uniform he often wore, its matching blue cape swirling down from his shoulders to his knees. "The snowy, cold days remind me of the winters I spent growing up in Connecticut," he said in the enthusiastic tone of voice he usually used when speaking about his New England boyhood.

Then he would go on to describe the times he and his father would go fishing through the ice. "Dad and I poked holes in the ice of one of the local ponds, set up tilts, and then waited for a pickerel or perch to nibble the bait." The number of fish they were able to catch, if they caught any at all on a particular day, seemed immaterial. The most important thing to them was the excitement of the process.

Throughout his life, Dad maintained a fondness for baked fish and other tasty seafood, such as boiled lobster and steamed clams, which he had eaten with his parents at their Connecticut home. One day he patiently explained to Mother, Howie, and me the procedure to prepare a typical clambake, a summertime feast that he remembered fondly from his boyhood. He even wrote down the instructions on a piece of paper:

> On the day of the bake, my brother, my sisters, and I would cut cheesecloth into squares and then put a peeled onion, a sweet potato, and a piece each of fish, chicken, and sausage into the packet. We also made packets of washed clams. Everything was placed on layers of seaweed and put in a tall aluminum can, then steamed over a fire. The results were delicious.

Although Mother enjoyed eating steamed clams, particularly in seafood restaurants, she didn't like making Dad's somewhat complicated meal. He usually had to wait until his reunions with family in Connecticut to partake of this feast. In Kansas, other events were far more bothersome than the difference between summer and winter temperatures, especially in 1939.

Even though the tide of the Depression was fortunately ebbing, reports about events in Europe buzzed in the atmosphere like bees at a picnic. "The Germans have overrun Poland," my father grimly told Mother one September afternoon.

On the first day of that month, Hitler's troops had attacked Poland from the north, south, and west, thus rendering it completely defenseless. Only two days later, Britain and France declared war on Germany. In the United States, dramatic changes were also taking place that year. Under the guidance of U.S. Army Chief of Staff General George C. Marshall, the army began increasing its membership, modernizing its equipment, and starting to prepare its troops for combat. This preparation meant that more and more officers would be needed to fill leadership roles.

It also caused a rumor to spread in officers' clubs throughout the United States that Camp Beauregard, Louisiana, would soon be the location of massive war maneuvers. That rumor turned out to be true. One of the participants in those realistic games of war was my dad, who graduated in February 1940 from the Command & General Staff School. His three months in Louisiana serving with the 21st Engineers would involve intensive training for a leadership position in a combat environment, precipitated by the storm of events in Europe and Asia.

The War Department ordered more than sixty-five thousand troops from various divisions and regiments of the U.S. Army to join this massive training operation. Tanks and other equipment lined the wide highways, and soldiers marched through both busy towns and open fields. Occasionally, soldiers could be seen riding atop mule packs, which was a sight the residents of Rapides County, Louisiana, would never forget.

Our street was silent and empty when Dad and many other men from our neighborhood left for Louisiana in late spring 1940. In the days and weeks that followed, my mother often joined other lonely wives at coffee get-togethers, where they could share their fears and concerns.

Because so many wives and children were left alone, a military policeman (MP) was appointed to patrol our area, giving us the secure feeling that the U.S. Army was taking good care of its dependents. We used to see the young corporal, a Southerner, stride slowly by our house in the evenings. Years later, my mother enjoyed telling the story about the time she opened the front door and called "Howdy!" to my brother, who went by that nickname then. Instead of hearing the voice of her son in reply, she heard a shy "Howdy, Ma'am" from the corporal, who happened to be walking by our house. Mother loved to tell this funny story about Fort Leavenworth to her guests.

Down at the Louisiana maneuvers, meanwhile, the weather became oppressive, as did the war reports that Dad and his fellow officers of the 21st Engineers were receiving.

In May, German troops swept into France by way of Belgium, a move that Dad and the other engineers found particularly distasteful. They were dismayed that the Maginot Line was a failure. The line, built prior to World War II, was named after French statesman André Maginot. It was a high concrete structure—about two hundred miles long—which was supposed to serve as a permanent defense system against German attack. Although it adequately covered the French-German frontier, the Maginot Line left the French-Belgian border uncovered.

The German army took advantage of this blatant oversight by breaking through the line's northern end using tanks on the ground and planes in the sky. They then continued their offensive around the rear of the line, thus rendering it completely useless.

In June, France surrendered. French Premier Paul Reynaud chose to resign rather than sign the surrender document, which would have been too humiliating. (My father met with Paul Reynaud during the Cold War, which is discussed in the chapter entitled *Helping to Fight Communism*.)

Reynaud's successor, Henri Petain, was more than happy to take his place, since it gave him the opportunity to form a puppet government in the city of Vichy, in the south. This move kept France divided throughout World War II between a zone in the west and north occupied by Germany and a puppet zone in the south that collaborated with the enemy.

Also in June, Germany successfully conquered Denmark, Norway, Belgium, Luxembourg, and Holland, Additional dramatic events were happening that month in Great Britain. After Neville Chamberlain resigned in May, brilliant, cigar-smoking Winston Churchill was appointed the new prime minister. On June 18, he delivered a notable speech before the House of Commons about the future of his nation. One purpose of speech was to energize the British people. Here are some of Churchill's words:

> Hitler knows that he will have to break us in this island or lose the war. If we can stand up to him, all Europe may be free and the life of the world may move forward into broad, sunlit uplands. But if we fail, then the whole world, including the United States, including all that we have known and cared for, will sink into the abyss of a new Dark Age made more sinister, and perhaps more protracted, by the lights of perverted science.
>
> Let us therefore brace ourselves to our duties and so bear ourselves that, if the British Empire and its Commonwealth last for a thousand years, men will still say, "This was their finest hour."

In the days ahead, German troops were not able to land in Britain—much to Hitler's disappointment and Churchill's relief. Its shores were highly fortified, and the use of radar in Britain helped the military spot potential invaders who attempted to arrive by ship. Churchill's relief was short lived, however.

Starting in July 1940, frustrated Germany sent its Luftwaffe bombers roaring through the sky to Britain, causing its terrified citizens to run repeatedly, week after week, into the safety of bomb shelters. Like crystal vases shattered by rocks, Britain's factories, airports, homes, ports, and buildings were broken apart by German blitz bombs.

Significant events were also happening in Howard Peckham's army career. In July, he received news that he had been promoted to major and would soon participate in a growing armored force. This force, which moved on treads, had historic roots in the United States Cavalry. The cavalry was made up of mounted horsemen who galloped their way through the wars of the United States, beginning with the Revolutionary War and ending during World War I, when a horse cavalry was shown to be impractical.

The Louisiana maneuvers, during which tanks had played an important role, had emphasized the need for a strong armored force within the army. The War Department thus created sixteen armored divisions during World War II. It selected Fort Benning, Georgia, as the home base for the 2nd Armored Division, which was activated there on July 15, 1940.

Among the core units attached to the 2nd Armored Division was the 17th Armored Engineer Battalion, whose job was, among other tasks, to design and construct the pontoon bridges across which heavy armor would be driven. The officer appointed to command the 17th Armored Battalion at Fort Benning was Howard Peckham, and Fort Benning was the destination to which we traveled in August 1940.

Not long after our car had traversed the Tennessee border and entered Georgia, my father announced that we were now in the peach-tree state. "We'll see some beautiful orchards," he stated enthusiastically. I was unable to show any interest in sightseeing at that point, however. My mouth felt as dry as desert dust. We all agreed that we should stop for refreshments, so my father parked the car in front of a drug store, where my brother and I gulped down icy Coca-Colas. Now, instead of experiencing the blazing heat of the Kansas plains, we were sweltering because of high humidity.

Upon our arrival at Fort Benning, I found out the location of the post's swimming pool and spent many hours there that summer, paddling around and jumping into the invigorating water. I lived in my own childhood world of water games and vigorous splashing, impervious to the fighting in Europe.

President Roosevelt, at the same time, was concerning himself with the resolute necessity of trying to prevent a German takeover in Europe. The takeover unfortunately rolled forward and could not be prevented. Furthermore, Japan, which he hoped would stay as quiet as a docile kitten, was roaring like a lion. In

September 1940, it attacked and occupied French Indochina. An agreement Japan had made with the Vichy government in France helped Japan accomplish this feat, thus putting it on the side of the Axis.

In 1940, a fight of sorts was going on in the United States related to Winston Churchill's June 18 speech before the House of Commons. In addition to energizing the British people, his speech aimed to secure aid from the United States. He was well aware that many people in "the Colonies" admired him; and he knew that Americans would be listening to his speech on their radios or reading it in their papers.

To a certain extent, President Roosevelt granted Churchill his wish for assistance. After using much persuasion and ignoring the protests of isolationists, the President successfully convinced Americans that our country should supply arms to our friends, the British. This was accomplished by way of the Lend-Lease Act, a document that allowed Congress to send badly needed supplies to Britain. At the same time, the Lend-Lease Act was worded in such a way as to keep the United States neutral in the war.

Members of the isolationist America First organization realized that this move by Congress brought the United States at least partly into the worldwide conflict, so they were outraged. The theme that it and other isolationists had preached was that the United States shouldn't get involved in foreign wars. My father considered himself to be at the service of the President of the United States; furthermore, my dad was in accord with the reasoning behind helping Britain.

During the months that Americans were arguing about the war, Adolf Hitler was planning a new conquest. For a long time he had wanted to capture Egypt as a means to gain access to the Suez Canal and hence the oil fields of the Middle East. To accomplish this goal, in February 1941 he appointed General Erwin Rommel to head the Africa Corps, an elite corps of men who charged fearlessly through the desert in big Panzer tanks. Rommel had several successes against the British, such as overtaking strategic locations in Libya. He even looked the part of a successful invader.

No commander made a more striking figure than he, as far as attire was concerned. Photographs showed Rommel standing defiantly in his medal-bedecked uniform and peaked Africa Corps cap, wearing tank goggles on his forehead and holding leather gloves in his hand.

Within several months an American general would arrive in North Africa whose impressive appearance somewhat matched Erwin Rommel's. This was George S. Patton, a graduate of the West Point class of 1909. First, though, George Patton had important work to do at Fort Benning. He was a colonel and a brigade commander when he first arrived at the post in 1940. General Omar Bradley, West Point class of 1915, was the post commander. (It's interesting to note that Omar Bradley was George Patton's boss at Benning, although their roles would be reversed later on, as the war progressed.)

George Patton could make other officers feel completely awed while they spoke with him, as if they were in the presence of an icon. A former cavalryman, he looked distinguished in the long shiny boots and riding breeches he often wore. These weren't just for show, however. Partly because of the military's long-time dependence on horses and its worldwide appreciation of them, dating as far back as feudal times, it was not unusual to see officers dressed that way—even those who hadn't ridden a horse in a long time.

This style of dressing was especially common among expert horsemen such as General Patton, who, in addition to having been a cavalry officer, was a skilled polo player. He seemed to adore horses.

My father, on the other hand, never expressed any interest in joining the cavalry or playing polo, and I never saw him atop a horse. Nevertheless, he did take riding lessons, and more than once he acknowledged the fact that horses performed a great service for the U.S. Army long before the advent of mechanized warfare.

For this and for many other reasons, Howard Peckham never became, and undoubtedly never wanted to become, an "image" of

George Patton. Their mannerisms and personalities were as different as a peach tree in a crowded orchard and a Georgia pine on a lonely hill. Another contrast between them was that my father might have used swear words on occasion when he was with other men, but not in mixed company, as George Patton was known to do.

My father did in any case admire the tough-speaking 2nd Armored Division commander, whose voice sounded a bit shrill at times. Dad explained this dichotomy when he once said "George Patton had a way of commanding respect." He implied that it was the meaning of General Patton's words that mattered, not the pitch of his voice.

Patton used that voice often. At Fort Benning, he had an amphitheater built where he gave speeches to the troops. Additionally, at least once a week he brought all his officers together so he could lecture to them about tactics and related subjects. H. Essame writes in *Patton: A Study in Command* about Patton's strong influence on the division:

> For a whole year from April 1941 the 2nd Armored Division maintained the full blast of the Patton drive. In the process he made every man in the division to some extent the image of himself.

During the period that General Patton commanded the 2nd Armored Division, he and his wife Beatrice were eager to make a good impression on the division's officers and their wives—who included my parents. As Blumenson writes in *The Patton Papers: 1940-45,* "Patton and his wife had a series of buffet suppers for all the officers and ladies of the division." For my ambitious father, attendance at such an important social event was imperative. It helped that the Pattons were gracious hosts who put their guests at ease, so my mother—a young and dutiful wife—probably enjoyed the event.

To assure its preparedness for war, the 2nd Armored Division, which was directly descended from the American Tank Corps of World War I, participated in realistic maneuvers. The first of these maneuvers, where divisions with names such as Blue and Red battled each other, started in the limpid spring of 1941 in Tennessee, near the towns of Tullahoma and Manchester. When my father received orders to attend these field maneuvers, he accepted the news with allegiance to the efficiency of the 2nd Armored Division.

In June, my father's attention turned to an invasion taking place in Russia, which the Germans had code-named Operation Barabossa. The Germans mistakenly believed their invasion of Russia on the twenty-first day of that month would be successful. They were very wrong. This defeat paved the way for Russia to join the war and open an Eastern Front.

German troops were humiliated by another unsuccessful invasion of Russia at the end of 1941, when they again stormed into that country like lions. They became entangled in a storm of another sort, however—the cold severity of winter. It ruined their efforts to capture Moscow and Stalingrad and gave the Russians an opportunity to mount a strong counter-offensive. The Germans were forced to retreat from the Eastern Front like lambs.

"Russia is a country in the eastern part of Europe, and its citizens have very little freedom," my teacher at the Benning Elementary School told the class one day soon thereafter. "Unlike the United States, it is not a democracy, which means its people cannot vote freely for a president." I knew that a uniformed man with a large moustache, named Joseph Stalin, ruled that country, because I had seen a picture of him. Russia didn't seem to be a pleasant place in which to live, but I was glad the huge country was on our side and not Germany's.

In September, my father took part in larger maneuvers than those that had been held in the spring. These were located in Louisiana, in the vicinity of the Sabine River between Carthage and Kirbyville. He was very familiar with the swampy atmosphere of this bayou state, having gone there on maneuvers while we lived in our Fort Leavenworth quarters.

Due to the large size of the endeavor (more than 200,000 men were to participate), my mother was very apprehensive; she feared the consequences of such a concerted war-preparedness effort on the part of the army.

The exercises started in blinding rain, but then the troops struggled with mud, stagnant water, and mosquitoes. Tanks had to forge their way in thick forests, and the men, who sweated in the humidity, frequently had to empty their sand-filled boots. Needless to say, my father was exhausted at the end of the maneuvers.

After striding slowly up the concrete walkway to our house and embracing my mother, he talked a bit about the rugged conditions he had endured. Then he added, "In spite of everything, morale was high, and the men learned important lessons about planning, tactics, and teamwork." They also learned how to move supplies efficiently, a task with which the army's Quartermaster Corps would be particularly concerned during World War II.

By mid-fall of 1941 the situation in Great Britain had become much more hopeful. Germany's Luftwaffe pilots, after a year of flying over Britain and dropping their dreaded bombs, no longer had the stamina to pummel and frighten Britain's citizens. A strengthened and determined force of Royal Air Force (RAF) fighters and bombers now was retaliating against the German planes, causing the blitz to dim like an overused lamp.

In October 1941, about four weeks after his promotion to lieutenant colonel, Howard Peckham was detailed to the General Staff Corps as Assistant Chief of Staff, G-3, of the 2nd Armored Division. As G-3, he was concerned with the dual functions of planning and operations. During the following month, the last peacetime maneuvers for the 2nd Armored Division were held in the Carolinas. In *Patton: A Study in Command,* H. Essame writes that in an exercise in North Carolina, "Patton and the 2nd Armored Division completely outshone all others."

Only one month later, the United States was shaken by what seemed like a worldwide tsunami. In spite of the preparedness of the 2nd Armored Division, no one at Fort Benning was prepared for the startling events that occurred on the otherwise peaceful

Sunday of December 7, 1941—especially not the wives and children. My mother was the first member of our family to hear the news. She had been listening to the radio when an announcer interrupted her program with a shocking report—the Japanese had made a sneak attack on America at Pearl Harbor in Hawaii. The next day, my tenth birthday, the radio broadcasted President Franklin Roosevelt's speech to Congress. Of particular concern to Dad were the President's words regarding our armed forces:

> **President Franklin Roosevelt:** Yesterday, December 7, 1941—a date which will live in infamy—the United States of America was suddenly and deliberately attacked by naval and air forces of the Empire of Japan....
>
> Indeed, one hour after Japanese air squadrons had commenced bombing in the American island of Oahu, the Japanese ambassador to the United States and his colleague delivered to our secretary of state a formal reply to a recent American message. While this reply stated that it seemed useless to continue the existing diplomatic negotiations, it contained no threat or hint of war or armed attack. The attack yesterday on the Hawaiian Islands has caused severe damage to American naval and military forces. Very many American lives have been lost....
>
> As commander in chief of the Army and Navy, I have directed that all measures be taken for our defense. . . .With confidence in our armed forces, with the unbounding determination of our people, we will gain the inevitable triumph—so help us God....
>
> I ask that the Congress declare that since the unprovoked and dastardly attack by Japan on Sunday, December 7, a state of war has existed between the United States and the Japanese empire.

On that very historic day most isolationists abandoned their protests, which suddenly seemed irrelevant and useless.

Up until this point, our lifestyle at Fort Benning had been idyllic. During our three-year stay, we lived first in attractive officers' quarters on Austin Loop and then in even better quarters on Miller Loop. The latter was a two-story stucco home almost identical to the other tidy homes on our block. To the right of the entry hall was a cozy kitchen that led to the dining room.

To the left of the hall was a spacious living room. Also off the entry hall was a long staircase leading to bedrooms on the second floor. My room, I was glad to learn upon first seeing it, had a view of lacy, green-leafed trees in a forested area across the street.

In springtime, purple wisteria growing abundantly on a tall trellis attached to the side of the house emitted a heady fragrance that faithfully greeted me whenever I approached it. Then, at the beginning of summer, my mother would transform our living room into a southern summer locale, an ambiance that remained until the fall. She would send our dark slipcovers and Oriental carpets out for cleaning and storage. Then she would put cool-looking white slipcovers on the furniture and full-size beige rugs on the floor.

Peacetime army life was indeed pleasant, especially in the languid atmosphere of the Deep South, where household help was both inexpensive and plentiful.

Because my mother enjoyed entertaining, she appreciated having help from Rosie, our heavy-set and jovial black maid. Rosie was also my confidante. On some afternoons after school I would sit on a stool in the basement and watch her iron the linen tablecloths. As she and I made small talk, usually about my day at school, her stout presence and the gentle whirring of a nearby fan made me feel cozy and comfortable.

Later, if my mother expected other officers' wives to stop by for tea, Rosie would place a freshly ironed tablecloth on our round mahogany table in the living room. On top of it, she would neatly arrange my mother's gleaming silver tea service and fragile china cups.

The bombing of Pearl Harbor made the social life infinitely less relaxed, and other changes at the post were rapidly becoming noticeable. Soon after the attack, Omar Bradley ordered Fort Benning troops to guard the bridges and electrical generating plants throughout the state of Georgia. Fears of sabotage or enemy attacks also resulted in the enforcement of air raid drills.

When we heard sirens at night indicating that a drill was about to begin, appropriately called a blackout, my father would often call out to my brother and me. "Turn off the lights!" he would shout. Then, like busy squirrels hunting for acorns, we would rush from room to room to check that they were all off. Then we would sit quietly in the bleak darkness of our home, as though sitting in a cave, until the signal came on again to indicate that the drill had ended.

During the early weeks of 1941, Irwin Rommel's successes against the British in North Africa were analyzed among 2nd Armored Division officers at Fort Benning, especially after the British started dubbing the sly German commander "the desert fox." After Pearl Harbor, armored warfare became more and more a topic of discussion, and many officers, including my father, were concerned that the U.S. Army's Sherman tanks would be no match for Germany's heavy Panzers.

The war was also a major topic of conversation among my classmates at the Fort Benning Elementary School. We children learned that the small countries of Hungary, Romania, and Bulgaria had passively joined the Axis powers of Italy, Germany, and Japan. As a result, games played against imaginary Axis soldiers became intense. A negative attitude towards Japan was particularly evident one day at recess when I naively revealed to a classmate, "The initials in my name, Jean Anne Peckham, spell JAP." From then on, I was teased about my unfortunate initials. This sort of teasing would not be a problem much longer at Fort Benning, however, because a new relocation would soon be headed our way.

In January 1942, General Patton, who had risen to the rank of two-star general, left Fort Benning for a new assignment. The general's leadership expertise had impressed the army's Chief of Staff George Marshall, who ordered him to command the Desert Training Center in California. There, in thousands of sand-covered acres about thirty miles east of Indio, General Patton was placed in charge of troops from several armored divisions, who would be trained to perform tactical maneuvers in a hot and arid desert environment. The harsh exercises, such as being forced to run for several miles in the sun while carrying rifles and wearing full backpacks, were needed to prepare the troops to face the hot desert of North Africa—and the Germans.

Willis Crittenberger, then a brigadier general, replaced Patton as commander of the 2nd Armored Division. As Assistant Chief of Staff, Lieutenant Colonel Howard Peckham worked closely with Willis Crittenberger and his Chief of Staff, Lieutenant Colonel Maurice Rose. All distinguished themselves later. Other later-renown staff officers included Senator Henry Cabot Lodge, Jr., a reservist on active duty who became a Republican candidate for Vice President of the United States.

Also in January 1942, those same staff officers received the discouraging news that Manila had fallen to the Japanese, a surrender that set the tone for other capitulations soon to follow. In February, the island of Singapore leaned forward precariously and then toppled to the Japanese, like a top-heavy brick wall. Also that month, the Japanese encircled Corregidor, the island in the Philippines on which General MacArthur, commander of the combined American and Filipino forces in the Philippines, had his headquarters. This encirclement put him and his family in an extremely perilous situation. Yet they found a way out of this predicament.

On March 11, just as dusk began to creep over the tadpole-shaped island, the general, along with his wife Jean, young son Arthur, and military escorts, discreetly boarded PT boats. Their destination, in accordance with orders the general received from President Roosevelt, was the island of Mindanao. From here, they were flown on a B-17 to Australia, where they were safe.

Jean, whom Douglas MacArthur married in 1937 in Manila, was his second wife, and the marriage was happy. Up until the time the Japanese bombed Pearl Harbor, the couple had enjoyed a reasonably pleasant life in the tropical, friendly atmosphere of the Philippines. It was a country they both liked very much.

The same cannot be said of his first wife, the former Louise Cromwell. She found it impossible to adapt to the Philippines after she and Douglas MacArthur moved there in 1922. In addition to not liking the tropical weather, she often said that Manila was too unsophisticated. A former socialite, she was used to the glamour of Paris and New York.

When Dad arrived in Manila in 1923, he undoubtedly heard rumors circling among his fellow officers, possibly during a social hour at the Army and Navy Club, that Louise's negative attitude was putting a strain on her marriage. Her complaints were often vocal, embarrassingly so. After the MacArthurs returned to the United States in 1925, the marriage continued to fall apart. It ended in divorce three years later.

FOX HUNTING: FT. LEAVENWORTH, 1940

In Australia, his first marriage only an unpleasant memory, MacArthur had time to ruminate about the war. He hated what was happening to the Philippines and felt chagrined that he couldn't prevent its fall. Combined American and Filipino forces on Bataan held out as long as they could, but the strongly armed Japanese vastly outnumbered them. On April 9, 1942, worn out by hunger and disease and reduced in number due to a high casualty rate, they surrendered. The Japanese then forced thousands of American and Filipino prisoners of war to march about sixty miles—without food and water—to a Japanese prison camp. Many prisoners died along the way, especially those who had been in poor health.

My father met a few survivors of that Death March. One of those was Colonel Edmund J. Lilly, who served under him in 1949 in Paris and whose daughter, Tori, was a schoolmate of mine at the American Community School. Before being captured, Edmund had commanded the 57th Philippine Scout Regiment. He then spent approximately forty months in Japanese prison camps, where conditions were harsh and often cruel.

DAD (THIRD FROM THE LEFT IN THE SECOND ROW) AND SOME OF HIS CLASSMATES AT THE COMMAND AND GENERAL STAFF SCHOOL: FT. LEAVENWORTH, 1940

In a conversation with Dad in Paris, Edmund said the Scouts were excellent fighters and that Philippine Division members, in spite of malnutrition, injury, and other hardships, performed valuable reconnaissance work. Edmund also firmly stated that the Regiment ably maintained defensive positions—that is, until they could no longer counterattack strong assaults by the Japanese.

(LEFT) JEAN ON THE BALCONY OF OUR QUARTERS *(RIGHT)* A SNOWY WINTER SCENE: FT. LEAVENWORTH, 1940

CRITTENBERGER STAFF: WILLIS CRITTENBERGER (IN THE MIDDLE), ASSISTANT CHIEF OF STAFF HOWARD PECKHAM (FAR RIGHT), CHIEF OF STAFF MAURICE ROSE (FAR LEFT), JOHN CABOT LODGE (STANDING 2ND FROM RIGHT): BENNING, 1942

Chapter 4

Old and New Kentucky Homes

Weep no more my lady, Oh! Weep no more today! We will sing one song for my old Kentucky home, for the old Kentucky home, far away.

—STEPHEN FOSTER

DURING THE EARLY MONTHS OF 1942, the Philippines, a country Howard Peckham had gotten to like and know very well as a young lieutenant, suffered from one capitulation to another. After General MacArthur left that country and found safety in Australia, President Roosevelt ordered Jonathan Wainwright to succeed him as the commander of the American and Filipino forces.

Then-Lieutenant General Wainwright took on this task with courage and hoped that fate would treat him well. Success was impossible to achieve, however. Only a few weeks later, he wrote the following words to Douglas MacArthur from Corregidor, "We have done our best, both here and on Bataan." Then he added, "Although we are beaten we are still unashamed," thus proving that his pride was still intact, in spite of defeat.

The next day, May 6, 1942, he surrendered to the Japanese. He was then held in prison camps for three years, during which he lived in squalor and a state of near-starvation. Those years were agonizing for his wife, too. Adele Wainwright worried about him unceasingly. When he was finally released she was shocked to see that he looked as thin as a skeleton.

I already knew a little bit about life in the Philippines then, primarily because of the two brass containers that went with us from one home to another. "They're called chow pots," Dad explained to me one day. "After meats, fish, and other foods were cooked, Filipino people could sit in a circle, reach into the pot, and help themselves." He had acquired the large souvenirs when he was stationed on the Islands as a young lieutenant.

In the spring of 1942 my father received new orders. So, at the end of May, our chow pots and other household goods were packed and placed in a large van. We then left Fort Benning in our four-door sedan. Then my father drove us on scenic narrow roads adjacent to the budding fruit trees of Georgia, the hills and dales of Tennessee, and finally the lovely blue-green pastures of Kentucky. Our final destination was Fort Knox, Kentucky, named after George Washington's chief of artillery. Here the United States maintains its gold bullion depository, located on a piece of valuable land that the Treasury Department acquired from the U.S. Army.

At Fort Knox, my father had an important role to play in an expanding and highly mechanized force known simply as the American Armored Force. At that time, then-Major General Jacob L. Devers commanded the Force. At his Fort Knox headquarters, Jacob Devers was responsible for expanding the Force, which he had commanded at that post since August 1941. Sixteen armored divisions were eventually created under the Armored Force.

Howard Peckham was assigned as Chief of Staff of the 8th Armored Division, which had been activated at Fort Knox in April 1942, only a month before our arrival. It was serving as a training division at the post. Here the division trained officers and enlisted men from other divisions, as well as its own troops.

My father's experience as Assistant Chief of Staff of the 2nd Armored Division prepared him well for this new assignment. His goal was to help bring the 8th Armored Division to a prominent standing among the various divisions. (Its war code name was Tornado.) During the early weeks of the 8th Armored Division's formation, it was jointly commanded by two men—Thomas J. Camp and Robert W. Grow—who were both brigadier generals at the time.

In his book *In Tornado's Wake*, author Charles R. Leach explains why Dad's commanders had separate responsibilities:

> To facilitate training, units of the Division were grouped under Combat Commands A and B. General Camp was assigned to head CCA; Brigadier General Robert W. Grow assumed command of CCB. General Orders Number 3, Headquarters, 8th Armored Division, dated April 1942, designated Lieutenant Colonel Howard L. Peckham Division Chief of Staff.

My father's assignment coincided with his promotion to full colonel. A few weeks later, both Thomas Camp and Robert Grow received new assignments. Brigadier General William Grimes, a former cavalryman, replaced them.

I didn't know anything about the large German Panzer tanks in Europe about which my father had once expressed concern, and I had certainly never seen one. I did see Sherman tanks, however. One day I stood very close to one that was on display at Fort Knox, and I recall feeling dwarfed by its big treads and complex-looking weaponry. Nevertheless, I climbed into it and smiled while a bald-headed sergeant walking by took my picture.

As fate would have it, I would never sit in one of those tanks again. Howard Peckham's stellar performance during an intensive one-month course at the Armored Force School brought about a change in his assignment. "I've received orders to report to Camp Campbell later this month," he informed my mother and me one evening in early July 1942. He had already told my brother. "Oh, no!" Mother sobbed, while pressing her head firmly against a wall in the stairway. She was still in the process of hanging drapes at the windows, and we had lived at Fort Knox for only three months. This was one of the few times I ever saw her cry when told we would be moving.

"I'm sorry, dear," Dad said sympathetically, "During wartime, officers are sent where the need for their leadership is the greatest." Feeling the need to behave like a gallant army wife, my mother regained her composure and began to pack.

In late July 1942, our furniture was again loaded into a huge moving van, and I started wondering what my future school might be like. We had moved to Fort Knox near the end of the school year, so I didn't attend classes there. I had enjoyed the vacation, though. For one thing, I always looked forward to the arrival of a bakery truck that came to our cul-de-sac twice a week to deliver newly baked bread and sugary cinnamon rolls. I was unhappy when these treats ended.

The large two-story, red-brick quarters in which we and other senior officers' families lived were luxurious, more so than any others in which we had previously lived. (Our cul-de-sac had the dubious distinction of being nicknamed "snooty loop" by some children living down the street from us.)

Big changes were also taking place that summer at Fort Benning, and other officers' wives—many of them wives of senior officers—were having to make adjustments, my father reminded Mother. For example, in July, Ernest N. Harmon—then a brigadier general—was transferred to Fort Benning to take over Willis Crittenberger's job as head of the 2nd Armored Division. His wife Leona packed up and went with him to his new job, something she would not be able to do later in the war, when his combat duties kept them apart for about three years. Years later, Ernest Harmon retired as a major general and wrote a book about his wartime experiences, titled *Autobiography of a Soldier.*

In August, General Crittenberger assumed command of III Armored Corps (later called XIX Corps) at Camp Polk, Louisiana. Josephine, his wife, had to adjust to the humidity and numerous mosquitoes. Much more difficult were the worry and loneliness she would feel in the future. During the following year, General Crittenberger left for assignments in England and then in Italy, the latter of which had more than its share of danger.

Josephine undoubtedly felt an enormous strain while her husband was serving in Italy—not only was he leading the IV Corps during its many days of fighting north from Rome and across the River Po, but their son, Townsend, was in combat in the European Theater at the same time. Tragically, Townsend did not survive the war. His father, a strong-faced man who had inherited the chiseled features of his Teutonic forebears, learned that Townsend, an army corporal, had been killed in tank action in Germany. One of the letters of sympathy he received came from General George Marshall, according to Forrest C. Pogue in his book *George C. Marshall: Organizer of Victory.* These are some of the words in that letter:

> I have just learned that your boy was killed in action. . . .You have my full sympathy. I am grateful for the contribution which you and your sons have made to the Allied victory over Germany. It is most distressing to me that Townsend was called upon for the highest sacrifice. I hope that your pride in his great service will be an eternal solace to you.

Those sympathetic words helped lift his morale, but they could never completely heal the pain that he and Josephine felt throughout the coming years.

Like his job at Fort Knox, Howard Peckham's assignment at Camp Campbell, a relatively new army installation (now called Fort Campbell), was in Kentucky. We would still be living in a pretty bluegrass state noted for its horse ranches, but the Camp had no available houses for dependents. Therefore, we would have to live in one of the nearby small towns.

No longer would we have quarters on a typical army post, I realized, as we had since I was seven years old. An army post was structured and efficient, a place where straight-backed uniformed men and women, who looked as if they had ramrods attached to their spines, walked at a quick pace on sidewalks located next to manicured lawns and immaculate parade grounds. At the post elementary schools I had attended, I was an "army brat," just like all the other pupils. I was not an outsider, as I believed I would be in this civilian environment.

Fortunately, my parents found an attractive place to live in the town of Hopkinsville, located sixteen miles north of Camp Campbell. Named for Samuel Hopkins, a Revolutionary War soldier and pioneer, Hopkinsville was caught up in the patriotic spirit of the times. Several of its residents offered to share their homes with army families, and my parents found one prospect that was especially appealing. They learned of a middle-aged married couple who had a few rooms for rent in their home. These rooms, formerly used by their now-grown children, had been converted into an apartment, where renters could enjoy privacy and yet have access to the yard and other amenities.

After showing my parents their property, the owners, Robert and Frances Fairleigh, invited us to move in with them. My parents gladly accepted, and soon thereafter we began to unpack the few items we had with us. My bedroom was tiny, as was my brother's, but my parents at least had a large bedroom-sitting room combination, where we spent much of our time. Our own furniture, which had always traveled with us to our far-flung temporary homes, was placed in storage.

At first, it seemed strange to me that we were "boarding" in someone else's house, but at least, I reasoned, we were living on an old, charming mini-estate with its own distinctive name: Fairlelond. Also, it was nice that we usually ate dinner with the Fairleighs in their big dining room, meals that were creatively prepared by their cook and served by their slender maid, who always wore a crisp white cap and apron. The property's grounds were vast and filled with flower gardens and vegetable patches, and I've never forgotten the taste of large ripe tomatoes we picked and ate right off the vine.

A favorite four-legged playmate of mine, who stayed in a backyard doghouse much of the time, was the Fairleigh family's rambunctious setter, Lady, who produced a large litter of puppies during our stay. Also in attendance was the frisky black and white shorthaired cat Howie and I acquired, whose name was Willie.

Robert and Frances Fairleigh were to become lifelong friends of my parents, my brother, and me. When I was confirmed at their church, Hopkinsville's Grace Episcopal Church, they served as my godparents. Years later, they sent my husband Bob and me a beautiful silver tray as a wedding present. My parents, brother, and I became regular churchgoers at Grace Episcopal, where Howie was often asked to carry the Crucifix to and from the altar.

Although Dad was a Baptist and Mother was an Episcopalian, their church attendance together had been sporadic until World War II. After Pearl Harbor Day, wartime fears and pressures caused many people to reach out to God for assistance, and my parents were no exception. They happily joined the rest of the congregation in reciting prayers and singing hymns. When the following words of hope echoed throughout the church, they temporarily forgot about the war:

> From war's alarm, from deadly pestilence,
> Be Thy strong arm our ever sure defense;
> Thy true religion in our hearts increase,
> Thy bounteous goodness nourish us in peace.

The move to Hopkinsville had been quite advantageous as far as my father's career was concerned. In late August 1942, he received a welcome promotion to brigadier general. He had accumulated an impressive array of complimentary efficiency reports from his superiors over the years, so gaining a star was a well-deserved step up the career ladder.

The population of nearby Camp Campbell steadily increased because of the war's escalation and the ensuing growth of the U.S. Army. At first, townspeople were concerned when flirtatious soldiers whistled at their daughters and tried to pick them up. "These naïve girls," as one society matron described them, "seem much too eager to respond to the boys in uniform."

But it didn't take long for residents of the town to make friends with the army. Like other military families, my parents learned to treasure the warm hospitality of the town and its leisurely pace. Soldiers were often invited to Sunday dinners at the homes of Hopkinsville's citizens, and several women of marriageable age acquired GI boyfriends.

For many soldiers assigned to the 12th Armored Division, training was so rugged that they had little time or energy for socializing. Their days consisted of long marches and endless combat exercises. "When the sun shines, dust unmercifully flies into their eyes," Dad said about their environment, "and when it rains, they have to trek through deep mud."

My father knew all of this firsthand because of his job as commander of Combat Command A, and he sympathized with the soldiers. The commander of the 12th Armored Division then was Major General Carlos B. Brewer. Brigadier General Henry C. Newton headed Combat Command B. When General Jacob Devers paid a visit, my father and the two other 12th Armored Division generals greeted his plane, gave him a tour, and updated him about the division's progress.

Dad's main task was to ensure that the division received training to prepare it well for its inevitable participation in battle. Learning how to load armored vehicles for sea transport, how to communicate in a tank environment, how to perform armor tactics and tank gunnery operations—all of these and many other topics were necessary components of armored warfare training.

Divisions are just one of the many components that make up the army chain of command. The following text gives a general description of all the components, starting from the smallest to the largest.

The numbers are approximate, rather than exact.

Squad: 10 soldiers commanded by a sergeant. Platoon: 35 soldiers commanded by a lieutenant. Company: 150 soldiers commanded by a captain. Battalion or Squadron: 1,000 soldiers commanded by a major or lieutenant colonel. Combat Command or Brigade: 4,000 soldiers commanded by either a colonel or one-star general. Division: 11,000 soldiers commanded by a two-star or three-star general. Corps: Two or more divisions, commanded by a two-star or three-star general. Field Army: Two or more corps commanded by a three-star or four-star general. Army Group: Two or more field armies commanded by a three-star or four-star general.

In World War II there were five types of divisions: infantry (containing sixty-eight divisions), armored (sixteen divisions), airborne (five), cavalry (two), and mountain (one division only). The division that suffered the most casualties during the war was the 3rd Infantry Division, to which Robert Shaw, my mother's brother, belonged. All but four of the sixteen armored divisions activated during the war were deactivated in 1945 or 1946.

Twenty-four corps were created by the end of World War II, and five field armies became operational by 1945—First Army, Third Army, Seventh Army, Ninth Army, and Fifteenth Army. The latter came to Europe just as Nazi Germany was about to collapse, so its primary focus was getting rid of areas of resistance that remained in parts of France. In the European Theater, there were two army groups, the 6th Army Group and the 12th Army Group. The U.S. Army has not used groups since World War II.

Although my brother heard glowing words about the army from his dad while we were living in Hopkinsville and knew a lot about it, his main interest was airplanes. In the spring of 1942, while we were still at Fort Benning, he had been thrilled when sixteen B-25 bombers took off from the *USS Hornet*, which was positioned not far from the Japanese coast. The pilot of one of those planes was then-Lieutenant Colonel James Doolittle. The pilots hurriedly dropped bombs on Tokyo, their destination, and then flew to the safety of China. Little damage was done to the city of Tokyo, but this heroic and dangerous mission partially avenged the bombing of Pearl Harbor and was a great morale booster.

Howie loved reading or hearing anything relating to planes and pilots. Now, in Hopkinsville, he was getting the news about other positive airplane-related developments: the massive and successful RAF bombings of key sites in Germany, launched by the British.

Mother, Howie, and I had no idea what my father's mission would be as the war progressed, but we did know that his promotion to brigadier general in had altered our lifestyle. One of the perks of his rank was the availability of a large sedan, for his own use and that of his family on certain occasions. The sedan was driven by a young and efficient soldier, and it certainly changed the way I was perceived by my schoolmates. I became a celebrity at school one afternoon when Mother arrived in the sedan to confer with my teacher. A few of my classmates, none of whom were the children of army men, stood at the entrance of the school to watch her emerge from the sedan and to stare at the general's star on the bumper plate.

In the early days of the war, not many men held that rank, but their numbers certainly increased as the war progressed. In later years, after my father acquired his second star, he modestly downplayed his rank. For example, I was a college student home for the weekend when I overheard a civilian guest say to him, "I suppose there aren't many of you generals in the army, comparatively speaking." Dad smiled at the man in an engaging way and then replied, "Oh, we're a dime a dozen."

Howard Peckham's genuine humility and sense of humor were two traits I always admired. He could be stern when he thought the situation required it, however. I once witnessed him giving a reprimand in downtown Hopkinsville. General Patton was known to publicly berate soldiers who failed to salute him or who looked disheveled. Like Patton, my father disliked seeing a sloppy-looking soldier, and one day he let it be known that he couldn't stand what he saw.

We were riding in the sedan that day and were only a couple of blocks from our downtown destination when he told the army driver to pull over by the curb and stop the car. "Yes, sir," the driver replied, as he followed the orders and parked the car. Dad then opened the car door and walked over to the sidewalk, where a decidedly unkempt soldier nonchalantly strolled next to some shops.

"I'm General Peckham," he brusquely said to the brown-haired man, while I sat slouching in the back seat of the car. "You look disgraceful. Straighten up that hat and tie right now, corporal!"

The soldier looked red faced, but he immediately did as he was told. Inwardly, I sided with the man for a while and felt embarrassed for him, but I admitted later to myself that my father had done the right thing. This was wartime, so the deportment and appearance of army soldiers were being scrutinized by the townspeople. Even more importantly, allies and foes were judging the appearance and deportment of American troops overseas.

In November 1942 welcome news came to 12th Armored Division Headquarters concerning North Africa. British and American forces had arrived in Algeria, and the American Western Task Force, headed by George S. Patton, had landed safely in Morocco. The news about General Patton was especially a relief to the officers who knew him personally and were aware of his plans to embark on this risky journey. His ship had crossed the dangerous Atlantic, where German U-boats roamed like sharks.

Also in November, the British, under the command of Field Marshal Bernard Montgomery, successfully launched an offensive at El Alamein, Egypt, which forced the German troops to travel westward, away from Egypt. The heavy responsibility for succeeding in the overall Allied North African engagement, called Operation Torch, had fallen on the capable shoulders of Dwight D. Eisenhower, who commanded all the sea, air, and land forces involved in the operation.

A decisive victory for the U.S. Navy was its defeat of the Japanese during the Battle of Guadalcanal. This operation, which ended in late January 1943, had been under the command of Admiral Chester Nimitz. This success provided an optimistic beginning to the new year.

One late winter afternoon my father remarked, "Many senior officers, from all branches of the armed forces, aren't planning strategy on European battlefields or commanding operations in the Pacific. They're working behind the scenes in Washington, often in cramped, temporary office buildings." The temporary buildings in which government offices did their work were in various places in Washington. They were on the Washington Mall, in front of the Lincoln Memorial, along Constitution Avenue, near Fort McNair, and in the grassy areas surrounding the Washington

Monument. The Pentagon had been constructed, but occupants were moving in at a very slow pace.

Dad's remarks were prophetic, because he was soon to be part of that harried Washington lifestyle. In the spring of 1943 he was ordered to report to the Fuels and Lubricants Division, a division of the Quartermaster General's office. For the first few months on the job, he would serve as deputy director of the division, commuting between Washington and Hopkinsville.

SHERMAN TANK ON DISPLAY AT FORT KNOX

His change in assignment coincided with the end of the war in North Africa. Leading up to this victory were the steady gains American troops had made after their disappointing defeat by the Germans at Kasserine Pass (February 1943). Another fortunate occurrence was that hundreds of British Matilda tanks and American Shermans had been able to push back the smaller force of German Panzers. Dad, who at the start of the desert campaign was concerned that the power and weight of the Panzers would place the lighter Shermans at a disadvantage, was relieved that the large number of Allied tanks used in the campaign made up for their smaller size. The Allies defeated Axis forces in Tunisia in May 1943, thus spelling the end of Hitler's dream of access to the

Suez Canal. Uncle Bob Shaw, who was serving with the 3rd Infantry Division in North Africa that spring, saw firsthand the downfall of Rommel's troops, as he writes in *Shaw Clan*:

"What a sight as the Africa Corps surrendered by marching their units, without guards, under their officers, to the POW camps." Considering the discipline Rommel had enforced on his elite corps, it's not surprising that they surrendered in such a controlled way. When the war later progressed to France, Irwin Rommel would again be a force to reckon with, as would the powerful German Panzer and Tiger tanks.

Uncle Bob and his 3rd Infantry Division went to Italy after leaving North Africa. Mussolini's arrest in July 1943 ended the power of Italy's Fascist regime, but, as the division would soon find out, fighting the Germans there was intense.

CHIEF OF STAFF HOWARD PECKHAM SPEAKING TO HIS FORT KNOX OFFICERS

In Kentucky, meanwhile, our moving day approached, and I received some bad news about it: Dad ruefully told me we couldn't bring Willie to Washington. Noticing the onset of my tears, he said, "We'll make sure he gets a good new home." Like fish propelled forward in a river, thousands of workers had been swept to Washington, so he explained that it would take us time to find a place to live. The day before we left, a carload of soldiers came to pick up Willie, and a bit later we learned he had become a mascot of their unit. I felt much better. Soon thereafter, my father drove us away from a friendly small town and towards a city where newcomers often lived in lonely anonymity.

COMBAT COMMANDER HOWARD PECKHAM

JACOB DEVERS BEING GREETED BY SENIOR OFFICERS (L TO R) BREWER, NEWTON, PECKHAM, AND RYAN: CAMP CAMPBELL, 1942

Chapter 5

Petroleum, Congress, and the U. S. Army

Any addition to our gasoline supply and our oil supply is of the utmost value.

— LT. GEN. BREHON B. SOMERVELL

UPON OUR ARRIVAL IN WASHINGTON, my parents' first task was to find a house that would meet their needs and tight budget.

Howard Peckham was not one of those officers who before the war sought a wealthy bride in order to give lavish parties and show off an expensively dressed wife. Some officers, especially new West Point graduates, were rumored to have done that. Although the financial success enjoyed by my mother's maternal grandfather Joseph Davis had enabled her family to live in luxury for a while, he lost his fortune long before my parents were married.

She did bring into her marriage an understanding of military social customs, however, as well as the resiliency and adaptability required to move frequently from place to place. Also, she had learned well from both her mother and stepfather the art of entertaining military officers and their wives, and she was aware of the need to observe correct protocol. Her military background became particularly helpful in socially conscious Washington.

Nonetheless, it didn't help my parents with their house-hunting efforts. On the army posts where we had previously lived, we resided in government-supplied housing. Although Fort Lesley J. McNair, located in a woodsy area adjacent to the Potomac, had officers' quarters, they were insufficient to fill the demand. The same was true of Fort Myer on the Virginia side of the Potomac, with its stately senior officers' quarters on a bluff overlooking the river. Not only was official army housing free, residents on army posts could shop for groceries at a nearby commissary and buy toiletries and many other items at the post exchange (PX). It's no wonder military housing was a popular commodity.

As a temporary solution, Dad suggested that we live in the small town of Falls Church, Virginia, which was within commuting distance of Washington. In those days, the town enjoyed a quiet, bucolic atmosphere, and a house was available there that my parents liked.

To get to the city each day, my father planned to drive through the Virginia suburbs and then across Key Bridge, one of the stately bridges that span the Potomac. He would take Howie and me with him, dropping us off at our respective schools near Georgetown—Gordon Junior High for me and Western High for my brother, the school from which he would eventually graduate. Dad would then drive to his job. We all agreed that it might be fun to reside in a country environment for a while, close to nature, so the idea of living in Falls Church was appealing.

"I hope you don't mind taking care of my cat," the owner said when we came to sign the lease. She was a thin, chain-smoking author who planned to travel for several months to do research for her next book. I believe she had lived alone in the house.

"Oh, no, that's fine," my father assured her. Howie and I really missed Willie, our cat in Hopkinsville, so we looked forward to taking care of a substitute.

As if the name Alice weren't unusual enough for a cat, this one's name was *Mister* Alice. "I added the 'Mister' to his name when I discovered she was a he," the owner explained. He wasn't neutered, and after we moved in, we learned that he was far from housebound. Every morning Mister Alice would leave the house to wander far and wide, perhaps in search of a new girlfriend or two. We sometimes feared we would never see him again, but he always reappeared at dinnertime.

In September I had to put aside thoughts of Mister Alice's wanderings and my Nancy Drew books, which I had voraciously read while lying barefooted on the couch that summer. Classes were starting for Howie and me, so our schedule on weekday mornings became hectic. After a quick breakfast, he and I would hurry out the door and jump into the car. Dad would then drive us to our schools and then continue on to his job.

For Dad, September would present new challenges related to his work in the Quartermaster General's office as Director of the Fuels and Lubricants Division. It would also take him inside the Senate Office Building and, hence, face-to-face with several of its august occupants. "I'll be spending time in the building where the senators preside over many of their hearings," Dad explained. "The topic of discussion is a project in Canada."

Known as the Canol project, for "Canadian oil," the project concerned an oil pipeline near the Yukon Territory, my mother's birthplace. The contractor was Bechtel-Price-Callahan. (On one occasion after the war, my father and Stephen Bechtel, Jr., president of the Bechtel Corporation and grandson of its original owner, lunched together at Trader Vic's in Oakland and discussed "the Canol project days.") The project was supported by then-Lieutenant General Brehon Somervell, Dad's tough boss from his WPA days, who submitted a directive on its behalf in 1942.

The U.S. Army and the War Department were in support of General Somervell's position and were convinced that oil products from this resource, in addition to their importance for national security, were needed to facilitate construction of an Alaskan highway. Secretary of War Henry Stimson was in favor of the project right from the beginning. He expressed this favorable attitude in a letter he wrote in May 1942 to Standard Oil of California:

> As a defense measure, our Government has decided to develop the oil resources at Norman, District of McKenzie, Canada, to

construct and operate a pipe line between that point and
Whitehorse, the Yukon, and to construct and operate a
refinery to produce 100-octane gasoline and other petroleum
products at Whitehorse, the Yukon. The products of this
refinery are needed for military use in that region.

He went on to say that consultants from Standard Oil should
be made available "to the officers of the United States and to the
designers of the facility." He wanted the wheels to turn quickly, it
seems, because he requested that these gentlemen be made
available "without delay."

The Secretary of the Interior, Harold Ickes, didn't fully
endorse the project back then, and he certainly didn't want to
rush into it. His reluctance is shown in exhibits produced at the
hearings, including two letters addressed to Mr. Stimson: the first,
dated June 3, 1942, admonishes the Secretary of War for not
consulting his office "before authorization of the project." The
second, dated less than three weeks later—June 22—discusses
"the hazards of the pipeline." It didn't help the situation that one
of these two strongly opinionated men, Henry Stimson, was a
Republican; the other, Harold Ickes, was a Democrat.

The Canol project did proceed, however. On September 11,
1943, Congressional hearings were begun for the purpose of
securing more money for the project. My father was called in to
testify before Congress on behalf of the U.S. Army. Other military
officers who would testify included Brehon B. Somervell, chief
supporter of the project.

The reputation of another man, though, stimulated Howard
Peckham's curiosity. "I've heard he's a tough interrogator," he
told us one evening at dinner. His comment concerned the
chairman of the committee investigating the National Defense
Program at the Canol hearings. The person assigned this job was
owlish faced and wore rimless glasses and, as someone once said,
he looked "more like an accountant than a senator."

This "accountant" of course was the senator from Missouri,
Harry S. Truman, who would soon become Vice President of the

United States in the next election, and later the President. His handling of investigations of the National Defense Program had no small part in ensuring that his benign, angular face and forthright manner would become well known in Washington's political circles. When he was in charge, he was well prepared. To avoid taking center stage too often, however, he let other senators dominate.

On the first day that my father walked up the steps to the Senate Office Building, where the hearings would be held, he noticed that the leaves on the surrounding trees were turning yellow and that the sky above the building was often "bright blue and as clear as spring water." No matter where he was, my father always seemed to be aware of nature's handiwork, as a result of his boyhood on a farm in New England.

My father was thoroughly briefed on the events that had transpired back when the project first started, but he did not officially become chief of the Fuels and Lubricants Division until the fall of 1943, when he succeeded Brigadier General William Covell as director of the division. Julius Amberg, special assistant to the Secretary of War, formally introduced my father to the subcommittee that had convened the hearings:

> MR. AMBERG. I may say that General Covell, who has been the Chief of the Fuels and Lubrication [Lubricants] Division of the Quartermaster Corps, is leaving for overseas and will not be in town after tonight. If you have any questions particularly for him, you think you might wish to ask him, I would appreciate your doing it tonight. He will be succeeded by General Peckham, who is here now.

Several pairs of curious eyes turned to look at my father, who would now be under scrutiny. My father was of the opinion that the project was important for national security, as did other U.S. Army representatives. They believed they had the proper facts to support their point of view. General Brehon Somervell was particularly insistent that it not be abandoned.

Serving on the Congressional committee investigating the Canol project, named the Truman Committee after its soon-to-be famous chairman, were some well-known senators: Tom Connally of Texas, James Mead of New York, Mon Wallgren of Washington, Carl Hatch of New Mexico, Harley Kilgore of West Virginia, Homer Ferguson of Michigan, Harold Burton of Ohio, Joseph Ball of Minnesota, and Owen Brewster of Maine.

The senators needed to know some valuable technical information, so they didn't hesitate to admit their lack of technical expertise. At a critical session on October 26, 1943, Senator Homer Ferguson of Michigan, a silver-haired former judge with distinctively dark eyebrows, wanted to know the length of a certain road in Canada. While enforcing his usual penetrating style, he asked my father that question, as well as one concerning the cost to drill a particular oil well:

SENATOR FERGUSON. How long is that?

GENERAL PECKHAM. The scale of this map is 1 inch, 200 miles.

SENATOR FERGUSON. The $290,000 is a certain percentage of $5,800,000?

GENERAL PECKHAM. Five percent.

Both answers came quickly. As I often discovered during our many long trips by car while I was growing up, there was no faster or better map reader than Howard Peckham. Before we took off to a new home, he would spread out a map on the car's hood and carefully study our route. We never had to worry about getting lost or arriving someplace late; inevitably, we arrived on time wherever we were headed, whether it was to our ultimate destination or some tourist spot along the way.

Answers to mathematical problems came easily to him, also, and I recall that he and I would occasionally sit in tall straight-backed chairs pulled up to our Governor Winthrop mahogany desk in the corner of the living room, where he patiently helped me with my math homework. At this brightly polished desk, my father also devoted time occasionally to his only hobby during the war—collecting stamps. I can recall the intense way he leaned over his albums while holding a large magnifying glass and peering at the information on a newly acquired stamp for his collection.

In addition to giving technical answers verbally, my father gave the committee pertinent information in written form. The full text of a memorandum he wrote was entered as an exhibit prior to the committee's adjournment one day. Rudolph Halley, Executive Assistant to Chief Counsel, and Herbert Friedlich, a representative from the Office of the Under Secretary of War, discussed it first:

COLONEL FRIEDLICH. May we have the letter, the memorandum? I would like to get it in the record here.

MR. HALLEY. Which memorandum is that?

COLONEL FRIEDLICH. The one I just gave you, the memorandum of November 19 on the subject Canol project, signed by Brig. Gen. H. L. Peckham. May that be an exhibit?

MR. HALLEY. Surely.

SENATOR FERGUSON. It will be put in the record.

The memo was filled with technical details and addressed to Herbert Friedlich of the Office of the Under Secretary of War, Room 3E739 at the Pentagon. It was marked Exhibit 1104 and entered into the permanent record.

A major point my father had written in the memo was that the Whitehorse Refinery, which was then under construction, would possess the necessary capacity to produce 100-octane gasoline, a product that was much needed in the various theaters of operation. In the following words, he explained how this product could be created:

> The refinery is comprised of two stages. The first stage will produce basic straight-run naphtha and unsaturated hydrocarbons; the second stage converts these unsaturated hydrocarbons into high-octane blending alkylates. By mixing these aviation gasoline products of the two stages and by adding 4 cubic centimeters of tetraethyl lead per gallon, it is possible to produce 100-octane gasoline.

Before the hearings ended, my father took advantage of the nice autumn weather to take us on our first major sightseeing tour of Washington. On a bright October weekend, he drove Mother, Howie, and me slowly throughout the city in one of the Chevrolets he bought over the years.

The city's many trees were gorgeous. They were ablaze with lively fall colors, as if they had been splashed with orange, yellow, and red paint. "Nature's bounty is quite impressive here," my father remarked. Even more impressive, at least to me, were the famous monuments and buildings.

When we drove by the Washington Monument, I stuck my head out the car window and craned my neck to get a good look at it. The tall pillar looked as thin as a fence post, and it seemed to touch the clouds. I felt lightheaded while my father drove around Dupont Circle, one of the complex circles in the city from which streets radiate like spokes in a tire.

A statue of Henry Wadsworth Longfellow, whose lyrical verses I would one day read in high school, sat in a small square nearby. The poet's furrowed brow and brooding posture made me think about the gloom that overcame wartime Washington once the sun had set. At night, the famous buildings and beautiful monuments seemed like dark shadows cast against an even darker sky. In my geography books, photographs had shown them to be basking in the glow of floodlights.

My father explained the reason for this dichotomy. "That's how Washington used to look at night, before Pearl Harbor Day." Then Dad said, "Because of wartime energy conservation policies, President Roosevelt has directed that unnecessary lights be turned off." The most famous floodlight of all, the one that had illuminated the Capitol building for such a long time, was turned off soon after the President's address to Congress on December 8, 1941, in which he had spoken about the bombing of Pearl Harbor and its consequences.

Before the start of World War II, Washington was a sleepy southern city—actually more like a small town. Pearl Harbor changed all that. People began moving to Washington from all over the country to take advantage of the need for government workers, and their families often came with them. This caused more and more cars to arrive, causing bigger traffic jams. In order to widen the shady streets to make room for the increasing traffic, a number of Washington's famous old trees along the sidewalks were roughly torn out, as if someone had ordered that they be punished for impeding the war effort.

The sightseeing tour, which ended when darkness enveloped the city, had been educational for Howie and me, and it provided a respite for my father from the heavy responsibilities of his job. For example, a few weeks later, Senator Harry Truman requested that a conference take place so that matters relating to the Canol project could be fully discussed.

My father would need to be fully prepared for that meeting, which occurred on December 9, 1943, according to *Army Service Forces Canol Project, Historical File RG 160.*

Among the approximately twelve attendees were Secretary of War Stimson, in whose office the conference took place; Harold Ickes, Petroleum Administrator for War; Ralph Davies, Deputy Petroleum Administrator for War; Julius Amberg, Special Assistant to Secretary Stimson; Donald M. Nelson of the War Production Board; and Howard Peckham, Director of the Fuels and Lubricants Division.

When the conference ended, my father was confident that he had effectively presented the army's point of view. Author Stephen J. Randall describes the conference further in a footnote to his fine book *United States Foreign Oil Policy Since World War I.* On page 195 of that same book, Randall writes that even though the military supported a strong oil policy, "there was a reluctance to see a major injection of government into the private sector." Then he writes these words about Dad:

> Brigadier General H.L. Peckham, for example, director of the fuels and lubricants division of the Quartermaster Corps, commented to the secretary of war [in a memo] that the department's view had supported a "frank discussion" on areas of potential Anglo-American friction. . . .

Even though my father believed that the United States should have a reasonable amount of control over petroleum sources abroad, in order to ensure its security, he also was cognizant of the need to maintain good relationships with foreign countries.

The red and gold leaves of autumn had long-since fallen from Washington's deciduous trees when, on December 20, 1943, my father's presence at the Congressional hearings finally ended. Now the skies were often steely gray instead of bright blue.

While my father was immersing himself in his office work, my mother and I prepared for the holidays. First, we did our Christmas shopping at the Hecht Company and Woodward & Lothrop department stores in downtown Washington, along with hordes of other people. Then we put a wreath on the door, a pinecone centerpiece on the dining room table, and a couple of big red bows on the fireplace mantel.

The customary nighttime illumination that had been turned off at the start of the war was particularly missed during the holiday season, lending an almost eerie effect to the sky in Washington. At the end of one long day, after darkness had fallen and my father had walked out of the Senate Office Building, he looked over at the darkened Capitol dome across Constitution

Avenue. "It seemed almost invisible against the dark sky," he told Mother and me. The air outside had been quite chilly, adding to the stark atmosphere.

On the evening the hearings ended, he strung lights on our fresh evergreen tree, which stood against the wall opposite the fireplace. Then Howie, Mother, and I hung bright ornaments on its green boughs, accompanied by Christmas carols emanating from our tall, wooden radio.

Dad seemed relaxed on Christmas Eve and in the days that followed, not only because he was enjoying the holiday season, but because he no longer had to face the Truman Committee.

The Committee tried hard to force abandonment of the Canol project, primarily because of economic reasons, but U.S. Army representatives, General Brehon Somervell in particular, worked diligently to represent their opposite viewpoints effectively. The army prevailed over the committee in these hearings and won its case for more funds for the project.

The dawn of a new year brought American families, including ours, back from the joy of the Christmas season to the grim reality of war. When Uncle Bob left for North Africa, his wife Bunny— the blonde and dimpled former Bernice Daniel—moved into the Colonial Village apartment of his parents in Arlington. In late January she learned that he had landed at Anzio with his 3rd Infantry Division and would now be continuing through Italy with the division. My parents were glad she was living with my grandparents and was also situated near us during the stressful months that Bob was in combat in North Africa and Italy.

A few days after we got the news about Uncle Bob, my father learned that General Dwight D. Eisenhower had just been appointed Supreme Commander of Allied forces in Europe. His appointment was a sure indication that plans for the D-Day invasion were now being intensified and that employees in the Fuels and Lubricants Division would be working longer hours and under greater pressure.

For Mamie, General Eisenhower's wife, the news of his appointment as Supreme Commander meant that she would be spending many lonely months in her Washington apartment. She had already known her share of grief. The Eisenhowers lost their first child, Doud Dwight, to scarlet fever at age four. Now their only other child, John, was a cadet at West Point. No one knew then when the war would end, so Mamie probably feared he might be sent into combat.

My parents were at this point looking at houses for rent in the city. Their search for one with a reasonable monthly rent as well as a good address finally bore fruit in March 1944, after we had been living in Falls Church for eight months. We were ready to say goodbye to Mister Alice and his owner. Because my father's workload would soon increase, he looked forward to living closer to his office. Our house at 3108 Cathedral Avenue was typical of those in the northwest part of Washington—a two-story brick colonial, with a small front yard divided directly in the middle by a no-nonsense, straight sidewalk leading to the front door.

Located on both sides of the front steps were trimmed, symmetrically placed bushes. To the right off the entry hall was a large living room that led to a sunroom, where the movers carefully placed our piano. My mother would spend much time there in the future. I can still picture her seated on the piano bench while she played and sang *Trees*, a song by Joyce Kilmer. It was a favorite of Dad's, and he enjoyed hearing her lilting soprano voice while she sang that song and others that he liked. In the months to come listening to her singing helped him get his mind off the war for a while, especially because the sunroom was furnished with a comfortable and cheerfully upholstered chair in which he usually sat.

The other rooms in the house consisted of a dining room and kitchen to the left of the entry hall and four upstairs bedrooms. The smallest of those bedrooms served as a den for my brother, who was a conscientious student. A long outdoor staircase, under which I would hold tea parties for my dolls in the summer, led to the backyard from the kitchen.

After the moving men left, we unpacked the dishes, silver, and mementos that had been in storage. It seemed to take forever.

My parents examined their favorite mahogany side tables and decided they would have to be refinished. They bore the visible nicks and scratches of too many moves. Unlike the southern army posts where we had lived for many years, household help in Washington was expensive and scarce; therefore, Mother didn't want to hire a maid. Because dust was scattered everywhere, we all pitched in to get the house in good shape.

Near the end of March, the yellow forsythia began to bloom beautifully on Cathedral Avenue. Spring then revealed all its glory, and near the end of April the city became a riot of color. The buds on the cherry trees encircled around the Tidal Basin burst open and exposed pink-colored petals, as did the dogwood trees—except for those whose petals were bright white. The purple azalea blossoms were my father's favorites among the city's spring flowers. The warmer weather brought our neighbors outside more often, whom my father would greet cheerfully as he strolled down Cathedral Avenue on weekends. "It's a good day for gardening, isn't it?" he would say as they puttered among their tulips and daffodils.

A well-respected Presbyterian minister was one of those neighbors. Peter Marshall, a Scottish immigrant known for his thought-provoking sermons at New York Avenue Presbyterian Church, where he was pastor, lived next door to us with his wife, Catherine, and only child, Peter John.

Little Peter John, a blond boy with a face like a cherub, often came over to our yard to talk to us. We pampered him not only because he was born in 1940 and was much younger than Howie and I were, but because we learned that his mother had been sick with tuberculosis ever since he was three years old. He often seemed lonely. Fortunately, Tennessee-born Catherine recovered, and in 1947 Peter Marshall was elected to the prestigious job of Chaplain of the Senate.

Down the street from us at 3000 Cathedral Avenue was Woodley, the large estate where Secretary of War Stimson lived. It was a beautiful property, filled with big magnolia trees and ancient elms. The southern colonial house, built in 1806, was situated on a hilltop and commanded a view as far as Rock Creek Park. It was one of Washington's historic mansions, and four presidents had used it as a summerhouse. Prominent dignitaries were frequent guests at the home, and journalists were often invited to dine with Mr. Stimson. His lawn was kept emerald green by sprinklers that often whirred loudly on hot days. Although my father attended meetings with the Secretary of War and corresponded with him, his work kept him so occupied that he had little time to keep up with what was happening at the Stimson estate or with other neighbors.

Dad's transfer to the Quartermaster Corps during the war brought him into one of the War Department's oldest supply agencies, which traced its origin to June 16, 1775. Its mission was to provide broad services to troops, from Revolutionary days onward.

In modern times, Quartermaster Corps laboratories were established, where scientific and technological skills were applied to enhance the effectiveness of all kinds of military supplies, from soldiers' olive-drab uniforms to gasoline cans.

For the purpose of its overall fuel planning, the Fuels and Lubricants Division acquired knowledge of current petroleum production in the United States and throughout the world. It procured petroleum products and issued them where needed. It also did valuable research on equipment and developed suitable containers to hold petroleum products. All the theaters of operation relied on its development, procurement, allocation, and research activities. In *Fuels for Global Conflict*, author Erna Risch describes another task of the division:

> The Director of the Division acted as deputy to the Commanding General, ASF [Army Service Forces], in his capacity as a member of the Army-Navy Petroleum Board [ANPB]. Since that Board was an agency of both the Army and the Navy, this third level at which the Division operated was the level of the Joint Chiefs of Staff. . . .

Through the ANPB, the army kept in touch with the navy in regard to procuring petroleum. The board also represented the military forces of the United States in matters concerning the British government. As a member of this board and deputy to the commander of the ASF, my father stood shoulder to shoulder on petroleum issues with General Brehon Somervell. They were united when dealing with the War and Navy Departments and with the irascible Petroleum Administrator for War Harold Ickes, who concurrently served as Secretary of the Interior. (Much to his credit, the heavy-jawed Mr. Ickes established effective policies for the wartime use and conservation of petroleum.)

In addition to serving the ANPB, Dad was War Department Liaison Officer for Petroleum. He worked on his combined functions in a temporary building where the Quartermaster General's office was located, just outside Fort McNair.

There was no scarcity of personnel to work in offices such as my father's. Office workers were pouring into the city all the time, especially young women from country towns who came to work as secretaries. If they had no activities planned at the end of their long workdays, the young women went home to inevitably cramped apartments. Sharing of homes and apartments was a necessity in overpopulated Washington, as amusingly depicted in the World War II movie *The More the Merrier.*

In April 1944, a dispute arose among representatives of the War, Navy, and Interior Departments relating to exploration of oil in Alaska. Secretary of the Interior Ickes felt an executive order was unnecessary, because subsoil and mineral rights in the Wide Bay area were under his jurisdiction and not the navy's. Oil exploration was greatly important to my father, but where and how to explore for this much-needed commodity was sometimes disputed among various departments.

Because of possible legal repercussions, my father believed it necessary to intervene in this dispute via a memo to the Joint Chiefs of Staff. As Erna Risch writes in *Fuels for Global Conflict,* he gave this recommendation:

In a memorandum, Brig. Gen. H. L. Peckham, Director of Fuels
and Lubricants Division, to Joint Chiefs of Staff, 12 April 1944,
recommended that competent legal opinion be sought to determine
the issues involved.

The same book describes a decision my father and Brehon
Somervell made in May to help the War Department and the
Department of the Interior reach a compromise in Alaska:

In a conference between the Commanding General, ASF, and
the Director of the Fuels and Lubricants Division, a decision was
made to divide the project, with the War Department undertaking
the operations at Wide Bay as previously agreed and the
Department of the Interior carrying out the geological, geophysical,
and other exploratory projects proposed for the other areas of
Alaska.

When the Alaska oil-exploration item was inserted on the
appropriations bill of the War Department, the pro-exploration
officials from that department held their breath in anticipation of
its acceptance. Congress had the last word, however. The item
was disapproved, and the War Department temporarily had to
abandon its search for oil in Alaska. Dad was disappointed, as was
Brehon Somervell.

Shortly after Pearl Harbor, the American economy began
changing from civilian pursuits to war production, like a
chameleon responding to a crisis by changing its colors. Many
new civilian agencies were created, such as the Office of Price
Administration (OPA). However, President Roosevelt found that
he couldn't rely solely on civilians. He desperately needed the
military's help not only to fight the battles, but also to procure
and allocate supplies efficiently and get the tanks and airplanes
built correctly.

Along with the civilian workers who flooded the city, there
was an influx of military personnel. More and more members of
the armed forces were ordered away from various army posts

and navy bases throughout the United States to work in the city's military agencies. Their presence was noticeable everywhere. You could see armed military guards standing as straight as tree trunks at the entrances to the most sensitive wartime agencies, such as those related to army intelligence. On cold winter days, army guards wore heavy olive-drab overcoats for protection from the elements. You could also see uniformed personnel scurrying to their jobs in the mornings along with hordes of civilians.

In regard to rationing of supplies during World War II, President Roosevelt stressed that military needs must be foremost in people's minds. After the United States entered the war, rubber was the first item to be rationed. The military needed it for its tanks, trucks, and other equipment, so Americans were asked to take their old tires to collection bins.

The military forces also needed various kinds of metal. I recall that Dad complimented my patriotism when I showed him a big, round aluminum ball I had made by squeezing empty wrappers from Juicy Fruit gum (my favorite brand) into silvery wads and pressing them one after the other into the growing ball. Later, I tossed the ball into a neighborhood collection bin.

Of course the military needed a tremendous amount of fuel. Mindful of his duty to set a good example for other citizens, my father was especially conscientious about conserving gasoline. He insisted that our family give up unnecessary drives. Our Chevrolet sedan had a gasoline-rationing sticker glued to its windshield, as did all other American family vehicles.

Among its other supply tasks, the Quartermaster Corps determined petrol, oil, and lubricant requirements of the United States ground forces, which were coordinated with those of the Army Air Forces and the U.S. Navy. (The United States Air Force was not a separate force until 1947.) The army, known for its fondness for acronyms, referred to these fuels and lubricants as POL.

There was an intricate chain of command on POL matters, which started in the office of President Franklin Roosevelt, the Commander in Chief of all the Armed Forces. Even though

President Roosevelt badly needed the help of the military in order to run the war smoothly, and relied on the chiefs of staff of the various branches to relay information to him, he made sure that military agencies were maintained under the direction of civilian departments, such as the Office of War Mobilization (OWM). The Secretary of the Interior, Harold Ickes, had ultimate authority over the military in regard to petroleum matters. Nevertheless, in regard to expedient decisions, exceptions were made. Risch notes this in *Fuels for Global Conflict:*

> Nothing . . . was deemed to limit in any way the authority of the War and Navy Departments to initiate or carry out directly without review or approval by the Administrator [Ickes] any action relating to petroleum or the petroleum industry which either Department considered a matter of military necessity or expediency and of such urgency as to require secret disposition.

The Fuels and Lubricants Division was fortunate to get highly experienced personnel on board, such as oil executives who joined the U.S. Army and then worked for the division. "Several of them had to undergo rigorous physical training to meet military standards," Dad once told me, adding, "It was sometimes quite a sight to see them struggling through the mud and other adverse conditions in order to meet the physical requirements." Yet by securing these knowledgeable people, the army was able to obtain "the benefit of every sound practice known to the American oil industry," as reported by the author of *Fuels for Global Conflict*. That book also describes the broad mission of the division:

> It directed the purchase, inspection, storage, issue, and distribution of all petroleum products, solid and gaseous fuels, and their containers, for which the [Office of the Quartermaster General] OQMG had procurement responsibility. . . . Thus the estimating of petroleum requirements for the entire United States

Army throughout the world, except petroleum used in aircraft, became the responsibility of the Fuels and Lubricants Division.

Although my father's division didn't estimate petroleum requirements for aircraft, it did estimate such requirements for Army Air Force (AAF) ground equipment. Huge requisitions from Dwight Eisenhower and from commanders in other theaters such as the Pacific came into the Fuels and Lubricants Division.

To escape temporarily from wartime pressures such as those mentioned above, and to enjoy the company of his family, my father would sometimes take us out for dinner at popular local restaurants. In wartime Washington, they were often noisy and packed with customers, and people stood in long lines waiting for tables. Nevertheless, we believed that the wait was worth it. My favorites were the Lotus, a Chinese restaurant where I celebrated my thirteenth birthday, and the Balalaika on Connecticut Avenue, where we listened to someone play a three-string, triangular-shaped musical instrument while we ate Russian pancakes.

(*LEFT*) THE ESTATE OF SECRETARY OF WAR STIMSON ON CATHEDRAL AVENUE (*RIGHT*) TWO WIVES, A MOTHER, AND A DAUGHTER ANXIOUSLY AWAITING THE RETURN OF THE SHAW BROTHERS FROM WAR (L TO R) BUNNY, BELL, VALERIE, AND ALTHEA, 1944

My father especially liked O'Donnell's Sea Grill on E Street, where he would order the New England specialties he loved, such as clam chowder and lobster. It was here that my parents, my brother, and I were dinner guests of Milo Boulton, the master of ceremonies for the CBS radio program *We the People,* a weekly show in which people came forward with stories of broad human interest. Mr. Boulton took us out to dinner as a way of expressing his appreciation to my father for joining the "impressive guest roster" (according to the press release) participating in the broadcast of April 23, 1944.

In a private room at the Wardman Park Hotel, my father had spoken into the microphone that evening about his work with the ANPB, a topic that was probably of particular interest to *We the People* at that time. Gulf Oil Company sponsored the show. His speech concerned the amount of gasoline required and used by U.S. Army vehicles in the European Theater. In particular, he talked about the gasoline needed on one day to perform a successful raid on German soil.

(LEFT) JEEP WITH A FIVE-GALLON GASOLINE CAN ATTACHED
(RIGHT) SKETCH OF MY FATHER, 1944

One of the other guests was entertainer Bob Hope. When we listened to a recording of the broadcast sometime later, I was delighted to hear him acknowledge Dad's presence on the program. (Mr. Hope recorded his portion in Hollywood, so we didn't have an opportunity to meet him.) Bob Hope, whom my father greatly admired for his tireless travels to military bases worldwide, spoke with affection about the military personnel he had met and entertained both in the United States and overseas.

Meanwhile, April and May witnessed the finalizing of plans for an upcoming event that would provide a major turning point in the war. On June 6, 1944, the U.S. Army, under the direction of General Dwight D. Eisenhower, invaded Normandy. D-Day would turn out to be one of the biggest days in history, and the Fuels and Lubricants Division had been anticipating it. My father was pleased that everything went according to plan on D-Day and the days immediately following it, as far as gasoline was concerned.

INFORMATION FROM CBS ABOUT DAD'S RADIO ADDRESS, 1944

As noted in *Fuels for Global Conflict*, before any vehicle was transported to Omaha and Utah Beaches, it was filled with a full tank of gas and carried an extra supply of gas in five-gallon cans. For example, jeeps carried two full five-gallon cans. Other vehicles, such as weapons carriers and small trucks, carried a larger quantity of extra gasoline in five-gallon cans. The proper amount of fuel for tanks and half-tracks also was determined in advance, to ensure that there was enough to last approximately six days. Also, as planned, gasoline reserves were on hand at the end of the invasion. Good fuel planning obviously played a big role in the success of D-Day and its aftermath.

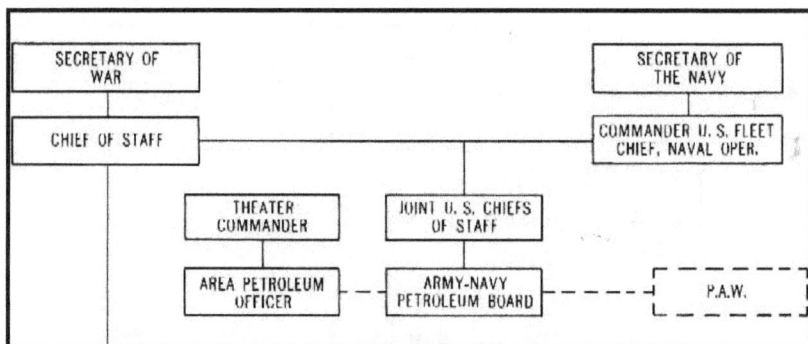

A DIAGRAM OF ANPB RELATIONSHIP TO THE JOINT CHIEFS OF STAFF, 1944
(U.S. Army Photo)

VEHICLES ARRIVING ON BOATS AND ROLLING ONTO SHORE: NORMANDY ON THE DAY AFTER D-DAY (U.S. Army Photo)

Chapter 6

Washington After D-Day

We promise we will get oil to our fighters on all fronts, at whatever costs, and at whatever sacrifices at home.

— HAROLD ICKES

RIGHT AFTER D-DAY, an adequate supply of gasoline, which Roland Ruppenthal refers to as "the lifeblood of modern armies," became a major concern to battlefield commanders in France. "During the late August and September [1944] pursuit of the enemy across France," writes Omar Bradley in *A Soldier's Story*, "gasoline formed the bulk of our tonnage." Indisputably, there was an incredible need for large amounts of fuels and lubricants during World War II. John K. Evans emphasized this need in an article he wrote, which appeared in the May-June 1944 edition of *The Quartermaster Review*:

> An army marches on wheels these days, and without fuels and lubricants those wheels bog down in a morass of despair and ultimate defeat. Even in the First World War it was said that the Allies floated to victory on a sea of oil. But that sea was merely a trickle as compared to the deluge of today.

Already buoyed by reports that the Allies had captured Rome on June 4, thus signifying the end of the Italian campaign, news of the success of the D-Day invasion gave much encouragement to Washington's war-fatigued citizens.

Miss Bertie Backus, the principal of Alice Deal Junior High (my new school), called an assembly soon after the invasion. When the entire student body had assembled, she asked us to pray for the continuing success of our military forces in Europe— and for a speedy end to the war on all fronts.

Near the end of June, several distaff members of the Shaw family began making plans for our annual family reunion, to be held in July. "The children deserve to have fun, and they need to enjoy a break from news about the war," my grandmother, Bell Shaw, reminded her daughters and daughters-in-law when they appeared hesitant about having a wartime reunion. Because of World War II, most of the women's husbands would be absent. But in the end, everyone agreed that in view of our country's D-Day success, and for the children's sake, it was time to resume a happy family tradition.

These gatherings, which my mother's relatives attended *en masse*, were usually held in Rock Creek Park, that green oasis in the heart of Washington, DC, where the grass smelled fragrant and trees as stately as statues provided a welcome relief from the heat. Here my brother, my Shaw cousins, and I would sit with our parents on long picnic benches and eat fried chicken, salads, biscuits, and big slices of fruit pie, food that my mother and aunts had prepared and then packed. More children would be born later, but at that time my Shaw cousins were Fred's daughter Valerie, Bob's daughter Merrily, and Barbara's children Jody, Molly, and Petey. We did have fun, as my grandmother had predicted. We took walks, played games, and ate heartily.

Other benefits were that the women became closer to each other, now that they belonged to a sisterhood of wives whose husbands were absent. And for Granddad Shaw, the day was an opportunity to remind everyone that he was the family patriarch, and that he still had strong shoulders on which they could lean.

Nevertheless, the husbands and fathers were greatly missed. A photograph taken that day shows the wives sitting next to what looks like framed pictures of their uniformed husbands, whose military duties prevented them from joining their wives and children at the gathering. Dad was on a petroleum-related trip to London. Bunny's husband Bob was serving in the European Theater, as was Bob's brother Dan. Frederick "Pete" Hinshaw, Barbara's husband, was serving in the Pacific Theater. (Fred "Buzz" Shaw was stationed in Maryland with the Chemical Corps, so he was able to join his wife Althea and daughter Valerie at the picnic.)

The photograph was a souvenir of the Rock Creek reunion, but it was also a reminder of wartime sacrifices. Additionally, it illustrates one family's rather unique devotion to military service.

For example, two of the men pictured were graduates of West Point: Dad and Pete Hinshaw. Two of the children would eventually graduate from West Point: Howie Peckham and Petey Hinshaw. One man was a retired brigadier general: Granddad Fred Shaw. Another man would eventually retire as a brigadier general: Uncle Bob Shaw. A third man would eventually retire as a major general: Howard Peckham. Also, two of the men rose to the rank of lieutenant colonel in the war: Dan and Buzz Shaw.

In Europe meanwhile, the success of the D-Day invasion was wreaking havoc on the morale of German forces. On July 15, Field Marshall Erwin Rommel, whom Hitler had appointed to command the German Army in France, gave the Führer a status report on the dire situation in France: "Allied troops will charge through Germany's defenses in France within the next few weeks," he declared. Then he added:

> The consequences will be immeasurable. The troops are fighting heroically everywhere, but the unequal struggle is nearing its end. I must beg you to draw the conclusions without delay. I feel it my duty as Commander-in-Chief of the Army Group to state this clearly.

Hitler refused to believe that Germany was on the verge of defeat, even when Erwin Rommel caused unexpected disarray in the command structure when he sustained an injury that month. This necessitated his recuperation in a convalescent hospital and required a replacement to be found for him. His successor was Field Marshal Gunther Von Kluge, who took over Rommel's job in France.

Von Kluge echoed his predecessor's gloomy predictions:

> In spite of intense efforts, the moment has drawn near when this front, already so heavily strained, will break. I consider it my duty to bring these conclusions to your notice. . . . my führer.

Meanwhile, the work of my father's Fuels and Lubricants Division maintained its steady course. Through written guidelines to commanders in the field, the division ensured that soldiers quickly decanted liquid fuel—brought by ocean tankers, rail cars, and trucks to assigned destinations—into fifty-five-gallon drums or five-gallon cans, depending on the need and location. Mostly for practical reasons, the War Department standardized the type of gasoline they used. With few exceptions, this was 80-octane, leaded gasoline.

To supplement the cans and drums in the European Theater, a pipeline system (called the Minor Pipeline) was begun in the area of Utah Beach about a week after D-Day. By mid-July, my father received word that the port of Cherbourg had been cleared, and that construction of the other pipeline system (called the Major Pipeline) would soon be started there. Eventually it would become the backbone of gasoline distribution on the Continent and would run overland from Cherbourg all across central France to Germany.

These pipelines were laid on the ground, or on trestles, and ran from distribution centers. The pipelines had the advantage of permitting gasoline to be sent over rough terrain. Also, they reduced congestion on the roads and carried gasoline over long distances by day or by night, in any kind of weather. On August 12, a flexible pipeline that ran under the English Channel pumped its first liquid ashore in Normandy. This was a British project, which brought gasoline and fuel oil from England to France. After the liquid came ashore, it was decanted and led into overland pipelines.

Especially good news came later that month to the Fuels and Lubricants Division. It was learned that on August 15, a force of mostly French and American troops had landed not far from Cannes. The invasion of southern France had thus begun. This force, the American 6th Army Group, was under the command of then-Lieutenant General Jacob Devers. (While serving in the 12th Armored Division as a combat commander, my father got to know the general and thought him to be an exceptionally capable leader.)

The group's timing couldn't have been better for our troops or worse for the Germans. Right after they learned about the D-Day invasion, German commanders made the mistake of sending many of their troops from the south of France to the country's north, so they could join the fighting up there. When the 6th Army Group started moving inland after arriving in southern France, it became apparent that many enemy soldiers had already left. The group therefore encountered only limited enemy resistance, thus enabling it to capture two important port cities—Marseilles and Toulon—and then quickly continue northward. In the vicinity of Dijon, these troops joined Allied troops who had landed in Normandy and were now traveling eastward towards Germany.

Two weeks later, other good news came to the Fuels and Lubricants when my father was updated about the construction of a portion of the Major Pipeline located twenty-nine miles south of Cherbourg.

A footnote in *The Quartermaster Corps: Operations in the War Against Germany* indicates that the news came to him from Major R. E. Boulter:

> On 16 July [1944] First Army began turning over its POL installations to ADSEC [Advance Section, Communications Zone], which it still regarded as one of its own subordinate units. On 25 July it finally became possible to bring a tanker ship into

Cherbourg, where ADSEC began decanting operations the next day. The first stretch of the Major Pipeline, twenty-nine miles south to La Haye-du-Puits, had already been laid, and on 1 August the first large inland decanting point was opened there. It was manned by three gasoline supply companies and a service company, and was soon decanting 250,000 gallons per day. [9]

[9]Ltr CO 210th QM Bn (M), (Maj R. E. Boulter), to Brig Gen Howard L. Peckham, 24 Aug 44 sub: Facts re Decanting and Depot Opns of QM Depot Q-6 at La Haye-du-Puits.

My father was heartened to receive this report about POL supply and about the good progress that had been made from mid-July to mid-August. In contrast, that was the same period during which Hitler was receiving ominous reports from his underlings about his probable downfall.

Later that month, a triumphant day arrived for France. On August 25 Paris was liberated, and General de Gaulle, leader of the Free French, returned from exile to become president of the Provisional Government. The tall, imposing general led a glorious parade down the Champs Élysées on August 26, which was greeted by smiles and cheers.

A few days later, my parents and other Washingtonians read newspaper stories about the many celebrations that that had occurred in Paris. *"C'est vrai! Nous sommes libre!"* a corpulent man apparently shouted as he ran out of a Montparnasse café. To celebrate the end of German rule, he eagerly hugged and kissed the first person he saw—a spindly elderly lady. Parisians shouted happily as they ran through streets washed by waves of glee.

U.S. Army pipeline engineers in northern France, meanwhile, were too busy to celebrate. The fast speed of the Third Army advance during the last days of August often outdistanced construction of the pipeline, even though the men worked fast and feverishly to put the sections in place. Sometimes they had to stop what they were doing and make repairs to the lines that had already been laid, creating frustrating delays. The lines west of

Alençon, for example, were shut down for repairs on August 29, and First Army was not able to draw gasoline there until September 2. By mid-September, the Major Pipeline, running southeast from Cherbourg, was still not adequate to move bulk POL requirements forward. Roland Ruppenthal writes about this crisis in *Logistical Support of the Armies*:

> At that time, the most advanced of the three pipelines was still twenty miles short of the Seine and was dispensing at Chartres; a second line was dispensing at Domfront; the third (for aviation gasoline) had reached Alençon.

Repairs to broken pipelines had been frustrating for the pipeline engineers, but George Patton encountered a problem concerning restrictions. During the August campaign east of the Seine, General Eisenhower restricted General Patton's Third Army to two thousand tons of gasoline per day. The needs of First Army were considered greater because of its larger size and larger number of armored vehicles. At first, Patton reacted philosophically to the news of his comparatively small ration. Later, when he saw what a problem this would be for Third Army in its efforts to advance, he was visibly upset. In his autobiography, *A Soldier's Story*, General Omar Bradley gives an account of the solutions Patton found to the dilemma:

> Although theoretically immobilized as the result of his scant daily gasoline ration, Patton funneled his driblet of fuel into a few tanks and rolled stubbornly ahead. Within the Third Army he deadlined thousands of vehicles and clamped ironclad conservation measures on the others.

Even though George Patton's thirsty tanks had swallowed up gallon after gallon of what the French called *"le sang rouge de guerre"* (the red blood of war), the above-described ingenuity on his part enabled him to meet the crisis effectively. A less-resourceful leader might not have been so lucky.

Even though the Fuels and Lubricants Division had procured and allocated enough gasoline for the European Theater, getting it from storage locations to the battle areas in time to meet the demand wasn't under the division's control. Possible fires or sabotage necessitated that gasoline storage facilities be situated away from the front lines. Nevertheless, my father sympathized with the affected battle commanders whenever deliveries of gasoline to the front lines were delayed by events beyond their control. Even the Red Ball Express, whose trucks carried supplies across France, couldn't have kept Third Army from running out of gasoline.

In early September, General Eisenhower agreed to increase Third Army's fuel allowance. As far as the outcome of the war is concerned, Roland Ruppenthal points out in *Logistical Support of the Armies* this important and encouraging fact: "POL shortages did not delay the final surrender." Nevertheless, earlier gasoline shortages on the front lines as well as pipeline delays had often been disheartening.

On trips to Europe, my father discussed issues like these with the chief quartermaster, then-Major General Robert Littlejohn, a broad-shouldered, athletic-looking former college football player and graduate of West Point's class of 1908. The meetings overseas were essential to my father's work, but Mother worried whenever he flew to Europe—she had heard about the awful rockets in the sky above London and knew they created a dangerous environment. After one trip, Dad told Howie and me confidentially, "My hotel had good views of the rockets, especially when I watched them from the hotel's rooftop." The news was exciting to us, but we cautiously avoided telling Mother about it.

During the weeks after D-Day, V-weapons were ablaze in the London sky like orange pumpkins in sunny fields. They had been ordered by Adolf Hitler, who was seeking revenge for the heavy Allied bombing of his industrial centers. First to rain on Britain were V1 rockets launched from northern France. In September 1944, when my father was in London, Hitler was already sending V2 rockets to that city. Because the Allies had captured Germany's original launching base in northern France, the Germans had to launch these new rockets from Holland. The V2 succeeded in having a fifty percent success rate by the end of the war, but by then it was too late. The defeated Germans had to leave many of them unused. It seemed that Britain's will to remain undefeated during the war had not only exhausted Germany's Luftwaffe, but had repelled its blitz bombs. And now, Britain was successful in foiling Germany's use of V-weapons.

In Washington, far away from the turmoil in Europe, I settled into a routine of school activities, homework, and family dinners. Dinner-table conversations were relatively formal in Washington, mainly because Dad would inevitably initiate our conversations and introduce topics. "Jeanie, how was school today?" he would ask, as he turned to look in my direction. He would be sitting in a high-backed chair at the head of the table, his eyes focused intently on me. His upper body would be as straight as an arrow, the same posture he had learned to use while dining as a young West Point cadet.

"Fine, Dad," would be my frequent response. Or, I would make a comment or two about certain aspects of my day. Then my father would introduce another topic. I knew he usually had his responsible job on his mind and that the briefcase he brought home every evening was crammed with papers he worked on after dinner, but his serious and rather strict demeanor in those days often made me feel a bit shy. It would never have occurred to me to argue with him about anything.

Many times he brought work home on weekends. On those occasions, Mother and I would often quietly leave the house and board a streetcar that traveled along Wisconsin Avenue in the opposite direction from my school. Georgetown, our destination, was an exclusive area on the verge of becoming an enclave for the well-to-do. Its quaint pastel-colored row houses seemed crowded together like rush-hour passengers in a subway car. We couldn't imagine it at the time, but one day many glamorous Washington socialites would entertain senators and congressmen here in old, lavishly remodeled homes. The area was exclusive then, but not to the extent that it later became. Mother and I would wander through the quaint antique shops and fancy markets, purchase a few small items, and then return home again on the streetcar.

In addition to ensuring that adequate fuel was procured and supplied to the theaters of operation, my father had another priority—making sure that enough gasoline containers were on hand. There were two main types of five-gallon cans. One was called a "jerrican," because it resembled the German version. (A common nickname for Germans was "jerry.") Another type was the "blitz." Dad recognized the need for flexibility, so adjustments to the number of cans needed in the European Theater were made constantly as conditions changed. He also considered the needs of the Pacific Theater (where fifty-five-gallon drums were being used and only a few cans) and requisitions by the other theaters, such as the Mediterranean Theater.

Wherever U.S. Army troops fought, having enough empty five-gallon cans available was a strong necessity. One remedy was to ensure that an adequate supply of reusable cans was on hand. Our troops delivered many of them to collection areas for refilling, but soldiers who were in the midst of battle had little time to deliver empty cans to those areas. To alleviate this problem, the U.S. Army assigned units of American soldiers to collect them. It also obtained the help of European civilians.

In this respect, farmers were especially helpful. They picked up empty cans they found lying near cow pastures and country roads and delivered them to designated places where they could be collected for refilling. The only problem was that some farmers ended up using the cans in their homes, possibly as storage containers for grain and other produce. Thus they gave them up with reluctance.

Young children were probably the best helpers of all. Parents recruited their sons and daughters to pick up empty gasoline cans, and the children probably enjoyed the task. It's easy to imagine boys and girls making a game of collecting them. In France, the Ministry of Education aided American efforts by awarding prizes to those children who were the most successful in picking up empty cans. Additionally, newspapers made appeals to their readers, and announcements were made on radio.

   After civilians picked up the empty cans and turned them over to the U.S. Army, quickly refilling them became an urgent priority. At decanting areas, soldiers would use power dispensers from railroad tank cars to fill the cans, as well as hand-filling methods. German prisoners of war were sometimes instructed to hand-fill the cans, so as to avoid unduly using American soldiers who were needed in combat. To lessen the risk of sabotage, guards closely supervised these prisoners and insisted that the cans be filled in wide-open areas. U.S. Army fire-fighting units were also on hand in case of bombings and subsequent fires.

   In the second half of 1944, when the War Department saw that the Allies were making strong gains in the war, production of new gasoline cans ended. Arrangements were then made to deliver cans manufactured in the United Kingdom directly to American troops in Europe. Roland G. Ruppenthal in *Logistical Support of the Armies* describes an order about which Colonel Carl E. Cummings informed my father:

> The chief quartermaster accordingly placed an order with the British War Office for nearly 4,500,000 cans to be supplied from U. K. manufacture by the end of 1944. Nearly 2,000,000 of them were intended for the air forces with the understanding that they would be turned over to the ground forces after their first trip in accordance with the practice of using them only once for aviation fuel.[37]

[37]Ltr. Cummings to Gen Peckham, 19 Sep 44, sub: Reqmts for 5-Gallon Blitz Cans, USFET 458-11 Cans 1943-45.

   From July 1944 onward, the whole issue of ordering cans required close collaboration between the United States and Britain, as did the matter of gasoline distribution to American units. Civilian agencies of the British government performed the distribution to our troops in the British Isles. The Fuels and

Lubricants Division in Washington dealt closely and frequently with officials in London concerning their cooperative efforts. Gasoline-can distribution was also a matter that my father discussed with General Littlejohn at a meeting they attended in London, which was held in September 1944. Authors Ross and Romanus write in *The Quartermaster Corps: Operations in the War Against Germany* that Dad offered at that time to give 7,000,000 surplus gasoline cans to the general:

> The latter snapped them up eagerly but it appeared that Peckham's figure had been overoptimistic. Littlejohn was willing to settle for 2,000,000 and suggested to General Feldman [the Quartermaster General] and Colonel Evans that the cans might be sent over empty, as filler or deck cargo. This seemed the only promising method of speedy delivery at a time when the QM tonnage allocation was threatened with a drastic cut, and when Littlejohn was trying to increase his imports of winter clothing. . . . But the Area Petroleum Service confirmed the need for 7,000,000 cans, and an official requisition for that quantity was submitted.

As a respite from wartime concerns, my parents attended church services often in Washington. My father particularly liked going to St. John's, the Episcopal church across Lafayette Square from the White House. Although he appreciated his Baptist upbringing and the faith it had instilled in him, he was feeling increasingly drawn to the Episcopal Church. Coming here for services was like attending a social event, due to the friendly conversations people engaged him in afterwards. "So glad you could join us," he would hear.

Everyone wanted to make the military members of the congregation, all wearing their uniforms, feel welcome. In view of their valiant service to America, the reception they received was well deserved.

At some point in November 1944, my father's days as Chief of Staff of the 8th Armored Division returned to the forefront of his thoughts. That's when he learned that the division, which had been through extensive training in the United States, had now joined the fighting in France.

In December, another of his former divisions, the 12th Armored Division, trekked through rugged land while fighting near Weislingen, a city in the Alsatian area of France. "It was a tough winter," Dad said years later about the division's hardships. "The men suffered almost as much from trench foot as from war injuries."

Overall, the progress of the war was becoming more and more encouraging. When the red leaves of autumn 1944 started falling on Washington's sidewalks, there were indications that Nazi Germany was also falling. The Allied armies were pressing forward against the Rhine, but Hitler's army didn't move aggressively towards them in defense. Instead, its discouraged soldiers, who were as tired as the brown leaves in Bavaria's forests, fought weakly in retreat. The roaring tide was turned in favor of the Allies, who now had strong prospects for luxuriating in the warm water of victory.

Although I was glad to hear about the positive war news, my primary interest after I turned thirteen was my social life. In that regard, my parents enrolled me in dancing classes sponsored by the Army and Navy Junior Assembly, which were held on Saturday nights at the Linthicum Hall on O Street. These were hosted by Mrs. Lloyd Shippen and Mrs. Fred Austin, and were intended for military officers' sons and daughters in their early teens. My father was pleased that one of the purposes of the classes was to teach us students "social graces," as well as the latest dance steps. I did reasonably well in both endeavors, but I didn't earn any prizes in either category.

In December of 1944, Fred, Bob, and Dan Shaw enjoyed a memorable reunion in Paris, and their timing couldn't have been better. Uncle Fred, who was stationed in Maryland with the Chemical Corps, happened to be in Paris on an inspection trip. Uncle Bob had seen heavy combat with the 3rd Infantry Division in Italy and France, so his division commander sent him to Paris for well-deserved rest, recuperation, and rehabilitation (RRR). Uncle

Dan, the host of the event, was stationed in Paris with the European Theater of Operations USA Communications Zone (ETOUSA COMZ). His job, aside from its enviable location, brought him some unexpected romance. At an office party one evening, he met an attractive WAC sergeant, Olive "Holly" Holliway, who became his wife after the war.

When a public information officer learned about the Paris reunion of three army-officer brothers, he arranged for an official photograph to be taken of them while they stood on a balcony of Dan's office at ETOUSA COMZ headquarters. Afterwards, the three brothers participated in a bit of Paris nightlife.

At the White House in December 1944, President Franklin Roosevelt thought about his army's advance towards Germany and smiled. He knew full well that after crossing the Rhine, the Allies would wear the crown of victory in Europe. The Third Reich would then become a deserving victim of its own dreams of glory.

The fact that Germany was facing a humiliating defeat was good news for Washingtonians to hear that Christmas season. The bad news was that the German army planned to fight to the bitter end. A battle that began in September 1944 in the Hurtgen Forest, located on the Belgian-German border, continued all the way through December. For American soldiers fighting there, it was a terrible "holiday" season. Sherman tanks had a difficult time pushing their way through dense terrain. Infantry and artillery soldiers fought bitterly in areas thick with trees and without pathways. Combat conditions were truly nightmarish, and there were many casualties.

Sadly, more loss of life was to come. On December 16, 1944, about half a million German soldiers made a surprise attack on our troops in the Ardennes region of Luxembourg and Belgium. Fortunately, Germany's weak strategic intelligence in this battle, the Battle of the Bulge, was no match for the inventive talent of the U.S. Army. The Americans fought hard and managed to secure victory, but at a very high cost. By the time the battle ended at the end of January, nineteen thousand American soldiers had lost their lives.

General Anthony C. McAuliffe, a graduate of the West Point June 1918 class (whom my father had first met when they were cadets), distinguished himself during the Battle of the Bulge. He became temporary commander of the encircled 101st Airborne Division. Under his leadership, the division fought on stubbornly from December 18 until it was rescued on December 26.

When the Germans demanded his surrender, the general's answer was "Nuts!" This single-word laconic reply has become legendary, and it is representative of America's confidence and strength at that juncture.

Early in January, only a few days after city workers had swept New Year's Day confetti off the streets of Washington, General Douglas MacArthur was given command of all American ground forces in Asia. Admiral Chester Nimitz took command of all naval forces. Dad presumed that these two leaders would start to finalize plans for the invasion of Iwo Jima, Okinawa, and possibly Japan—the best prize of all.

For me, the new year provided an opportunity to see some famous Hollywood celebrities in person and collect a few autographs. On a chilly January day I waited patiently at the entrance of the Shoreham Hotel, where some famous stars were staying who had come to celebrate the President's Birthday Ball. This event, at which guests danced in exclusive hotels, such as the Shoreham adjacent to Rock Creek Park, always brought many Hollywood stars to town.

The balls actually started back in the thirties for the purpose of raising money for polio treatment programs and facilities. This subject was close to President Roosevelt's heart, because he, too, had been a victim of the disease. When he was a young man, he swam in a contaminated swimming pool, which left him crippled. He never fully recovered from its debilitating effects. In fact, they even worsened as the war progressed.

In his inaugural address on January 20, a weary-looking President Roosevelt, who had recently been elected to his fourth term in office, reminded Americans that he and they were "passing through a period of supreme test." He resolved that "it is

America's purpose that we shall not fail" and that "we shall work for a just and honorable peace, a durable peace, as today we work and fight for total victory in war." The President deemed that the time had come to meet with Allied leaders, so two conferences were arranged early in 1945.

Malta, a sunny island off the west coast of Africa and a colony of Great Britain, was selected as the location for the first international meeting, to be held in January. Among other officials who arrived for the conference was a group of senior American military officers, who supplied pertinent information to be discussed. Brigadier generals in the group, including Howard Louis Peckham, provided backup support to military attendees above them in rank, such as Brehon Somervell.

The main purpose of the meeting was to discuss strategy for bringing World War II to a satisfactory end. Several topics were discussed, including tentative dates for ending the war with Germany and with Japan. The assurance of an adequate supply of petroleum products overseas was the topic with which my father was the most concerned.

After returning to Washington, Dad described what he had seen during a tour of the island. In a small shop in the old town of Medina, he bought a crocheted doily with the word "Malta" embroidered on it, which he later gave us as a gift. I had it framed, and it still hangs on my wall along with other framed souvenirs that I value highly.

The second conference was held from February 4 to 11 at a resort on the Black Sea. (Like most of the generals who had been at the Malta Conference, my father did not attend.) It was here, at the Yalta Conference on the Crimean Riviera, that Franklin Roosevelt, Winston Churchill, Joseph Stalin, and other Allied leaders gathered to complete agreements relating to postwar concerns. Among these agreements was a declaration that territories liberated from Nazi Germany be permitted to have democratic elections. Because this declaration seemed to be reasonable enough, all three parties agreed to it. At that time, no one would have guessed that Joseph Stalin would betray the countries of Eastern Europe or that the United States would be involved for decades in a Cold War.

Unfortunately for Poland and the Baltic States of Latvia, Lithuania, and Estonia, the declaration never saw the light of day. When the conference ended, Stalin slyly made sure that elections in those Baltic countries and in Poland were rigged in favor of officials of Soviet-controlled parties. Sadly, this betrayal by Stalin opened the door to future Communist domination in Eastern Europe. Throughout most of Europe, it was becoming as clear as Slavic crystal that Stalin could not be trusted.

Washington, in the meantime, temporarily brushed aside the problems Stalin was creating abroad and concentrated instead on America's victories.

FAMILY REUNION IN ROCK CREEK PARK
(L TO R) MARION PECKHAM; HOWARD PECKHAM IN FRAME; BUZZ SHAW; GRANDDAD SHAW; VALERIE SHAW; BELL SHAW; BOB SHAW IN FRAME; ALTHEA SHAW; JODY HINSHAW, BARBARA HINSHAW (HOLDING SON PETEY), AND MOLLY HINSHAW; BUNNY SHAW, JEAN PECKHAM; MERRILY SHAW; PETE HINSHAW IN FRAME; HOWIE PECKHAM, AND DAN SHAW IN FRAME: WASHINGTON, 1944

(LEFT) PART OF MAJOR PIPELINE ON AN IMPROVISED TRESTLE BRIDGE
(RIGHT) CAMOUFLAGED PUMPING STATION NEAR A PIPELINE: FRANCE, 1944

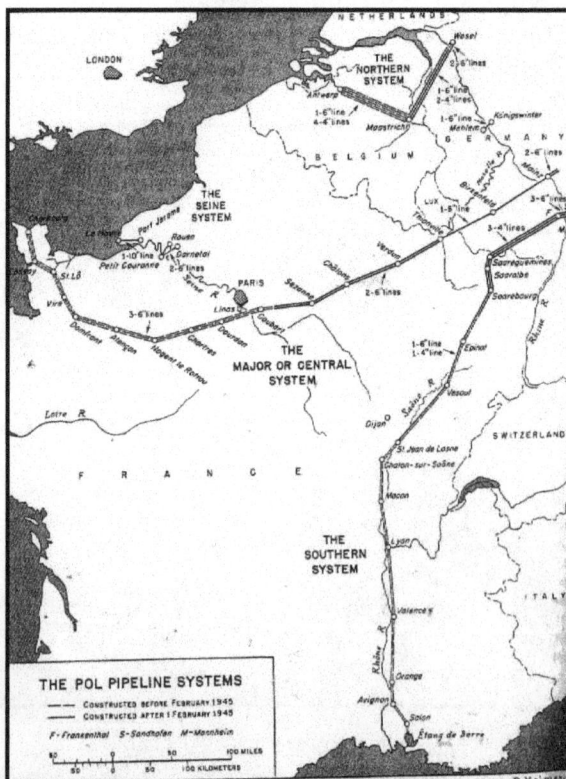

MAP OF THE POL PIPELINE SYSTEMS RUNNING EAST FROM CHERBOURG
AND NORTHEAST FROM SOUTHERN FRANCE, 1944 (U.S. Army Photo)

JEAN WITH DAD AT HER BIRTHDAY DINNER: WASHINGTON, 1944

THE SHAW BROTHERS AT THEIR WARTIME REUNION (L TO R) BOB, BUZZ,
AND DAN: PARIS, 1944

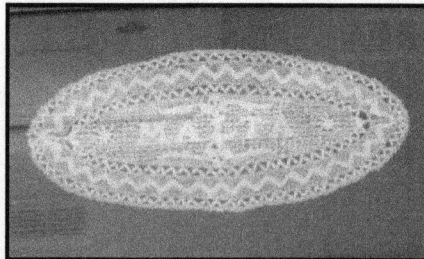

(TOP) MEMO FROM ANPB TO THE JOINT CHIEFS SHOWING TWO COPIES TO DAD, 1944
(BELOW) DOILY THAT DAD BROUGHT HOME FROM THE MALTA CONFERENCE, 1944

Chapter 7

Marching on the Road to Peace

*Among the men who fought on Iwo Jima, uncommon valor
was a common virtue.*

—ADMIRAL CHESTER W. NIMITZ

JUBILANT NAVY DEPARTMENT EMPLOYEES clapped loudly when they learned that American troops had recaptured Bataan and rescued the gaunt, thin survivors of the Death March. That was in February 1945. During the following month, they cheered again when the Marines took Iwo Jima, a small but strategically important island where the Marines had been engaged in a fierce battle. Japan had especially wanted to maintain control of Iwo Jima's airfields, which had now slipped out of its hands like eels slipping out of a boat on Miyako Bay.

Not cheerful at all was the news that my father received in March. It concerned Maurice Rose, who had served with him on General Crittenberger's staff at Fort Benning. Both he and Dad were lieutenant colonels then.

Maurice Rose had made a swift advance to major general during the war, and on March 30 he was commanding the 3rd Armored Division, to which he had transferred. While he was seated in his jeep at the head of a column and leading his division on an attack of a German training center near Paderborn, his driver turned a corner and accidentally ran into the rear of a German tank. The tank commander then opened his turret hatch and, while pointing his machine gun at the general, shouted at him to surrender. General Rose leaped out of the jeep and put his hands in the air. The German tank commander, however, was dissatisfied and kept gesturing towards the general's pistol. When the general lowered his right hand to release his belt and drop the holster to the ground, the commander apparently thought he was drawing his pistol. While screaming angrily, he fired his weapon at the general's head and instantly killed him.

The general's aide and driver, who were witnesses to what occurred but were fortunately able to escape the scene, reported the information to their superior officers. The details then spread throughout the upper echelons of the army.

Maurice Rose had risen from the ranks. As a result of the valor and leadership expertise he had shown in North Africa, and then in Italy and France, the general had been awarded several medals, among which were two Silver Stars, a Bronze Star, a Purple Heart, and a Distinguished Service Cross. He left behind a wife and four-year-old son. It was his second marriage, and it seemed full of promise. He is buried at the United States cemetery in Margraten, Holland, six miles east of Maastricht.

For my dad, the sad news about Maurice Rose was alleviated by the good information that the Fuels and Lubricants Division received that spring. By mid-March the Major Pipeline across France had extended to Thionville, where it supplied Third Army. By mid-April, it had reached Mainz. At the same time that gasoline was flowing like golden rivers through increasingly lengthened pipelines, trucks and C-47 transport planes brought vast supplies of it to the forward areas.

In Washington, meanwhile, the yellow forsythia bushes on Cathedral Avenue started to bloom in radiant splendor, proof that another glorious Washington spring had arrived. The fact that the war seemed almost over made the new season seem as hopeful as beams of sunrise shining on the Potomac.

On Thursday, April 12, however, lighthearted enjoyment of spring temporarily ceased. Instead, waves of shock flowed over the city of Washington and its citizens. I was alone in the house after school listening to music on the radio when the program was suddenly interrupted.

An edgy voice suffused with emotional pain announced that President Roosevelt, while he was on a visit to his home in Warm Springs, had died there of a cerebral hemorrhage. For people who didn't realize how sick the President had been, the grim news was shocking. I can remember turning off the radio and then rushing down Cathedral Avenue to share the news with a neighbor.

The truth about his disability was easier to hide in those pre-television days. He needed to hold on to someone to walk from his chair to a waiting car, it's true, but he was often photographed in a seated position. A blanket would be draped over the metal braces that supported his legs, hiding his infirmity. He had recently looked a bit haggard, but people attributed that to the stress of the war and his having returned only a few weeks earlier from the tiring Yalta Conference.

On Friday the thirteenth of April, an unlucky day for the superstitious, the nation awoke to find itself with a fresh, new leader. "We have to go to the assembly hall," a classmate told me when I arrived at Alice Deal Junior High that morning. There, in the hall that was often as empty as space, I joined the rest of my school's students to hear principal Bertie Backus ask us to pray for America. In a short speech filled with emotion, she implored us to put our faith in Harry S. Truman, who would now lead our grieving country.

The next day I joined crowds of mourners who lined the route between Union Station and the White House. I stood there patiently for quite a while. Finally the flag-draped coffin of the President came into view, lying on a caisson headed towards the White House for the funeral services. I was too far away to see very much, and sometimes I balanced unsteadily on the tips of my toes to get a better view. I will never forget hearing the sound of horses' hooves and the sobs of many people in the crowd, however. One mourner was heard to murmur, echoing the sentiments of other Americans, "Our country will be lost without him."

Monday was a workday, so the citizens of Washington ended their mourning and resigned themselves to the homey style of Harry Truman. They knew he was taking over from a formidable predecessor.

There was still a war to be won, though, and Mr. Truman needed all the support he could get. After a short stay at Blair House, the new President—along with his wife Bess and college-bound daughter Margaret—moved into that famous white mansion at 1600 Pennsylvania Avenue, the wide avenue where groups of mourners had recently stood.

In Germany, meanwhile, a series of strategic Allied events triggered the final collapse of Germany's Third Reich. From the west, British, French, and American troops moved quickly towards Berlin. Concurrently, Soviet forces converged on that city from the east. The Allies had thus surrounded their densely populated, concrete prey like spiders encircling a fly. Now there was no doubt that Germany was doomed, a fact that even Hitler finally admitted.

Unable to face the inevitable dire consequences of defeat, Hitler committed suicide in his Berlin bunker on April 30, less than three weeks after the death of President Roosevelt. Germany surrendered to the United Nations on May 7.

From Europe, General Eisenhower forwarded the good news about the official surrender to a tired but very happy President Truman in Washington. The next day, which was V-E Day, my parents and other Washingtonians heard the now-familiar voice of the President as he announced the end of the war in Europe. Speaking from the Radio Room of the White House, he began with these memorable words: "This is a solemn but a glorious hour."

Later in his speech, he reminded his audience that victory was only half won and that much work still lay ahead. Although my father didn't yet know that he would be heading the American Graves Registration Command (AGRC) in Europe and would be returning home American dead of the European Theater, he was grateful to hear the President remind people of the tragic losses of life in that theater.

President Truman spoke about the sorrow and heartache abiding in many American homes due to "Hitler and his evil band." Here are the President's words:

> Our rejoicing is sobered and subdued by a supreme consciousness of the terrible price we have paid to rid the world of Hitler and his evil band. Let us not forget, my fellow Americans, the sorrow and the heartache which today abides in the homes of so many of our neighbors—neighbors whose most priceless possession has been rendered as a sacrifice to redeem our liberty.

The deaths of innocent European civilians caused by the Nazis were also becoming more known. At the end of April, Nazi atrocities became quite evident to members of the 12th Armored Division when they began the sad task of liberating Nazi death camps in the vicinity of Landsberg, Germany. At close range, the soldiers saw the interiors of Dachau's "subcamps," as they were called, and many of the division's men made commitments to spread the word far and wide about the horrors they had seen.

During the same period that the 12th Armored Division and other American armored divisions were ending their campaigns, bellicose partisans in sunny Italy were gathering strength and momentum. To express that anger, they stormed into Milan and liberated the city. Then they took justice into their own hands by arresting and shooting Mussolini on April 28, 1945. In an instant, Italy's once-revered Fascist dictator died amidst the heat and hatred of gunfire.

Elsewhere in Europe, the war was winding down like an overused Bavarian clock. On May 6, General Patton's Third Army, which had begun liberating parts of Western Bohemia in the middle of April, liberated the Czech city of Pilsen, located about forty-five miles southwest of Prague. This Western Bohemian city, known more for its excellent beer and fine architecture than for its place in World War II history, was the largest city liberated by Third Army. The Russians freed other areas of Czechoslovakia from German control, including the capital city of Prague.

Life in Washington on V-E Day, May 8, went on pretty much as usual. Victory in Europe was an important milestone, but the celebration was fairly quiet for Washingtonians who had lost family members in the war or still had loved ones fighting in Asia. They packed Saint John's and other churches to pray for an end to hostilities. A bright glow lit the sky above the dome of the Capitol that night, evidence that the pre-war floodlights and illumination had returned.

My father had the opportunity to get an up-close look at the newly illuminated sky in June 1945. Once again, as he had done during the war, he walked determinedly near the Capitol's steps to testify before Congress. This time, ten members made up a special committee investigating petroleum resources, in addition to the committee's chairman, Senator Joseph O'Mahoney of Wyoming, an influential Democrat.

In his capacity as the liaison officer for petroleum, my father delivered the following opening statement on behalf of the War Department:

> The interest of the War Department in the subject of this particular hearing is that there should be available in case of future war sufficient available petroleum for all interests of a national defense. The present war has demonstrated that the success of air, land, and sea operations is dependent upon the availability of petroleum products. It has been necessary to mobilize the entire petroleum-producing capacity of the Allied Nations in support of the war effort, and without our resources the situation would have been desperate indeed. . . .

He then provided statistics about United Nations petroleum production, saying that his data didn't include Russia. This prompted Henry S. Fraser, chief counsel to the committee, to ask why Russia was excluded. "Because we do not have good information with respect to production of crude oil in Russia," my father replied. When a puzzled Mr. Fraser asked why not, my father explained that the Petroleum Administration for War

(Harold Ickes's office) was approached for the information but that they didn't have it.

Again, Henry Fraser asked why not, to which my father answered, "I do not know." Mr. Fraser, determined to find out the reason for Russia's elusiveness, vowed to look into the matter. Of course, elusiveness and lack of cooperation on the part of Russia would become more and more commonplace as the Cold War progressed.

Discussion then abruptly turned to Nazi Germany. Senator O'Mahoney pointed out that a major portion of the German war effort was fueled by synthetic oil made from coal. "That is true, Senator," Dad said amiably, not realizing he was ushering in a debate between Senator O'Mahoney and another attendee, Alfred White.

"That was reserves stored up over a long period," added Mr. White, Chief of the Petroleum Economics Division of the Bureau of Mines.

"Oh, no," Senator O'Mahoney countered. "It was being manufactured day by day." The senator added that the testimony on the following day would reveal up-to-date information secured by American scientists in Europe. "They have just returned from Germany, and they will report to this committee tomorrow on what they learned in the German plants."

Concerning any future wars, my father pointed out that the United States could be in serious danger if it were to become overly dependent on synthetic oil factories for liquid fuels, especially if its enemies had ample supplies of easily obtainable liquid petroleum. "The destruction of Germany's synthetic oil plants and refineries by strategic bombing was an important factor in the military defeat of that nation," he said. After more discussion, he stated these conclusions:

> American companies should continue to increase their ownership and production of foreign oil. Aside from the financial benefits to these companies, such ownership and production would give the United States a greater participation in world oil affairs. . . .

In determining the amount of foreign oil which should be imported into the United States, careful consideration must be given to the effect upon domestic production. Importation which would depress the domestic market price for crude oil to the extent that the capital and resources of domestic companies would be depleted with resulting injury to the domestic industry would be unwise for reasons hereafter stated. . . . Increases in domestic reserves must, to a large extent, be dependent upon the exploration and development activities of our domestic companies. Only in this way can there be an increase in the known oil resources of the United States.

The activities of domestic companies have been and are also important from the standpoint of scientific and technological developments. Only if there is a healthy domestic industry with a fair chance of profit can we anticipate a full utilization of American business ingenuity in the exploration, production, and refining of oil.

Senator O'Mahoney responded by saying, "That is what one might call a very well-balanced statement, General." My father then thanked him for his kind words. Other words of appreciation for Howard Peckham were yet to come.

Before the committee was adjourned for the day, Mr. White turned to Senator O'Mahoney and said, "Mr. Chairman, I would like to compliment the general for his splendid presentation." The senator agreed by saying he had been "very grateful" for my father's presentation.

Obviously, these hearings were quite different from the earlier combative ones concerning the Canol project, as far as my father was concerned. The fact that victory in Europe had been achieved undoubtedly intensified the feelings of good will expressed by the committee towards the army and especially the Fuels and Lubricants Division. The division continued its work until victory was assured.

In Asia, meanwhile, the last major conflict of World War II in the Pacific was nearing an end. In June, the Japanese halted their stubborn resistance on Okinawa, thus ending the horrific three-month Battle of Okinawa.

At this stage in the worldwide apocalypse, a tired world refocused its attention towards peace. During the same month that the Battle of Okinawa ended, representatives of fifty countries met to draw up a charter that would promote security, international cooperation, and peace among nations. On June 26, at the War Memorial Opera House in San Francisco, where the meeting was held, all fifty representatives signed the charter, after many hours of deliberation. As fate would have it, a lively President Truman, not a sickly and now deceased President Roosevelt—who had steadfastly guided America through most of the war—witnessed the historic signing of the charter. The document was officially ratified two months later, thus giving birth to the United Nations.

The name of the organization was not new, though. President Roosevelt had coined it early in the war, but at that time he used it in reference to nations that pledged to continue their fight against the Axis.

There was little time for President Truman to rest on his well-deserved laurels, however. From July 17 through August 2, the President attended the consequential Potsdam Conference in Germany. A primary issue discussed at the Conference, which was also attended by Joseph Stalin from Russia, Winston Churchill and Clement Attlee from Great Britain, and other Allied leaders, was the apportionment of defeated Germany.

The Allies decided that Germany would be divided into four zones, to be occupied by the military forces of France, Britain, the United States, and Russia. According to the agreement, Russia would occupy the Eastern Zone, where Berlin, the capital, was located. Berlin itself would also be divided into four sections. Russia was to occupy East Berlin, which would become the capital of Russian-occupied East Germany. The United States, France, and Britain were to occupy West Berlin.

My father strongly believed in the demilitarization and de-Nazification of Germany, as agreed upon by the attendees of the

Potsdam Conference. Unknown to him at the time, however, was the fact that dealing with the Russians in the Eastern Zone would become difficult for the United States in the future. He would learn this through personal experience when serving in Europe from 1947 to 1950 (discussed in a later chapter).

Early on the day preceding the official start of the Potsdam Conference, a loud boom was heard in the vast, barren New Mexico desert. This ominous sound meant that the first atomic bomb had been successfully detonated and was now ready to be used. Of course the President couldn't hear the boom, since he was in Europe, but he was certainly aware that this test would occur. He had approved it, and soon he would be ready to approve the use of the bomb in the war with Japan.

To avoid the unnecessary loss of American life, especially in view of the high American casualty rate suffered during the recent Battle of Okinawa, the President ordered that an atomic bomb be dropped on the Japanese industrial city of Hiroshima. So, on the bright morning of August 6, it was done. Not until after a second atomic bomb was dropped three days later, on Nagasaki this time, did the Japanese agree to surrender unconditionally.

Because the bombs caused the deaths of so many innocent civilians, the bombing still continues to be debated. Had the decision been wise? Had it indeed been necessary? Not everyone thought so, including one of Dad's closest friends, Bonner Fellers, who graduated with him in the West Point class of November 1918 and eventually retired with the rank of brigadier general.

General Fellers was of the opinion that the Japanese probably would have surrendered soon anyway. Even today, Americans are divided on the issue. In a postwar article reprinted in *Reader's Digest* and copyrighted by the Veterans of Foreign Wars, the outspoken Bonner Fellers wrote that "the atomic bomb neither induced the Emperor's decision to surrender nor had any effect on the ultimate outcome of the war."

He knew a lot about Asia. His first tour of duty there was in the Philippines from 1936 to 1938, when he served as staff officer for General Douglas MacArthur. As Frazier Hunt writes in *The*

Untold Story of Douglas MacArthur, Bonner Fellers created "almost overnight" a Reserve Officers' Training School in Baguio. He also served as personal liaison officer between Douglas MacArthur and Manuel Quezon, President of the Philippines. One occasion Bonner Fellers especially liked to recall was the time he and President Quezon called on Douglas MacArthur to congratulate him on the birth of little Arthur, his newborn son. He again served as staff officer to MacArthur in the Philippines during World War II. According to D. Clayton James in *The Years of MacArthur*, they met with each other, either individually or in a group, thirty-seven times between 1941 and 1945.

Several senior officers, such as George C. Marshall, praised the skill of Bonner Fellers in other locations where he was stationed. As General Albert C. Wedemeyer writes in his memoir *Wedemeyer Reports*, General Marshall considered Fellers to be "a valuable observer" and praised the competence he had shown in the North Africa Theater from 1940 to 1941.

Bonner Fellers was known to be candid, however, in his criticism of British desert-war tactics. In that same memoir, Albert Wedemeyer, who had been a strategic planner in North Africa, writes about a conversation he had then with American Ambassador Alexander Kirk concerning the matter:

> He talked to me at length about Bonner Fellers, our Cairo military attaché. Kirk had a high regard for Fellers' ability as an intelligence officer but felt that he was overzealous in the performance of his duties in a way that unnecessarily antagonized the British.

My parents, brother, and I knew the Fellers family well. Mother and Dad found the blunt-spoken Bonner and his wife Dorothy to be charismatic and sociable. Nancy, their only child, was a few years older than I, and we stayed in touch over the years. In Washington, her personality was often as bubbly as the soda pop she offered us teenagers whenever we came to her house as guests.

In 1963 Bonner Fellers showed his affection for my parents in an explicit way by serving as a pallbearer at my mother's funeral. He proved to be a good friend again, at a much happier time, when he and Dorothy served as attendants at the wedding of my dad and the former Evelyn Hemenway, which was held in Washington's National Cathedral.

Another of Dad's friends from the West Point class of November 1918, Leslie Richard Groves (known as Dick by his classmates), had a far different view of the atomic bomb. Upon their graduation, both were commissioned into the U.S. Army Corps of Engineers. Before entering Army Engineer School after graduation, both traveled to France and Germany with other engineering classmates to visit the battlefields. Also, both graduated from the Command & General Staff School at Fort Leavenworth and were promoted to brigadier general in 1942.

From that point on, their careers branched in different directions. My father transferred to the Quartermaster Corps and went to Washington in 1943 to run the Fuels and Lubricants Division, which I described earlier. Leslie Groves, who stayed in the Corps of Engineers, went in 1942 to New York City to become the military director of an engineering district that would soon evolve into the Manhattan Project. He selected the code name "Manhattan" because the district's headquarters were located in the skyscraper-filled burrough of Manhattan. The three primary sites he chose for development of the atomic bomb, however, were either small or remote. These were Hanford, Washington; Oak Ridge, Tennessee; and Los Alamos, New Mexico.

Robert S. Norris, author of *Racing for the Bomb,* relates Leslie Groves's view of the decision to drop the bomb on Japan:

> Groves's personal feelings about the bomb were not complicated: He never had any moral doubts, at the time or afterward, about using it. From the outset he believed that the bomb could be decisive in ending the war and saving American lives....

Nevertheless, the subject of using the atomic bomb during World War II continues to be debated, even today.

The summer of 1945 was historic because Japan saw two of its cities shattered by an atomic bomb, and also for the reasons I previously described: San Francisco witnessed the signing of the United Nations Charter, and Potsdam hosted the important Potsdam Conference.

Washington, meanwhile, crawled through another languid summer until August 15, when a joyful celebration awakened it from its lethargy. On that day, V-J Day, Washingtonians kissed and hugged each other and happily danced in the streets. The Japanese had surrendered, and the months of worrying and sacrificing were over.

Not everyone felt cheerful on that day, however. I had just gotten home after dancing around on F Street with friends and other celebrators when the sound of Mother's crying brought me into the kitchen. She was sitting at our square, wooden breakfast table. If it hadn't been for sugar rationing, she might have been mixing batter for muffins or some other sugary treats; but now she seldom did this. When I asked what was wrong, she said, "Just think of all the soldiers who died in that terrible war. They won't be coming home."

Her words were prophetic in light of my father's future assignment. Two years later he would be sent to France, where he would be in charge of sending home thousands of those victims about whom Mother cried that day. Sadly, they would be coming home in caskets. In retrospect, then, her tears on V-J Day were neither unreasonable nor inappropriate.

The ceremonial aspects of the Japanese surrender were held on September 2, 1945, aboard the battleship *USS Missouri*, which was temporarily anchored in Tokyo Bay. The ship was flying under the flag of Fleet Admiral Chester Nimitz, one of the signers of the surrender instrument and the man who had commanded the United States Pacific Fleet during the war. Other signers of the surrender document included General Douglas MacArthur and representatives of several Allied nations. The Japanese foreign minister, Mamoru Shigemitsu, signed the document on behalf of the Emperor of Japan.

In 1946, Dad was an invitee to a social function where he acquired an autograph from Admiral Nimitz, who was attending the same event. When Dad gave it to me, I was pleased to see that the admiral had signed his name with the same pen he used to sign the surrender terms. His message was lighthearted, however, and it reflected the joy of victory. The postwar joyful celebrations and partying continued during 1946.

RAILWAY TANK CARS FILLING HUNDREDS OF GASOLINE CANS: BELGIUM, 1944
(U.S. Army Photo)

Meanwhile, the Quartermaster General sat quietly at his desk in Washington and thought long and hard about President Truman's Proclamation concerning the American war dead. The repercussions of that document were becoming more and more etched in his mind. He knew that a somber and yet extremely important task for him and for the Quartermaster Corps waited just around the corner.

GASOLINE IN 55-GALLON DRUMS DROPPED NEAR A BEACH IN THE PACIFIC, 1945
(U.S. Army Photo)

(LEFT) THE ARMY-NAVY CLUB IN WASHINGTON
(RIGHT) 8TH ARMORED DIVISION TANK ON A STREET IN PILSEN, 1945
(U.S. Army Photo)

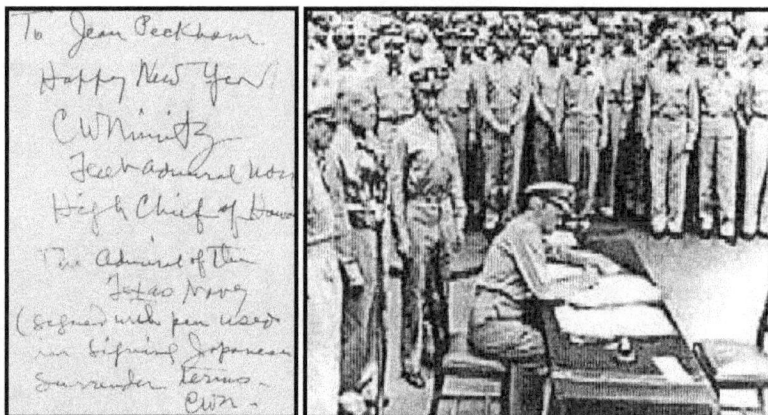

THE AUTOGRAPH JEAN RECEIVED FROM ADMIRAL NIMITZ AND A PHOTO OF HIM SIGNING SURRENDER DOCUMENTATION ON THE MISSOURI

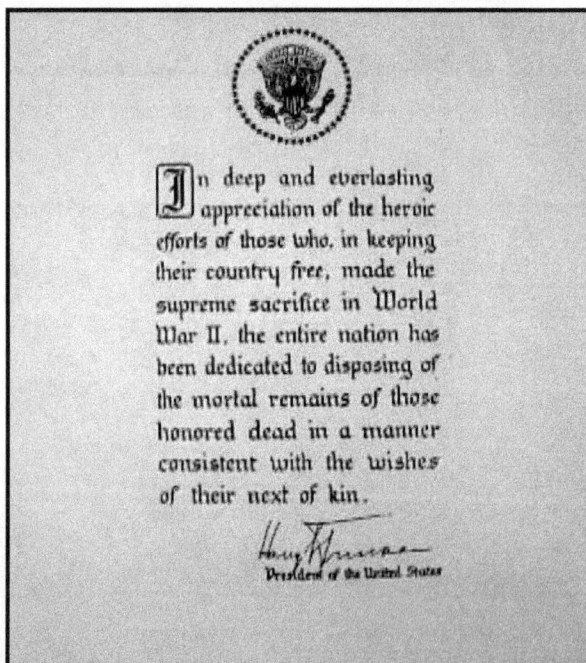

PRESIDENT TRUMAN'S PROCLAMATION ABOUT THE AMERICAN WAR DEAD, 1946

Chapter 8

Freedom Is Not Free

The atom bomb was no "great decision." It was merely another powerful weapon in the arsenal of righteousness.

—HARRY S. TRUMAN

IN OUR NATION'S CAPITAL, the atmosphere changed considerably after V-J Day. For one thing, the nightlife was far more relaxed. My parents were among those who ate in good restaurants more frequently after the war, and they were thankful to be seated in rooms that were much less crowded and not so hectic. Also, it was much easier to get reservations. Both of them liked seafood, and often they ate at one of the quaint, brine-smelling restaurants near the Potomac River.

Their first course was inevitably a big round plate of raw oysters or steamed clams on the half shell, which they loved. Mother didn't like to prepare New England-style clambakes, but she did enjoy eating clams, especially in restaurants.

Whenever I joined my parents for a seafood dinner, I turned my head away when the raw oysters or steamed clams arrived. "Mmmm, don't those look good," my father would say. I thought they looked slimy and unappetizing, so he wasn't able to inculcate this passion in me.

Military social gatherings in Washington were also more relaxed. My parents attended private parties at homes of old friends, such as Dorothy and Bonner Fellers.

Formal military events were often held at the large Army-Navy Club, which occupied an entire eight-story building on 17th Street. The building's exterior was graced with attractive awnings above tall, arched main-floor windows. Inside were a tastefully furnished dining room and a variety of banquet rooms. Women attended private parties in the banquet rooms and ate in the dining room as guests, which Mother did on many occasions.

On the first floor officers such as my father could sit in big chairs and exchange stories about places in which they had served. Granddad Shaw enjoyed playing bridge there after he retired. Most areas on that floor were closed to women, since it was definitely a men's club in those days.

Also off-limits—to me, at least—was the estate of Secretary of War Henry Stimson, just down the street from my house. I made an exception to Dad's "no trespassing on the Stimson property" rule soon after V-J Day, however. One sunny afternoon, my friend Claire Ordway stopped by to tell me she noticed several official cars parked in front of the property.

Claire, the hazel-eyed daughter of Colonel Godwin Ordway, lived a couple of blocks away on Woodley Road. I agreed with her suggestion that we find out what was happening, so we hurried down the street and arrived at the estate just when someone was heading up the driveway. When Claire asked the driver what was going on, he replied, "There's a garden party being given in honor of General Dwight Eisenhower." At that point, she and I boldly decided to join the festivities.

After striding up the hill, we stood for a short while at a polite distance, watching the smartly dressed people as they gathered in small groups on the green lawn. Then a kind-faced waiter led us over to General Eisenhower—who was seated in a comfortable-looking garden chair—so that we could get an autograph. When we approached him, a broad easy smile lit up his face. I responded with an awkward revelation, "My father's in the army, too."

The general made no comment and then started signing his name on a piece of paper that I had handed to him. Then I said a few words about another subject, and Claire joined in the conversation. After he had given each of us an autograph, we thanked him and walked away. But we were still within hearing distance when we heard him casually remark to another guest, "Nice kids, aren't they?" We were naturally thrilled to hear this comment from someone who had become such a worldwide hero, and I felt less embarrassed by what I perceived as awkwardness on my part.

Later, I told Dad about the party-crashing venture. When I mentioned that I had told General Eisenhower about his being in the army, my father said, "Well, I hope you didn't tell him my name." I felt relieved when I noticed a mischievous smile cross Dad's face as he spoke.

The kindly Secretary of War occasionally strolled down the Cathedral Avenue sidewalk, as noted by next-door neighbor and future author Catherine Marshall in her book *A Man Called Peter*, but I don't recall ever having seen him there. He died in 1950 at the age of eighty-three, after a distinguished career of service to his country.

After V-J Day, President Truman slowly re-entered the Washington social scene. His social calendar became full during the 1946-1947 season, as if to make up for the time lost by wartime asceticism. My parents were among those senior officers and their spouses who attended an Army and Navy Reception, hosted by President and Mrs. Truman at the White House. Like most professional army officers, my father was apolitical and didn't vote during presidential elections. He felt he should serve every American President with honor, regardless of the man's political affiliation.

My parents admired the Trumans. My father appreciated the President's spunk and lengthy service to his country, especially the years he spent in the army during World War I. The President was commissioned a first lieutenant and served with the Field Artillery in France. He was discharged as a major, but was a member of the Army Reserve Corps from 1927 through 1944, where he rose to the rank of colonel.

My father and the President also had in common the fact that both were farmers' sons and got teased about their piano playing. (Dad only knew a couple of songs by heart, one of which was a German drinking song that he played and sang rather loudly. I'm sure the President's repertoire was much larger.)

Mother felt sympathetic towards Bess Truman, who had lost her father to alcohol and suicide when she was a teenager. The First Lady was reluctant to reveal that fact when her husband was running for the highest office in the land. Now she was coping with the many pressures, especially the social responsibilities, of being a President's wife.

In addition to an increased social life, Washingtonians were attending the city's various cultural events more often. The free Watergate concerts resumed after the war, for example. Held along the Potomac River, the concerts drew big crowds in the summertime. Throngs of Washingtonians would find relief from the unrelenting humidity while they listened to the music. My father was one of those people who enjoyed evenings spent at these relaxing concerts.

The pace of my father's job was still rapid, in view of postwar concerns about the availability of petroleum. This topic was discussed in several Quartermaster Corps and War Department meetings that he attended. Congress was especially interested in the subject.

On the bright autumn day of October 5, 1945, Dad walked purposefully down a long hallway in the Senate Office Building. He was there to give further testimony to the committee that was investigating petroleum resources. After locating the appropriate room, he appeared in front of outspoken Joseph O'Mahoney of Wyoming, the committee chairman, before whom he had testified in June. Burnet R. Maybank, Senator from South Carolina, was also present, as was Henry S. Fraser, who still served as the chief counsel to the committee.

Sporting rather grim facial expressions, they faced Dad and several representatives of governmental departments, who sat at a long, leviathan-sized table.

As a representative of the War Department, my father made several introductory comments. He stated that the department "addresses itself primarily to the military aspects of petroleum requirements" and that civilian aspects could be more effectively dealt with by other agencies. He then gave statistics comparing World War I gasoline consumption with that of World War II. Among other facts, he noted why the percentage of consumed aviation gasoline keeps increasing.

He said that in order to meet the demands of the United Nations (the term "United Nations" was being used even before the organization was formed) for petroleum products during World War II, it had been necessary to restrict nonessential uses and to plan and supervise throughout the world "the production of petroleum and the manufacture and distribution of refined products." About the peacetime requirements of petroleum, he noted the following:

> Ample quantities of lubricants equal or superior to those used by our enemies have been available to the Allied Nations throughout this war, but research into the chemistry of synthetic products has opened a vista to new lubricants with qualities and characteristics superior to those of the petroleum lubricants now available. Consequently, our lubricants industry also may be revolutionized in the future.

With regards to the dire but not unrealistic possibility of a future war, he reported the following: "The armies, navies, and air corps of the United Nations in this war just ended have used all the petroleum products that were available. "

He pointed out that if the scale of a future war were greater than this one, and if the forces involved were more highly mechanized, the United States would need more proven and developed reserves of oil that could be more readily drawn upon "than we have had heretofore." He emphasized that the United States needs to keep ahead of the rest of the world in research and development of petroleum products.

As a member of the Army-Navy Petroleum Board, Dad was of course well aware that the U.S. Navy would need to be adequately prepared for its peacetime requirements. Navy consumption was also high during World War II—about equal to the U.S. Army—because big navy ships burned so much fuel oil. Knowing that a representative from the Navy Department would testify later, my father pointed out that whenever possible the army and navy used identical specifications and cooperated closely with each other. He added that their technical staffs were "constantly working together, through the Army-Navy Petroleum Board and other agencies, to simplify the petroleum supply of both services."

By the end of my father's testimony, the expressions on the faces of the senators had softened considerably. They liked what they heard, but also, unlike my father's testimony during the war, the main emphasis of these 1945 hearings was on postwar requirements of petroleum instead of immediate wartime needs. Just a few weeks earlier V-J Day had been celebrated. Therefore, the atmosphere in room 318 of the Senate Office Building, the room in which the hearings were held, reflected the coordination of peacetime efforts.

Peace also created optimism in regard to troop reduction overseas. After the Allies liberated the countries controlled by Nazi Germany, President Truman determined that great numbers of American troops were no longer needed on the Continent. Consequently, the United States (as well as Britain) sent home thousands of troops in 1945. Publicly, but maybe not privately, my father and other army officers saw no danger in diminishing our forces overseas. As one of his friends said, "Our boys have done a superb job and deserve to come home." Soviet Russia, on the other hand, still maintained a large military force in the countries it had liberated after the war.

Another fuel item needed during the war has not yet been discussed here, due to the emphasis placed on crude oil and petroleum products. The Fuels and Lubricants Division, however, also procured and allocated coal. It accomplished this work through its Solid Fuels Branch.

Along with other tasks, the branch had to deal with the leader of the United Mine Workers of America (UMWA), Mr. John L. Lewis, whose frequent scowl was more pronounced than his bushy eyebrows. His demands for higher pay for miners resulted in miners' strikes, so he was no friend of either the U.S. Army or the President of the United States. The War Labor Board believed such strikes hindered the war effort and violated the wartime "no strike" rule. To miners, though, John Lewis was a hero.

The Solid Fuels Branch fulfilled its mission, in spite of difficulties brought about by strikes and the consequent losses in coal production. Fortunately, it received admirable help and cooperation from mining representatives of our Allies in Europe. Although coal requirements in the United States were reduced by 1945, they increased overseas that year. Risch writes about this increase in *Fuels for Global Conflict*:

> On the other hand, during the last year of the war, the shipment of coal overseas to supply military and essential civilian needs increased sharply. In August 1945, War Department exports reached a peak of approximately 700,000 tons a month, which were procured and loaded under the direction of the Solid Fuels Branch of the Fuels and Lubricants Division.

After the war, my father received recognition for his service as director of the Fuels and Lubricants Division. For ensuring the smooth flow of petroleum and other fuel-related products during the war, and for procuring these products and then allocating them to the United States military forces from October 1943 through September 1945, my father received the Distinguished Service Medal (DSM). The DSM is awarded to those who perform "exceptionally meritorious service in a highly responsible duty."

On the day of his acceptance, my father said he was very happy to have contributed "to the significant wartime efforts of the Quartermaster Corps." Early in World War II, the petroleum administrator for war, Harold Ickes, said he promised to get oil to our fighters on all fronts, in spite of costs and sacrifices at home.

Risch elaborates on his promise and the role of the Fuels and
Lubricants Division in helping to fulfill it:

> This was a promise the Fuels and Lubricants Division took to
> itself and acted upon so effectively that it was successful in meeting
> every request for petroleum products.

In January 1946, a few weeks after I turned fourteen, my
father was assigned to duty as Director of Procurement in the
Office of the Quartermaster General (OQMG). Procurement, as
defined by the Joint Chiefs of Staff, ran the gamut from obtaining
services and supplies for the army to handling financing and
contracts related to selected contractors.

In February he was asked to speak about the subject of
procurement before students at the Industrial College of the
Armed Forces, located at Fort Lesley J. McNair in Washington. The
student body consisted of military officers and federal officials
who were studying national security preparedness from the
standpoint of economics and industry. They were known to be a
tough audience that asked probing, and at times tricky, questions
of its speakers.

My father accepted the challenge, and his speech was well
received. I suspect he was glad when the challenging question-
and-answer segment was over, however. His remarks included
the following:

> Mobilization for modern war is a gigantic task. The expansion
> of an army from peacetime to wartime strength places colossal
> demands upon industry.
>
> The speed with which industry is able to meet those demands
> might determine the final outcome of the war. . . .
>
> We entered World War I without a plan for the mobilization of
> industry. The bitter experiences of those days illustrated the
> necessity for making provision, in future national defense plans, for
> industrial mobilization as a concomitant to the mobilization of
> manpower. . . .

By the summer of 1940 Quartermaster procurement planning officers had extensive records indicating the actual and potential productive capacities of the firms in their areas for manufacturing the particular items to be purchased. . . .

The Fuels and Lubricants Division of the Quartermaster Corps officially ended its existence as a separate entity in April 1946. Then, all of its personnel, functions, and property were transferred to the newly created Supply Division, a postwar division. In their book *Operations in the War Against Germany*, authors Ross and Romanus describe both the relative ease with which the Quartermaster Corps furnished petroleum products during World War II and the overall success of its wartime operations:

> While the higher echelons responsible for determining priorities and providing personnel tended to neglect clothing, general supplies, and at times even food, they exerted every effort to smooth the flow of petroleum products. Chiefly for that reason, these products were usually supplied in adequate quantities. . . .
>
> An operation of this magnitude, supported from a base over 3,000 miles away, inevitably developed temporary shortages and local crises, but Quartermaster operations as a whole were outstandingly successful.

Although my father was busily engaged with his responsible work that spring and summer, he made it a point to drive my mother, brother, and me to Connecticut for our annual Fourth of July gathering at Granddad's. My father especially looked forward to this short vacation, since it allowed him to be with his father again and escape temporarily from the pressures of Washington.

It turned out to be a wonderful five days of pleasant reunions with relatives and excellent meals. Grandmother Whiting was no match for Frances, Granddad's first wife, in regard to knowing fancy recipes; but she was able to create meals composed of fine country cooking. In accordance with our longtime New England tradition, her dinners inevitably included corn on the cob and baked beans.

Also during our stay at Granddad's, my brother, an eighteen-year-old newly licensed pilot, took me on my first airplane ride. I recall that only a short time after we arrived at the local airport and signed in, the two of us leaped into the plane and then sat alone in a small Piper Cub, which, when it became airborne, dipped and swayed like an eagle caught in a windstorm. At the end of our half-hour flight, we landed smoothly at the airport. My brother went on to be a great pilot, but I can remember stepping shakily onto the ground.

Because of his love for planes, Howie was excited to hear about my father's next assignment. After half a year as Director of Procurement, Dad received orders to report to Army Air Forces (AAF) headquarters in Washington, where another challenge awaited him.

The commanding general of the AAF then was General Carl A. Spaatz, who had been transferred to Washington earlier that year after commanding U.S. Strategic Air Forces in the Pacific. My father would have the title of Air Quartermaster. Efficient and expedient air dropping of supplies to troops required much cooperation between the Quartermaster Corps and the AAF, and Howard Peckham would have a large role in the process.

Until six months before Pearl Harbor Day, the air forces were known as the Army Air Corps (AAC). In view of the increased role of air power that occurred during World War II—at that time under the command of legendary General Henry "Hap" Arnold—it seems only fitting that the word *"forces"* was substituted for *"corps."* As the Axis learned throughout the war, American planes and their valiant crews became "forces to be reckoned with."

In the meantime, the Cold War was dangerously sliding forward along an icy path. My father and his army friends now questioned openly the wisdom of having brought our forces home so soon from Europe, as our government had ordered. More and more, Russia was using its huge military force to extend Soviet influence in countries it had liberated. Many of its troops were still stationed in those countries, so by establishing puppet governments in these "newly freed" lands, it was able to dominate them in a nonviolent manner. By the end of February 1946, Soviet-controlled governments had been formed in Estonia, Latvia, Lithuania, Albania, and Bulgaria (Eastern Europe), as well as in Poland, Hungary, and Romania (Central Europe). This situation particularly worried Prime Minister Winston Churchill, who spoke about it on March 5 in a speech he delivered at Westminster College in Missouri. These are some of his words:

> A shadow has fallen upon the scenes so lately lighted by the Allied victory. Nobody knows what Soviet Russia and its communist international organization intends to do in the immediate future, or what are the limits, if any, to their expansive proselytizing tendencies....
>
> From Stettin in the Baltic to Trieste in the Adriatic, an iron curtain has descended across the Continent. Behind that line lie all the capitals of the ancient states of Central and Eastern Europe. Warsaw, Berlin, Prague, Vienna, Budapest, Belgrade, Bucharest and Sofia, all these famous cities and the populations around them lie in what I must call the Soviet sphere....
>
> I do not believe that Soviet Russia desires war. What they desire is the fruits of war and the indefinite expansion of their power and doctrines....

To ensure the avoidance of war, Churchill stressed the importance of maintaining peace by adhering faithfully to the Charter of the United Nations. The Charter, with its emphasis on mediation of conflicts between nations instead of warfare, seemed to outline the perfect road to ensuring a peaceful world.

President Truman, after hearing the electrifying words of his British visitor, left Missouri and returned to Washington, which knew little about an "iron curtain," a then-unfamiliar term. Most Washingtonians were only barely concerned, if at all. Now the city's citizens were busily making plans for a joyous Cherry Blossom Festival, which would resume at the Tidal Basin later that spring. Hundreds of Washingtonians and tourists alike would again view graceful cherry trees, whose pink blossoms would be reflected on the surface of the basin's shimmering water. Before the war, this festival, with its music and pageantry, had been one of the city's most cherished annual events. Wartime conservation measures had now ended, thus adding to people's joy. Beautiful gardens and buildings throughout the city were again awash with floodlights, making the postwar nighttime atmosphere as radiant as moonbeams.

Winston Churchill's speech in Missouri may not have rattled Washingtonians in celebratory 1946, but the bleak war years were often foremost in the thoughts of those who had lost loved ones in the war. World War II was also on the mind of Harry Truman, especially on May 16, when he approved and signed an important document with the unassuming title of Public Law 383. A portion of it reads:

> BE IT ENACTED BY THE SENATE AND HOUSE OF REPRESENTATIVES OF THE UNITED STATES OF AMERICA IN CONGRESS ASSEMBLED, That the Congress hereby declares it to be in the public interest to provide for the evacuation and return of the remains of certain persons who have died since September 3, 1939, and whose remains are buried in places located outside the continental limits of the United States and could not be returned to their homeland for burial due to wartime shipping restrictions, and to centralize in one agency the task of evacuation and return of such remains.

The law authorized the Secretary of War to implement the return of the World War II dead to their homeland for interment "at places designated by the next of kin, or in national cemeteries, provided such remains are entitled to interment therein." The deceased eligible for repatriation under the law included:

> (a) members of the armed forces of the United States who died in the service; (b) civilian officers and employees of the United States;

(c) citizens of the United States who served in the armed forces of any government at war with Germany, Italy, or Japan and who died while in such service and who were citizens of the United States at the time of such service; (d) citizens of the United States whose homes are in fact in the United States and whose death outside the continental limits thereof can be directly attributed to the war or who died while employed or otherwise engaged in activities contributing to the prosecution of the war; and (e) such other citizens of the United States, the return of the remains of whom would in the discretion of the secretary of war serve the public interest.

I didn't know anything about this document then—which authorized the return to the United States of thousands of fallen soldiers—or its impact on my father's army career.

At that time, my family had to contend with its own grief. My grandmother Bell Shaw died in May after her breast cancer spread uncontrollably. A mastectomy was performed too late, mostly because she was a faithful Christian Scientist and delayed getting treatment. Bell received comfort from a practitioner of that religion who came daily to pray with her, but when the pain became too much to bear, she dismissed the practitioner and began taking the painkillers her doctor had prescribed.

During the time we were dealing with the loss of Bell, Mother had medical problems of her own, which required a complete hysterectomy. Her operation took place in July while I was away at Camp Sequoya, overlooking Lake Sycamore in southern Virginia. I had never been away from home for such a long time, so I often felt homesick when I walked on the unfamiliar hilly terrain surrounding the camp.

My father called me the day after my mother's operation to assure me that all was fine, and he continued to update me in the days to follow. When I returned home from camp, Mother and I hugged each other tightly.

From that moment onward, my rebellious teenager phase—which began soon after I turned thirteen—quietly ended.

In January 1947 I reached a milestone of sorts in my studies by graduating from Alice Deal Junior High, where I had completed seventh through ninth grade. Because of my December birth date, my school years often ended during the busy, chilly middle of the year instead of in warm, mellow June.

Therefore, classes began almost immediately at Woodrow Wilson High School, where I started as a sophomore. Soon afterwards, I joined a sorority and made a lot of new friends; I also began to date. High school life was challenging and fun, so when Dad came home one early spring evening with news of his next assignment, I was far from pleased.

"I've been ordered to Paris, France," my father stated in a matter-of-fact tone of voice, adding, "I'll be in charge of the American Graves Registration Command." From my perspective, the timing was bad. Europe and its people would be so different from anything or anyone I had ever known. At that time, I seemed to be blending smoothly into the landscape at Wilson High, and I certainly wasn't ready to be uprooted.

My parents made a plan that seemed workable. My father would leave in May for Europe, as scheduled. In July, Mother would give Howie a big sendoff to West Point, which he would enter as a freshman. I would finish my sophomore year at the end of December.

"Jeanie and I can spend Christmas with Howie at West Point," Mother told Dad, "and then join you early in the new year." My brother's lowly plebe (freshman) status required that he and the other members of his plebe class remain at the Academy for the holidays.

Howie had been overjoyed when he first received news of his West Point appointment, and my father was delighted that his son would be attending his alma mater and following in his footsteps. Mother, however, had mixed feelings about it. The World War II photographs and newsreels that showed young officers leading their men on the battlefields of Europe and Asia, where they risked and often lost their lives, were still too fresh in her mind. My mother's fears for her son, who would be commissioned a second lieutenant upon graduation, were intensified when she received my father's first long letter to us, which came in the mail soon after his arrival in France.

More than ever before, she thought about all the mothers who had lost their sons during wartime when she read these words that my father had written:

> This year I will be in charge of Memorial Day ceremonies at all the United States cemeteries in Western Europe. All of them will have a service with joint participation of army chaplains and local clergymen. Flowers will be placed on each grave by local schoolchildren, and there will be a miniature American flag at each gravesite.

After Memorial Day had passed, which of course had been solemnly observed in our area at Arlington National Cemetery, Dad wrote us details about the Memorial Day ceremony in which he had participated at Hamm Cemetery, located in the wooded hills three miles east of the city of Luxembourg. He wrote:

> Thousands of people, mostly Luxembourgers, many of whom had arrived on bicycles, listened to the stirring music of American and Luxembourg military bands and watched the impressive theatrics of the U.S. Army Drum and Fife Corps.

Soon before he and the other dignitaries arrived, the excited crowd surged forward at times and had to be held back by policemen, he wrote. A motorcycle escort accompanied my father's car to the cemetery as well as automobiles that contained members of the Luxembourg Royal Family, General Lucius Clay, Prime Minister Pierre Dupong of Luxembourg, and General Pierre Koenig (Chief of French forces in Germany).

My father wrote that the reviewing stand from which he spoke was decorated with flowers and evergreens and by American and Luxembourg flags. As host, he was the first one to speak, in French then in English. He described Hamm Cemetery and the other resting places of American fallen soldiers in Europe. Dad also expressed his sincere appreciation to the people of Luxembourg. In these words, he then described for Mother and me the speakers and officials who followed him:

> Following my speech were those given by Generals Clay and Koenig and by Prime Minister Pierre Dupong. There were a few other participants, including U.S. Army chaplains who offered prayers....
>
> Next came the impressive wreath-laying ceremony, in which members of the Luxembourg royal family participated along with several civilian and military officials....

The firing squad fired three volleys over the graves, Dad wrote, and a bugler stationed near the reviewing stand played *Taps*. Another bugler situated back in a wooded area echoed his playing. Just as the guests were leaving, twenty-five P-51s flew very low over the cemetery in battle formation.

My father was in charge of this ceremony and others like it all over Europe that day, so he was gratified that everything had gone so smoothly. He was even more pleased that the people of Luxembourg had shown their gratitude to the U.S. Army for liberating them from the Nazis, evidenced by the presence of a large crowd and the many bouquets of beautiful flowers placed at the gravesites.

To provide us with more details, my father also sent us a phonograph record containing his radio address to the United States from Luxembourg on that Memorial Day, which was broadcasted after the ceremony. Although it was intended for all Americans, it was particularly aimed towards those citizens whose loved ones had died in the European Theater. After being introduced by Henry Cassidy, a commentator with NBC, my father spoke in a clear, strong voice. These are his words:

> The American Graves Registration Command supervised the significant ceremony which was held today at the American

Cemetery of Hamm, just outside the beautiful capital city of Luxembourg.

Similar Memorial Day ceremonies were held in all of the other 36 cemeteries which are under the supervision of this command. At Lisnabreeny in Ireland; at Cambridge and Brookwood in England; at Malmö, Sweden; Munsingen, Switzerland; in our three cemeteries in Holland; four in Belgium; and twenty-four in France—in each of these cemeteries, also, there was an impressive and dignified ceremony.

Some 156,000 men and women of the United States lost their lives in the European Theater during the course of World War II. This is more than half of the fatal casualties suffered by our country. Of those who lost their lives in the European Theater, 144,000 are now resting in these cemeteries.

Many of the cemeteries were established during combat, often, of necessity, upon the battlefields themselves. After V-E Day, the American Graves Registration Command was formed. Landscape architects and horticulturists were brought over from the United States to give technical advice with respect to the planting of shrubs, grass, and flowers. These battlefield sites have now been developed into the beautiful park-like resting places where our ceremonies have been held today.

The search for our 12,000 who have not yet been found is continuing. All means are being used to obtain information that might lead to their recovery: posters; appeals in newspapers and on the radio; the local governments—all are used to make known to the peoples of these lands over here that the Army is searching for its missing. Trained investigators and search teams take the information that is supplied and often find many leads themselves.

During 1946, our search and recovery teams covered an area of approximately one and one-quarter million square miles. They penetrated three hundred miles beyond the Arctic Circle. They recovered our dead from the Islands of the Azores, a thousand miles off the coast of Portugal. Their operations extended through Czechoslovakia and into the Ploesti oil fields of Rumania. No clue that might lead to the recovery of an American has been overlooked. No clue that may lead to the recovery of an American will be overlooked.

To establish positive identification of our dead, the experience of American police departments has been combined with the discovery and development of our own identification experts.

Scientific sensors and equipment are in constant use: the fluoroscopes, the x-rays, infrared photography, measuring devices of all types—all of these are used in our identification procedures. All care is taken to ensure that identification is positive. Unless it is positive, no identification is accepted.

I think you would like to know that the chaplains of the American Graves Registration Command visit all of our cemeteries frequently, and that religious services are often conducted in the cemetery chapels by the local people. From the outset, the peoples of the liberated countries have shown in many ways their gratitude for your sons and husbands and fathers. Not a day goes by that does not see groups of grateful people of Holland, Belgium, France, and Luxembourg visiting the cemeteries.

Soon the program for the return of our soldiers who lost their lives in World War II will begin. And those whose next of kin elect to have them returned to the United States will begin the long, long journey home. The program is scheduled to begin in the early fall of this year, and many of the men and women to whom we have paid our respects today will be in family burial plots or in national cemeteries in the United States when Memorial Day of 1948 comes around.

I wish to assure you—all of you who have loved ones in our cemeteries over here—that my command will never forget the reverence and respect to which they are entitled. Our preparations have been extensive to ensure that the greatest care shall be given to all of your deceased, whether they are to be returned to their homeland or are to remain over here in the lands that they fought to liberate. I want all of you to know that the American Graves Registration Command will do its part to fulfill its obligations to those who died in the service of our country.

My father's speech was followed by one given by Her Royal Highness, Grand Duchess Charlotte of Luxembourg, the reigning sovereign of that tiny, picturesque nation. After briefly describing her homeland, Mr. Cassidy introduced the Grand Duchess:

> The ruling family of Luxembourg is the House of Nassau, related to the royal family of the Netherlands. And the reigning sovereign is Her Royal Highness, Grand Duchess Charlotte of Luxembourg. The Grand Duchess is a regal but retiring mother of six children. She rarely appears in public. She was represented at this morning's ceremony by her husband, Prince Felix, and by her oldest son, Prince Jean, who is heir to the throne. But she has consented to transcribe for NBC a Memorial Day message to America. The next voice you hear will be that of the Grand Duchess of Luxembourg.

Grand Duchess Charlotte spoke in heavily accented English and quite emotionally at times, so the old tape I have of the radio broadcast is not as clear as I would have liked. Nevertheless, here are the most intelligible words:

> The great American nation, which has so generously advanced the cause of freedom for all other peoples, great or small, is not alone in its vigil. All over Europe and even the earth, men and women bend their heads in a silent tribute to those who gave their lives that we might live. . . .
>
> At the Hamm Cemetery, thousands of American soldiers of every rank who fell in the battle for the Ardennes lie beneath their wooden crosses. With them lies their courageous commander General Patton. There they sleep, surrounded by the affectionate devotion and the boundless gratitude of my people. Their last resting place will remain forever one of the sacred charms of Luxembourg. . . .
>
> Memorial Day has always been a day of remembrance and contemplation. Since the war, the wounds of the dead have taken on an even deeper significance. The endless rows of crosses are a

constant reminder of the last unspoken message of the young heroes of this gigantic struggle. . . .

It is up to us, the survivors, to make every endeavor that their sacrifice should not be in vain. Let us recall John McCrae's immortal lines from *Flanders Fields*:

> To you from failing hands we throw
> The torch; be yours to hold it high.
> If ye break faith with us who die
> We shall not sleep. . . .

But they can sleep in peace . . . with the help of God, until humanity has been spared the horror of war.

Mr. Cassidy ended his commentary with these words:

That was the Grand Duchess of Luxembourg. And this has been a moving experience for the members of the European staff of NBC who were proud to bring you a profound Memorial Day experience in the words of Grand Duchess Charlotte and General Peckham. . . . Americans at home are now being consulted as to whether the bodies will be left here or returned to America. If they are to go home, General Peckham's command will take them in full dignity. If they remain here, the people of the Grand Duchess will be honored to watch over them. Either way, those of us who observed today's ceremony are sure they are in good hands. This is Henry Cassidy in Luxembourg.

An announcer then closed the broadcast by saying:

NBC has presented "Memorial Day Overseas," with Grand Duchess Charlotte of Luxembourg, Brigadier General Howard Peckham, Henry Cassidy, and Paul Archinard of NBC's overseas staff. This is NBC, the National Broadcasting Company.

My father wrote this comment to Mother and me, "You will find the speech given by the Grand Duchess to be extremely moving and heartfelt." It certainly was. Also, listening to Dad's speech gave us a better picture of what his job entailed, and it was reassuring to hear that the AGRC was doing everything possible to help ease the pain of the next of kin. In late June, he wrote again and gave us more information about his job:

> One of my tasks is to visit the cemeteries in Europe to direct and inspect the work being done, such as the adequacy of transportation to and from the sites. I also must ensure that construction and grading operations are efficient.

Dad submitted to the Quartermaster General's office in Washington on June 11, 1947, a list of five methods to be used for grading, from which the best option would be selected. The first option was by local contract, with the contractor furnishing all machinery, personnel, and spare parts. The second was again by local contractors, but with the U.S. Army furnishing equipment and spare parts. The third was by use of U.S. Army Engineer troops. The fourth was by contract with an American firm, with that firm furnishing machinery, personnel, and spare parts. The fifth method was by contract with an American firm, but with the U. S. Army furnishing equipment and spare parts.

Steere and Boardman write about Dad's preference in *Final Disposition of World War II Dead: 1945-51*. It later became the adopted method.

> General Peckham anticipated the eventual choice of the first option as the most feasible since a preliminary survey had revealed that in France, Belgium, and Holland, several reputable contractors with ample heavy equipment and trained personnel were anxious to bid on the project. The possible use of this procedure in England was also under investigation.

On a windy day in September 1947, Dad marched to a speaker's stand at St. Laurent American Cemetery in Normandy. He was accompanied by American Ambassador to France Jefferson Caffery, Deputy Commander of EUCOM Lt. Gen Clarence R. Huebner, and French officials. They were there to pay homage to soldiers buried at St. Laurent who were to be unearthed that fall. "They will be returned to the United States, per the request of their next of kin," Dad explained to the crowd of spectators. He also explained that the cemetery would be reopened as a permanent resting place. Although the wind swept away the rain clouds while my father spoke, it unfortunately rustled the heavy silk flags of various veterans' groups.

When in Paris, Dad generally had dinner at his hotel, the Wagram, and turned in fairly early. Occasionally he attended social events, and he once met a fairly well-known actor at a party. Dad asked the actor for an autograph to send to his daughter "for her collection," and the man was glad to oblige. He wrote, "To Jeanie. Wish you were here tonight with your Dady. Sincerely, Wallace Beery." I don't know if the lovable character actor always spelled "Daddy" that way, but I prized his note.

Quite a few Hollywood stars, entertainers, and other well-to-do Americans traveled on vacations to postwar Europe, where they took advantage of the favorable exchange rate to dine in expensive restaurants and stay at luxurious hotels.

Members of elite Paris society were not hesitant to invite Hollywood celebrities to their lavish parties. For many other Europeans, including people in other areas of France, life was grim in homelands still devastated by war and poverty. Help was on the way, however. In June 1947, retired General George C. Marshall, who had served as American Secretary of State since January of that year, spoke at Harvard about a plan to rebuild the war-devastated countries of Europe. These are some of his comments:

> It is logical that the United States should do whatever it is able to do to assist in the return of normal economic health in the world,

without which there can be no political stability and no assured peace. Our policy is directed not against any country or doctrine but against hunger, poverty, desperation, and chaos. Its purpose should be the revival of a working economy in the world so as to permit the emergence of political and social conditions in which free institutions can exist.

Not long after General Marshall's speech, the United States government launched a program that was appropriately named the Marshall Plan, after him. Through its policies, the devastated economies of Europe could be rehabilitated, which would result in stabilized economies.

The Marshall Plan tied in well with President Truman's doctrine proclaiming that countries in need of financial assistance should be helped so as to stop them from turning to communism. Financial stability, both Truman and Marshall believed, would ensure the survival of democracy.

In the fall, a few weeks after General Marshall gave that historic lecture, Dad wrote a letter to Mother and me praising the way Howie had made it, with flying colors, through a traditional rite of passage that summer—Beast Barracks, a rugged course of six weeks during which the plebes at West Point arose before dawn, spent very long hours participating in military drills, and endlessly answered "No, Sir" and "Yes, Sir" to questions barked at them throughout the day by upperclassmen, who had been sent to haze them. Although the plebes learned a lot about discipline, the routine was very often demeaning. Howie was undoubtedly glad when academic classes began in September.

Dad's letter also described what was currently transpiring with the AGRC. "Among the other duties I have already told you about," Dad wrote, "I am busily making preparations for the journey home of our war dead from their current resting places."

The first shipload of American war dead from Europe, more than five thousand caskets, arrived in New York City in October 1947. They had left from the dock-filled city of Antwerp, Belgium, which was the primary port for the deceased of that zone in

Europe. General Lucius Clay, United States Military Governor in Germany and Chief of the European Command (EUCOM), paid homage to them before the flower-bedecked USAT *Joseph V. Connolly* slowly left port on October 5. On that day, wherever the American flag flew over U.S. installations in Europe, it was flown at half-staff.

Preceding the ship's departure, Dad wrote, his office had sent a list of the deceased's names by air courier to the Quartermaster General's Office in Washington. My father then explained the reason for this expediency: "The list enables their families to be contacted and permits arrangements to be made for subsequent transportation of the deceased within the United States." He added that the same procedure would be followed for later shipments.

We always looked forward to my father's informative letters about Europe. He and Howie occasionally received letters from my mother and me, but they didn't learn about everything that was happening at 3108 Cathedral Avenue. I wouldn't have known how to tell them, so I kept to myself news about the disconcerting change that I noticed in our daily routine. Sometimes after she returned from the grocery store, Mother would discreetly remove bottles of liquor from her bags of groceries. And she frequently invited Claire Ordway's mother, Christine, and a couple of other army wives to our house for highballs.

More often than not, she drank alone. Even though she didn't show any signs of intoxication, a feeling of apprehension nagged at me from time to time when I noticed this changed behavior on her part. Most of the time, it didn't affect me—and I wouldn't have wanted to worry Dad about it.

Like the snow that sometimes covered Cathedral Avenue's sidewalks in the wintertime, my apprehensions melted away during our last two months in Washington. What I wouldn't have known at the time is that Mother would continue to struggle with a drinking problem for the rest of her life.

December ushered in some pleasant events. On December 8, I celebrated my sixteenth birthday with a party at my house attended by a group of my schoolmates. Mother and I then began planning for a Christmas reunion with Howie.

On the day of our departure, December 23, we took a taxi to Washington's Union Station. Here we joined throngs of people who wandered throughout the cavernous building—many with gaily-decorated packages tucked under their arms. Anxiously, they approached information windows or scanned departure schedules under the high, arched ceiling.

The train we boarded took us to New York City, where we transferred to another train for the fifty-mile ride through the rolling hills of New York State. After it screeched into the West Point station, we immediately searched for Howie's familiar face among a sea of young men dressed in gray uniforms. When we spotted him, I saw that his posture was ramrod straight, due no doubt to obeying orders of first classmen and bracing on command. He looked more mature, I thought. After we greeted and embraced him, my brother helped us check into our guest quarters and gave us our schedule for the week.

First on the agenda was a tour of the Academy grounds, led by one of Howie's classmates. My mother knew the area well, having lived at West Point as a young wife when my father was an engineering instructor there. Several of the huge stone buildings, such as Washington Hall and the Administration Building, looked sturdy enough to be there until the end of time, and their Elizabethan style reminded me of pictures I had seen of castles in Europe.

Early on Christmas Eve, we went to the cadet chapel, which sat high on a hill overlooking the parade ground. In addition to the pine trees that surrounded it were some tall slender trees whose bare branches reached vertically upwards, as if to mimic the hands folded in prayer within the chapel. Inside the imposing Gothic-style structure, where we attended a concert of Christmas music, the sonorous voices of the cadet choir seemed to resonate among the arches high above me, bringing to mind the time Dad said, "One of my favorite activities at the Academy was singing in the choir." Then I remembered with pleasure the Christmas Eves when our family attended church services together. I also recalled the times that Dad joyfully sang his favorite carol, *The First Noel*.

The following day, after driving past the clock tower and ivy-covered academic buildings, my mother, brother, and I joined other dinner guests to feast on moist turkey and all the trimmings at the home of dapper Colonel Thomas D. Stamps of the military history department. At the end of another party the next evening, one of the cadet guests walked me home. We carried on a polite conversation while strolling under tall pole lamps that cast a soft glow on the ground around us. Snowflakes that gleamed like pearls quietly fell on the shiny visor of his cap and on the gray cape of his uniform. It all seemed quite magical.

An especially pleasant event for me during our week's stay was the dance—or hop, as they called it—at Cullum Hall. While I was walking through the hall's imposing entrance that evening, framed on each side by a bronze cannon and tall Grecian columns, I thought about teenagers in past eras who had danced with young cadets at West Point, glamorous belles whose spectacular hourglass figures were enhanced by tightly laced corsets.

I also thought about West Point graduates who became generals during the Civil War and donned either the Blue or the Gray, a list that includes Robert E. Lee, Ulysees S. Grant, George A. Custer, William T. Sherman, and Thomas "Stonewall" Jackson. In spite of feeling overwhelmed by the presence of so much history and tradition, I enjoyed twirling on the dance floor with several cadets.

On our last night, December 28, Mother and I attended an ice show put on by the cadets—a plebe Christmas tradition. The next morning we packed quickly in order to catch the train back to Washington. Fatigue overwhelmed me on the trip home, but it wasn't an unpleasant kind of tiredness. I looked forward to telling my father about my idyllic stay at his alma mater.

That would be happening soon, because on January 1, Mother received a tentative date for our voyage to Bremerhaven. My father wrote that he had arranged a mid-February departure, which meant we needed to prepare right away for our trip. This included getting our furniture delivered to the storage warehouse Dad had selected and packing items we would need in Europe.

We also had to get shots at the Pentagon medical center, but finding it wasn't easy. "I think we're supposed to turn left here," my mother said hesitantly after we had made a wrong turn somewhere within the maze of corridors. We did find it, though. According to my diary, my inoculations included smallpox and typhoid vaccines.

(LEFT) (L TO R) HOWIE, PETE CLAY, AND SANDY VANDENBERG ENJOYING A NIGHT OUT BEFORE THEY LEAVE FOR WEST POINT, 1947 *(RIGHT)* CULLUM HALL AT WEST POINT

In early February, after saying goodbye to Claire, Christine, and other neighbors, we packed our remaining belongings and left Cathedral Avenue behind us. A few months later, I got a letter from Claire extolling the virtues of Hawaii, Colonel Ordway's next station after leaving Washington. I wrote her saying that I, too, was living in a noteworthy place. In fact, I was there during one of the most decisive epochs in its history.

BELGIANS HONORING THE FIRST SHIPLOAD OF AMERICAN WAR DEAD FROM EUROPE:
ANTWERP, 1947

STARS AND STRIPES ARTICLE SHOWING CLARENCE HUEBNER AND DAD MARCHING SIDE-
BY-SIDE AT ST. LAURENT: NORMANDY, 1947

(**The caption below the pictures reads:** American and French officials march to a speaker's
stand in St. Laurent Sur Mer cemetery of U.S. World War II dead. In the center foreground,
carrying hat, is U.S. Ambassador Jefferson Caffery. Behind Caffery are Lt. Gen. Clarence R.
Huebner, deputy EUCOM commander, and Brig. Gen. Howard L. Peckham, commander of the
American Graves Registration Command.)

Chapter 9

An In-Depth Look at the AGRC

We are going to have peace even if we have to fight for it.

--DWIGHT D. EISENHOWER

MOTHER AND I WERE AGAIN SCHEDULED to board a train bound for the state of New York, as we had done at Christmastime. This time, however, it was to be an overnight ride on a Pullman.

February 17, 1948, found us hurriedly re-examining our tickets amidst the hustle and bustle of Washington's Union Station and then climbing into the train. This was my first time sleeping on a Pullman, and due partly to the clanking of the wheels on the railroad tracks and also to my excitement about sailing to Europe, I didn't sleep much that night.

It was early morning when we arrived at our destination, Fort Hamilton in Brooklyn. We wearily prepared our suitcases and were then driven to our guest quarters on the post. The accommodations were quite comfortable, and our meals in the typical U.S. Army cafeteria were excellent.

When our sailing date of February 24 finally arrived, we went to Staten Island, where our U.S. Army transport *Harry Taylor* was docked. Giving Mother, me, and the other passengers a royal sendoff as we walked up the gangplank was an army band, which enthusiastically played sentimental and patriotic music down on the dock.

A friendly guide directed us to our stateroom.

Not long thereafter, the anchor was pulled up and our transport slowly glided away from the pier. The *USAT Harry Taylor,* I learned after reading a souvenir booklet given to each of us passengers, was built in 1944 and was named after a general who had served as an executive officer of the Engineer Corps during the First World War. I read that in 1945, the ship sailed from Marseilles and was headed to the Pacific war zone by way of the Panama Canal when its captain learned of the Japanese surrender. When the news was received, the ship's bow turned joyfully towards New York, the booklet proclaimed.

The ship's postwar assignment was to carry military troops and members of military families to Germany as part of the occupation forces. Some of the passengers, such as my mother and I, were bound for other places in Europe.

Our journey was often rough, due to the frequent storms at that time of the year in North Atlantic waters. In my diary on the morning of February 28 I wrote: "I couldn't sleep because we were rocking so much. The waves looked like huge snowcapped mountains." During breakfast a bit later, I was fascinated to see the way our juice glasses frequently wobbled or slid across the table, and to hear the noisy rattle of cereal bowls and other dishes. Fortunately, I didn't get seasick.

On clear days my favorite pastime was standing near the railing to watch the dark-blue ocean as the ship's bow cut through it like a huge pie knife, particularly after a storm had recently abated. When the waves turned over, I would see a lovely shade of aqua.

I found several good ways to pass the time. I never missed the movies shown in the auditorium on our deck, which one rainy day included *The Red Danube* with Walter Pidgeon and Janet Leigh. I also enjoyed reading books and magazines borrowed from the ship's library, which I read while relaxing in a deck chair. I had another reason to visit the library besides a literary one, as I wrote in my diary: "One of the enlisted men working behind the library counter is really good-looking. I like talking to him." I talked to him too often, probably.

Because this was primarily a troop ship, many fire drills were scheduled in which we family members needed to participate. The ship had seven decks, and the troops—soldiers who were traveling without families—were not on our deck but on a different one.

Mother and I didn't follow the instructions correctly during our first abandon-ship drill. In our haste to get to our proper station within the time allowed, we ended up standing at attention on the troop deck, lined up with hundreds of soldiers. We should have been with the other hundred or so family members on another deck, but it was too late to get there after we discovered our mistake. She and I laughed about that incident several times in the days that followed. Like Dad, my mother loved jokes and laughter, even when the jokes were on her.

After nine days at sea, a series of exciting events took place indicating we were approaching Europe. On March 3, I spotted a fleet of graceful Irish fishing boats. At six o'clock the next morning, our ship picked up a pilot boat at Dover on the English Channel. Not long afterwards, we entered the North Sea, where we could see a few small English vessels.

On March 6, the port city of Bremerhaven in northwest Germany came into view. We gently entered its bleak harbor and pulled up beside a long wooden pier, where lively music played by a U.S. Army band greeted us. It was the same kind of music we had heard during our sendoff twelve days earlier, only less sentimental.

"Have fun in Europe!" I called to my new friends Johnny and Jo Ann Howard as we all headed towards the gangplank. Like most of the other passengers they would be living in Germany, where their father, an army lieutenant colonel, would be a member of the Army of Occupation. Many families had preceded them. The first dependents after World War II had arrived in Bremerhaven in 1946.

Due to the nuances of army protocol, my mother and I were instructed to be the first to leave the ship. Even though my father wasn't a passenger, he would be meeting us on the dock, and he outranked the officers who had traveled with us, as well as those who were on the dock patiently waiting for their dependents. In Washington I hadn't received the kind of privileges we would receive in Europe.

German dockworkers looked at us with curious stares as I self-consciously made my way down the gangplank. People standing at the bottom of the gangplank also watched us, as did our fellow passengers, who stood on the ship's deck. Dad rushed to meet us and greeted us with hugs and kisses. He had made a brief visit to Washington about four months previously, so it hadn't been very long since we last saw him.

It all seemed unreal. An army car with a general's star on its bumper plate was waiting for us near the area where my father met us, and the driver slowly took the three of us on our way. When military personnel walked by, most snapped at attention while saluting Dad, and he looked very important when he returned their salutes from the car window. He wasn't the casually dressed father in postwar Washington who had helped me with my math homework in the evenings—he was a senior officer in the European Command (EUCOM), and he belonged to a conquering army with headquarters in a vanquished land.

When the car started traveling farther away from the docks, I felt more than ready to be on dry land again; however, I was emotionally not prepared for the ghostly sight of downtown Bremerhaven as our car and driver took us through it. The docks looked largely unimpaired, fortunately for the transport ships, but the buildings in the downtown area had been completely shattered by Allied bombs, and nothing had really been done about rebuilding them yet. In some areas the city looked like a giant concrete pancake, where no buildings stood.

I told my father that seeing the piles of rubble was a shock, and he agreed with me that the damage had been extensive—but necessary. "Strategic targets, such as railroads, oil refineries, bridges, and industrial sites, were intentionally bombed by Allied pilots," he explained, "but they purposely avoided hitting docks that could be used by our ships after the war, such as those here."

The trains seemed to be working fine now, and we boarded one that began carrying us through Germany. I then saw more of the rueful damage done to that nation, destruction that the Allies had needed to inflict in order to win the war. Throughout the countryside, which I described in my diary as looking "torn up," industrial buildings opened up to the late-winter sky, and we saw big dumps of bricks and concrete everywhere. All that remained of many houses was a lone wall or perhaps a gutted frame.

Aside from the devastation, danger still lurked in some parts of the Siegfried Line, a defense system of fortifications built by the Germans along their country's western frontier. We personally were not in danger, but AGRC recovery teams certainly were, as my father explained:

> Minefields exist in dense parts of the Siegfried Line that haven't been cleared. In addition to being dangerous, this situation creates time delays for AGRC teams searching those areas for fallen Americans.

Searches for our soldiers were also difficult in the thick brambles of the Hurtgen Forest, where there were still several mines. Dad described this problem in a status report he wrote for the *Occupation Forces in Europe Series: The Third Year, 1947-1948*, published by the Army Historical Division (1949):

> An operational problem in the West Wall [Siegfried Line] area of Germany arose from the fact that the area was mined by the German forces and later re-mined by the Allied forces. Search and exhumation operations were therefore difficult. In the area of Aachen, for example, additional American tanks and American remains were found as more mine fields were cleared.

I didn't think further about the Siegfried Line or the Hurtgen Forest while our train clanked through the land of Wagner. I was too busy observing people through our compartment's window, such as the dour-faced men and women who seemed almost lifeless as they shuffled along on the often-broken pavement. The bitter air of winter had undoubtedly added to their misery. Even the younger ones, perhaps still in their twenties or thirties, appeared withdrawn, as if they were carrying a heavy burden. The women's apparel added to their sullen appearance. Most wore scarves tied snugly around their heads, as well as heavy, thick stockings and clunky-looking shoes.

At one point during that long night, U.S. Army personnel led us off the train at a railroad station and into an army car. The car and soldier driver then took us through part of Germany that was far away from Bremerhaven, but maybe my fatigue only made it seem that way. We were probably going from one station to another, but my diary doesn't mention the exact reason for this dreary, fog-shrouded journey. Someone from Dad's office in Paris had made efficient transportation arrangements, but nothing could have been done about the weather. We traveled for several scary miles through opaque fog, and the car's headlights cast long beams of light to guide us as we rolled carefully on our way.

On March 7, we boarded a crowded train that took us through Belgium and then into France. The scenery made me feel as if I had awakened from a bad dream into a new, bright day. I saw green pastures, tiny homes, and horse-drawn carts, which, when viewed all at once, looked like settings on a stage. In my diary I described the scenery as "just beautiful." The train ride gave me the chance to compare the French people with the Germans, and I noticed several obvious differences. Some of this contrast would have been noticeable without World War II, but most of it was due to the negative effects of Germany's defeat and surrender, as well as the deplorable conditions in which many of its people lived.

For example, the Frenchwomen that I saw wore shoes and stockings that looked much less bulky than those of the German women. Temperamental contrasts were even more striking. French passengers who boarded the train seemed refreshingly lively. They engaged each other in animated conversations, hands flying this way and that, and they often shouted something like

"Mais oui!" to a companion. When fellow passengers squeezed by me as I walked in the train's narrow corridor, they would cheerily say *"pardonez-mois"* or simply *"pardon."* Unlike the few Germans with whom we spoke, they seemed to enjoy talking with us. "The fraternization ban imposed on American military personnel has been lifted," my father told us later, "but friendly conversations between Americans and Germans are still strained." Friendships between American GIs and their German girlfriends were an exception, however. "They seem to like each other quite well," my father said with a sly smile.

After our train had whizzed adjacent to the small villages of northeastern France, it clanked its way noisily through the city suburbs and finally, on March 9, into the Paris station, where the car and driver sent from my father's office were waiting for us.

Dad immediately started acting as our guide after my mother and I settled ourselves into the backseat. When we drove down the famous Champs Élysées, where victorious armies throughout French history have marched in glorious parades, he pointed out that American soldiers had been among those who marched here in August 1944 to celebrate the liberation. "Paris opened its heart to them," he told us.

When our drive along the Champs Élysées ended, our car brought us to the wide Place de la Concorde. Here I saw the thin obelisk that points towards the sky and two round fountains on either side of it that gaily spouted streams of water, offsetting its austerity. They were surrounded by several monuments, which represented various cities in France. "The Hôtel Wagram on the Rue de Rivoli is right around the corner," my father said while I was busily admiring the fountains.

The hotel, named after a battle in which the French under Napoleon had defeated the Austrians, had been my father's home ever since he arrived in the city. Greeting us as we walked into the lobby was the pink-cheeked, smiling concierge, who gave us our key and helped us with our bags. We then rode in a small cage-like elevator that crept slowly up to my father's floor. While leading us into the large sitting room of his suite, he said, "I'm sure you'll like the view." Then he pulled open the heavy drapes that covered the room's two tall windows, which faced the busy and fashionable Rue de Rivoli. I walked onto the small balcony off one of the windows to get a good look at the rectangularly shaped Jardin des Tuileries Park across the street.

I could see the bare limbs of slender trees on which new spring buds would soon open. I could also see paved areas where, in late spring, children would launch tiny sailboats into a serene pond, and young couples would walk hand in hand alongside flower gardens as colorful as rainbows.

In the coming days, I often looked down from that balcony. I would see prosperous-looking Frenchmen, most of whom wore what appeared to be good-quality business suits, rushing to the Metro or hailing taxis. Also, I would observe stylishly dressed women strolling down the Rue, some undoubtedly on their way to Rumpelmeyer's café to enjoy its famous tea and pastry. They were wearing long dresses, the hems of which seemed to touch the pavement. "I see the 'new look' is in vogue here like it was in Washington," I naively said to Mother after I stepped back into the comfortable sitting room. (The "look" started in Paris, of course.)

From these observations and others that I made during my first weeks in the city, it seemed to me that Parisians had bounced back well from World War II. However, I would soon see for myself that residents of Paris, especially those who could afford to frequent the shops and cafés near the Champs Élysées, were not typical of postwar French citizens.

Many parts of France were economically devastated by the war, thus causing political instability. Much to the distress of President Truman and Winston Churchill, France and Italy were experiencing growth in the influence and membership of the Communist Party. For much of Europe, where communists had already taken over, it was too late. In fact, the month before my mother and I arrived on the Continent, Party members won a parliamentary election in Czechoslovakia, thus putting that small inland country under complete control of the Communist Party. It became the last nation in Europe to slide like a stream of water behind the Iron Curtain.

Partly to counteract the growth of communism in Europe, President Truman signed a notable document in April 1948 establishing an agency that would be set up to administer the Marshall Plan's recovery program. The agency that evolved was called the Economic Cooperation Administration (ECA). Paul G. Hoffman, who had formerly been the chairman of the Studebaker Corporation, was appointed to head the ECA, with headquarters in Washington. The administrator of the ECA program in France, from 1949 to 1950, was Barry Bingham. His son, Barry Jr., was a schoolmate of mine. (He was in tenth grade at the American School in Paris when I was a senior.)

For the most part, the plan was warmly received in France, where news about its goals and progress spread widely. *"J'aime beaucoup le Plan Marshall"* or *"Le Plan Marshall est terrifique"* are typical comments I heard when I told people I was an American. The good effects rendered by way of the ECA in France were dramatic. French farms and factories were rejuvenated because of the goods they got from the United States, such as wood, coal, and tractors. French business owners benefited from advice they received from American technical and economic consultants. Under the Marshall Plan, which was in effect for about four years, the United States gave Western Europe several billion dollars in recovery aid, which helped to restore industrial expansion, agricultural production, and financial stability. It also brought political stability, thus lessening the influence of the Communist Party. Even defeated Germany benefited greatly from the plan.

By April 1948 I still hadn't visited Germany, except for our trip through the green-forested countryside on our way to France. The Howards, whom I had met on the ship, were my only friends there, I thought. So I was surprised when an envelope addressed to me arrived in April, mailed from Bamberg, Germany.

When I opened it, I saw that it was a letter from the soldier who had worked in the ship's library, with whom I had chatted on several occasions. I had never told him I would be staying at the

Wagram, but I was pleased to hear from him. The subject matter of his letter primarily concerned army life in Bamberg.

It was also romantic in places, a fact that my father quickly noticed. "The man is undoubtedly much older than you are," he firmly remarked after I had excitedly, and rather naively, shown the letter to my parents. Then Dad let me know that the soldier was off-limits and that I was not allowed to reply to his letter. Somewhat reluctantly, I followed his instructions, thus ending a potential relationship. This was the first time I noticed that Dad had more than a passing interest in who my friends were. It was an eye opener. Several new and interesting experiences soon followed this disappointing incident, and my fond memories of that shipboard romance (of sorts) slowly faded away.

Dad hosted a party at the Hôtel Celtic in April. The hotel, located two blocks up from the Champs Élysées near the Étoile, was essentially an AGRC hotel then. At the party, he officially introduced my mother and me to several AGRC officers and their wives. Many Department of the Army civilians under my father's command also attended the party.

According to *Occupation Forces in Europe Series: The Third Year, 1947-1948,* the AGRC workforce consisted of approximately 1,500 military personnel, 3,300 civilians, and 2,600 local resident laborers. I saw Dad beam when a couple of guests complimented me on my appearance. It was a treat for me to receive attention from people who worked for him, and I was glad he seemed proud of me. When I was a schoolgirl in Washington, I never had an occasion to meet the people who worked for him at the Fuels and Lubricants Division.

A few weeks later, a reception was held in honor of my parents at Isle St. Germain, the AGRC depot on the Seine River. This was where Paris-based AGRC soldiers were billeted and had their mess hall. It's also where our theater (for stage shows), PX, commissary, and dentist were located. My parents and I rode to the occasion in an army car, accompanied by an official military escort. When we and the motorcycle outriders swung through traffic on streets near the Seine River, even Parisians who were otherwise blasé turned and looked at us with curious stares. It was as if we were celebrities. The reception at the depot was warm and congenial, and I was beginning to feel that life in Europe would be both interesting and fun.

We were not in Europe to have fun, however. Reality would be brought to the fore only a few days later, when I was in Howard Peckham's office at AGRC headquarters, where I had come to learn more about his work and meet the clerical staff. AGRC offices were located in the former Hôtel Astoria, at the corner of Rue de Presbourg and 131 Avenue des Champs Élysées. "This map shows the location of the temporary cemeteries," Dad said as he pointed to a map on the wall of his spacious office.

I learned from him that graves registration activities of the Quartermaster Corps in the European Theater began in December 1941, when the United States asked the British War Office about burial facilities for our military personnel expected to arrive in 1942 in Northern Ireland, where they would aid the British in their defense of that part of Ireland. Sadly, as was expected, American lives were lost after the men arrived in that area of Ireland. These burials had been in swampy ground in local cemeteries, but the U.S. Army negotiated with the British and secured a plot of land at Lisnabreeny, a suburb of Belfast. That's where the Americans were reinterred (not permanently, though, as I will explain later).

All through the war, graves registration soldiers diligently picked up our dead and transported them by trucks to temporary cemeteries. Moving them quickly was a big priority. This was especially true when the dead lay on main highways, where they could be seen by troops moving in their direction.

The victims who died during the initial landings on D-Day, so graphically depicted in the movie *Saving Private Ryan*, were buried as quickly as possible on the beaches and then later brought to temporary cemeteries (primarily St. Laurent-Sur-Mer).

In Europe, the command known as the American Graves Registration Command-European Area (AGRC-EA) was created in 1945. In the preface he wrote for L. R. Talbot's book *The Story of*

American Graves Registration Command in Europe and Africa, published in 1955, Major General Robert Littlejohn writes how and why the command was created. He was still serving as Chief Quartermaster of the European Theater in 1945 when it all began. Here are his words:

> I came home with General Eisenhower on his private plane in June 1945. On this trip he and I discussed the problem of Graves Registration, cemeteries, etc....
>
> We agreed that a separate command should be set up to do the job in the ETO....
>
> As a result, I was relieved as Chief Quartermaster, ETO, in the fall of 1945 and assigned as Commanding General, American Graves Registration Command with station in Paris....
>
> I organized this new command with an allotment of military personnel given me by General Eisenhower. Civilians were employed to the fullest extent....

Before formalizing the organization's establishment, the two generals discussed the main reasons for creating the AGRC in Europe. Among these were that American troops were quickly being repatriated to the United States after the war, leaving many temporary cemeteries understaffed. Also, there was a need to consolidate graves registration functions under one command, instead of leaving them in the hands of the various armies (such as Seventh Army). An official document to establish the AGRC-EA resulted from those discussions. It had the title "Establishment of Command" and became effective October 1, 1945.

In regard to the subsequent performance of the AGRC in Europe, Littlejohn indicated that he was quite pleased with its work. In his preface to Talbot's book, which he composed at his Maryland home in 1955, the general writes:

> I think I can truthfully say, without fear of contradiction, that the performance of the American Graves Registration Command in the European Theater was one of the greatest jobs ever performed

by the Quartermaster Corps and the Army anywhere at any time in any war. . . . I salute the commanders who followed me for their accomplishments for which I only pointed the way, to wit:

Brigadier General John C. Odel
Brigadier General Alfred B. Denniston,
Major General Howard L. Peckham

Right after V-J Day, any Americans who had been buried temporarily in Germany were brought back to Allied territory. German prisoners of war were used for certain hard-labor jobs, but they were forbidden to handle American war dead. My father would have considered such action on their part to be a serious breach of U.S. Army policy.

One of the first tasks of the newly established AGRC was to conduct extensive searches for our war dead in the liberated areas of Europe, where local labor was used, and in the French, British, and American zones of Germany. (Later, this book describes problems involved in searching for our dead in the Russian zone.)

Thousands of permanent reinterments were to be handled under the Return Program. When my father was put in charge of the Return of the Remains Program, he faced a responsibility far bigger than that of the two other AGRC commanders who followed General Littlejohn, Generals Odel and Denniston.

Now, while pointing to a large map of Europe, my father described the thirty-seven temporary American cemeteries that were located throughout the Continent. Just as in World War I, most Americans who died in the European Theater lost their lives in France, where there were twenty-four temporary cemeteries by the end of the war. As was the case in the other Western European countries, these were located near the battle sites where the soldiers had perished. Two neutral countries had American cemeteries on their soil. "Near Malmö, Sweden, thirty-eight American fliers died when their planes crashed," my father said, adding somberly, "The site in Switzerland contained the remains of sixty-six fliers whose planes were forced down in that country." The cemetery was closed in January 1948, and he had taken part in the closing ceremony. Three other countries stayed neutral in the war—Spain, Portugal, and Ireland. The temporary cemetery in Lisnabreeny was under AGRC supervision. There were no American cemeteries in Spain or Portugal.

At the time of that first visit to Dad's office, the temporary properties were in the process of being returned to their owners because of a document approved by President Truman on August 5, 1947. This document, which was an amendment to Public Law 368, empowered the Secretary of War to acquire foreign land for permanent American military cemeteries. The amendment's approval officially enabled the AGRC to start returning thousands of war dead to the United States and to start reburial of thousands of other Americans in ten permanent sites in Europe.

My father worked hard to maintain good relations with the host countries, so he insisted that temporary sites be given back to those countries in an orderly condition. In this respect, he required the complete demolition of the AGRC's temporary structures, as noted in *Occupation Forces in Europe: 1947-1948*:

> The Commanding General, AGRC-EA, emphasized that temporary cemetery sites were in no circumstances to be left in a half demolished condition. Complete demolition [of structures erected by the AGRC] was required even though the project entailed greater expense.

All ten permanent sites had an association with a nearby battle or engagement. "Each is being graded and constructed under the direction of the AGRC," my father said. All would be on the site of a former temporary cemetery, except for St. Avold in France, which was being built on new ground.

Three countries would have one permanent cemetery each, which were given the names Margraten, Hamm, and Cambridge. Margraten Cemetery in The Netherlands was chosen as the burial place of primarily Ninth Army casualties. Hamm Cemetery in

Luxembourg was selected as the resting place of mostly Third Army casualties. Cambridge Cemetery in England became the predominant resting place of members of the United States Army Air Force (USAAF) and victims of the Battle of the Atlantic. In addition, the dead who had been interred at Lisnabreeny were reburied at Cambridge when the former was closed. Belgium would have two permanent cemeteries, which were named Henri-Chapelle and Neuville-en-Condroz. They became the resting places of predominantly Ninth Army casualties who died during the advance of our troops into Germany.

Five permanent cemeteries were to be located in France— Draguignan in the south, Épinal in the northeast, St. Avold near the German border, St. James in Brittany, and St. Laurent in Normandy. These five were selected as the resting places of predominantly First, Seventh, and Third Army casualties.

St. Laurent in Normandy, now called Normandy Cemetery, is probably the best-known American cemetery in France, due to its connection to the history of D-Day. It is movingly shown in the opening and closing scenes of *Saving Private Ryan*. In one of the film's other scenes, the actor who plays General George C. Marshall (Harve Presnell) is heard repeating the comforting words that Abraham Lincoln spoke in a letter to the bereaved mother of five fallen Civil War soldiers. These same words were appropriate when Presnell, playing General George Marshall in the film, used them to comfort the next of kin of World War II:

> I pray that our Heavenly Father may assuage the anguish of your bereavement, and leave you only the cherished memory of the loved and lost, and the solemn pride that must be yours, to have laid so costly a sacrifice upon the altar of Freedom.

It is certainly true that George Marshall, then Army Chief of Staff, wrote personal letters to many next of kin, trying to comfort them as best he could. As I mentioned earlier, Willis Crittenberger received a letter of consolation from General Marshall when his son, Townsend Crittenberger, was killed in World War II.

My father's voice that day when I first visited his office was suffused with compassion for the next of kin who had lost loved ones in the European Theater. "I made sure my office complied with their preferences," he said. In regard to those preferences, the Memorial Division of the Quartermaster General's Office had a ranking system to determine whose wishes would receive first priority in selecting a burial site. It was followed in this order:

> If the deceased was married, the surviving spouse has first preference. If the husband or wife has remarried, or the parties were divorced or separated prior to the death, then the preference passes to sons who are over twenty-one years of age. If there is no son over twenty-one years of age, the preference passes to the daughters who are over twenty-one years of age. If there are children under age, or there are no children at all, then the right to dispose of the remains passes to surviving relatives in the order of their relationship to the deceased.

The Quartermaster General's Office in Washington sent letters to the next of kin expressing sympathy and also asking whether they would prefer that their loved one be reinterred in a permanent site in Europe or returned to the United States. Answers to those questions were then relayed to my father's office in Paris. In either case, it wasn't an easy choice for the next of kin to make. If they chose the European alternative, visiting the site in the years to come could be expensive and time consuming. Choosing the second alternative could reawaken the sorrow the next of kin felt when they first received news of the loved one's death. The war had ended more than two years earlier, so time had softened the blow for some family members.

Each alternative had advantages, however. My father knew that the sites in Europe could transmit peace and tranquility to the families who visited them. Also, the sites would be kept looking beautiful. "Those who choose the first alternative can be assured that the site will be well maintained in the future," he often said.

For family members who chose reinterment in the United States, personnel at distribution centers were available to help them. The AGRC had arranged for employees to be hired at those centers, and it had ensured that proper facilities were set up at the port of New York to greet incoming ships. Then Dad said, in a quiet, solemn voice, "Before the arrival of the ships, next of kin are notified so they can arrange for private services to be held." He of course knew how emotionally painful those services would be for the families.

U.S. to Honor War II Dead in 37 Cemeteries

By JONATHAN LEVIN
Staff Correspondent

PARIS, May 23—High ranking military, diplomatic and civil officials of the U.S. and host nations headed by Gen. Lucius D. Clay EUCOM commander, will lead this year's Memorial Day ceremonies honoring the 144,000 American World War II dead buried in 37 temporary military cemeteries in Western Europe.

Every cemetery, no matter how small, will have its own individual service with joint participation of U.S. Army chaplains and local clergymen. Thousands of school children will place flowers on the graves.

In many instances, Lincoln's Gettysburg Address will be read. Ceremonial wreaths will be placed and the rites will be concluded with the firing of rifle volleys and the sounding of taps. At each graveside will stand a miniature American Flag.

Clay to Speak at Hamm

Clay will be the principal speaker at Hamm Cemetery, in Luxembourg, where Gen. George S. Patton, Jr., wartime commander of the 3rd U.S. Army, is buried with soldiers of his command.

Brig. Gen. Howard L. Peckham, new commander of the American Graves Registration Command, which is in charge of Memorial Day ceremonies in the U.S. cemeteries in Western Europe, will introduce the EUCOM chief.

Clay will be accompanied by Gen. d'Armée Pierre Koenig, commander-in-chief of the French Zone of Germany, and Ambassador Robert D. Murphy, U.S. political adviser in Germany.

STARS AND STRIPES ARTICLE ABOUT MEMORIAL DAY CEREMONIES IN WESTERN EUROPE (1947) AND MY FATHER'S ROLE IN THEM

When I left my father's office that day, I had a good understanding of the AGRC's work in Europe. Looking back at that work from the perspective of time, I truly believe that nothing is more heroic than giving one's life for one's country. More than 400,000 Americans lost their lives while serving in World War II, the biggest war in history. Nearly 300,000 of those fatalities were battle deaths, according to the most reliable almanacs. The *Encyclopedia Britannica Almanac, 2004 Edition,* gives the figure of 292,141 for persons killed in battle and 115,185 for those who died from other causes, such as accidents. Many victims were buried in one of the fourteen permanent American cemeteries overseas (ten under my father's command, two in Italy, one in North Africa, and one in the Philippines).

Besides military personnel, a few eligible civilians, such as members of the press and Red Cross, are buried in American military cemeteries on foreign soil. Also, more than two hundred army nurses died in combat, seventeen of whom are buried in United States overseas cemeteries. This is noted in *V for Victory: America's Home Front During World War II.*

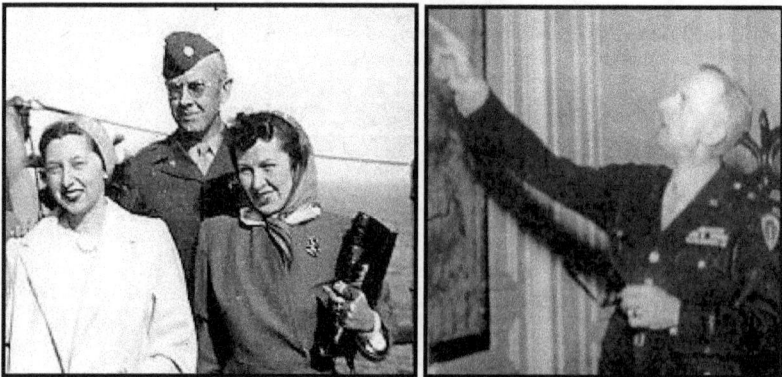

(LEFT) JEAN WITH LT. COL. AND MRS. HOWARD ABOARD THE TRANSPORT SHIP
(RIGHT) DAD IN HIS OFFICE DESCRIBING HIS AGRC WORK, 1948

My father's job with the AGRC was expected to end whenever the return of remains to the United States and the reinterments in

Europe had been completed—by 1951 at the latest. Then all of the American World War II cemeteries in Western Europe, as well as those in the Philippines, Italy, and North Africa, would be transferred to the care of an agency whose headquarters were in the United States but which had offices all over the world—the American Battle Monuments Commission (ABMC). Even before the transfer, an important interrelationship existed between the army's AGRC and the ABMC, an agency of the U.S. Government.

The firm of Harbeson, Hough, Livingston and Larson of Philadelphia, chosen to make the final layout plan for St. Laurent, completed its work in February 1948, considerably later than had been expected, but in sufficient time to permit AGRC engineers to prepare the necessary detailed grading plans. Following this step, invitations to bid on the grading work were issued to several French contracting firms. The successful bidder was not able to begin actual operations until June 1948 because of a delay in the receipt of the right of entry from the French Government. Grading and construction operations ended early in November 1948.[34]

[31] AGRC-EA, Engineer Historical Record of the Design and Development of the U. S. World War II Cemetery at St. Laurent sur Mer, France, p. 2.
[32] *Ibid.*, pp. 4, 6–7.
[33] *Ibid.*, p. 10.
[34] *Ibid.*, pp. 16–17.

PARAGRAPH FROM *FINAL DISPOSITION* DESCRIBING AGRC WORK AT ST. LAURENT, 1948

MARGRATEN CEMETERY IN HOLLAND BEFORE REINTERMENTS

AN AGRC PARTY AT THE CELTIC HOTEL FOR OFFICERS, DEPARTMENT OF THE ARMY
CIVILIANS, AND THEIR GUESTS, 1948

AGRC SOLDIERS' MESS HALL DECORATED FOR THANKSGIVING (DAD IN THE MIDDLE, COL.
KELLOGG FAR LEFT, JEAN FAR RIGHT): ST. GERMAIN DEPOT, 1948

Chapter 10

Life in Postwar Paris

April in Paris, chestnuts in blossom, holiday table under the trees.
April in Paris, this is a feeling no one can ever reprise.

--E.Y. HARBURG AND VERNON DUKE

THE PERMANENT AMERICAN MILITARY cemeteries of World War II would not be transferred to the ABMC until sometime in 1951, but much cooperation already existed between my father's AGRC headquarters and the ABMC office in Paris. A lot of this good will was due to the engaging personality of the army officer working in that office as the organization's representative.

An intense and unassuming man, Colonel Krueger preferred to use his nickname instead of his given name, Walter Krueger, Jr. His father, General Walter Krueger, was one of the army's most respected officers, who had reached his prominence by advancing through the ranks.

Dwight Eisenhower greatly respected General Krueger, as he writes in *Crusade in Europe*:

> A private, corporal, and sergeant in the late 1890s, he had an Army-wide reputation as a hard-bitten soldier. But through more than forty years of service he had kept pace with every military change, and few officers had a clearer grasp of what another war would demand of the Army; few were physically tougher or more

active. Relentlessly driving himself, he had little need of driving others—they were quick to follow his example.

Benny Krueger, West Point Class of 1931, seemed rather bookish, especially when he wore his round-lensed rimless eyeglasses. Unlike his dad, he didn't seem at all like a "hard-bitten soldier." Upon first meeting him, my father pleased him by saying, "I was honored to participate in the 1941 Louisiana maneuvers with your dad."

Benny lived in Paris with his wife Betty, a glamorous woman who wore her prematurely gray hair swept back in a bun, and their six-year-old daughter Carol. Like my parents, the Kruegers enjoyed attending shows at Isle St. Germain, where American stars would often perform.

They also liked to give dinner parties. I especially recall an evening in March 1948 when my parents and I were invited for dinner at their spacious apartment. I had not yet been there, so I looked forward to the evening. Near the end of our excellent dinner in the formal dining room, a tray of fresh fruit was carried to the table along with a plate of soft Camembert and a variety of bite-size crackers.

Later, while Dad and Benny enjoyed after-dinner liqueurs in the living room, Betty took Mother and me on a tour of the beautifully furnished apartment. What impressed me most was the row of perfume bottles on her dressing table, lined up like glass soldiers standing at attention. They varied in size and shape, but all of them were labeled Shalimar—her favorite scent. To an impressionable teenager like me, Betty Krueger seemed highly sophisticated.

In addition to being hospitable, the Kruegers were good sports. On another spring evening, they and I piled into the car belonging to the provost marshal, Dirk ver Hulst, after we learned that a raid was imminent in his search for AWOL soldiers. Joining us was Elianne, an attractive, thirtyish Frenchwoman and a member of the prominent de Courgolay family. She was Dirk's "fiancée" (although his divorce wasn't final yet).

Along the way to our destination—Mimi Pinzon's, a cheap dance joint—we picked up a husky white-helmeted MP from police headquarters. Off we all went like a posse descending on a pack of outlaws to Mimi's, where the deserting soldiers were known to be hiding out. We "observers" stayed safely outside in the car while Dirk and the MP went inside. "Three soldiers were caught," I later reported in my diary. I could just imagine the startled looks on the faces of the "ladies" inside as the deserters were hauled away.

The first American I met in Paris was my father's young aide, Lieutenant Paul Smith, who came up to our Wagram suite the day after Mother and I arrived. My father referred to him by his nickname, Smithy. Paul graduated from Officers Candidate School (OCS) and had been a paratrooper with the highly regarded 82nd Airborne Division during the war.

After accompanying Dad to meetings and on inspection trips, Paul (who was probably in his late twenties then) told me: "Your father has so much energy. Sometimes it's hard to keep up with him." Dad was always a fast-paced walker.

When Paul was ordered to report to an assignment in the United States, his replacement was Lieutenant James Murphy, whose tall, thin physique was just the opposite of Paul's short, stocky one. James stepped right in and seemed to enjoy his new job. I remember that he and his cute wife Jo laughed good-naturedly at songfests around our piano, especially when my father would glance in their direction and sing a solo rendition of *Who Threw the Overalls in Mrs. Murphy's Chowder?*

Among other traits, aides were chosen for their diplomatic skills. No one knew this better than Howard Peckham, having been an aide himself in his bachelor days. He felt paternalistic towards his aides, who went with him almost everywhere. They often accompanied him to solemn and impressive ceremonies at various military cemeteries throughout Europe.

Other attendees at those ceremonies were American military personnel, European dignitaries, local townspeople, and family members of attendees as well as family members of the deceased.

It was an honor to hear my father speak of gratitude and sacrifice as we stood near rows of crosses and stars. The first memorial ceremony I attended was on March 14, 1948, at Hamm Cemetery, just outside the capital city of Luxembourg. Members of the Luxembourg royal family were in attendance that day, as was the case in 1947 when Dad gave his Memorial Day radio address from that country.

Crown Prince Jean (*pronounced "John" in French*), the son of Grand Duchess Charlotte, sat in a tall chair on the ground in front of the reviewing stand. Like many members of European royalty, he wore a military uniform and cap, and his chair was placed between an American flag to his right and Luxembourg's flag to his left. Accompanying him were some of his country's soldiers, who stood in perfectly straight lines during my father's speech. Upon the abdication of his mother in 1964, the attractive prince, with his distinctively thin face and brown moustache, became Grand Duke of Luxembourg.

Other dignitaries, as well as American military personnel and local townspeople, also attended the colorful and touchingly formal ceremony. The date of the event was significant, as Dad explained. "Three years earlier, on March 14, 1945, Third Army troops moving north of the Moselle River turned to the southeast and joined forces with Third Army troops moving south of the river. Their combined strength enabled them to steadily advance and clear the entire west bank of the Rhine," he said. On March 22, they crossed the Rhine at Oppenheim, which led the way to the last offensive of the war in Europe.

Soon after our visit, Hamm Cemetery was closed temporarily to visitors, in order that reinterments could take place. The same procedures were taken at the other cemeteries, on varying dates and according to various schedules. Hamm had been one of Third Army's largest cemeteries.

George Patton had forcefully led the Third Army all the way from Normandy to Austria. After serving under the legendary general in 1940 and 1941 and seeing him briefly again years later, it seemed ironic to my father that his next encounter with George

Patton would be at Hamm Cemetery. Only this time, the general was one of the victims buried here; and he had lost his life not on the battlefield but as the result of an awful vehicle accident near Heidelberg, Germany, in December 1945. In accordance with the wishes of his widow, Beatrice, he was buried here instead of in the United States. "It seems fitting that he was laid to rest alongside his heroic troops," Dad remarked. Before his death, General Patton gained the fourth star he had coveted.

During our drive back to Paris, we stopped in Reims to visit General Dwight Eisenhower's former headquarters, located inside a technical college. A guide with a welcoming demeanor led us into the room where a document had been signed on May 7, 1945, to establish Germany's official military surrender. Allied officers had undoubtedly looked on quietly and with a sense of relief while General Gustav Jodl, commander in chief of German forces, signed the document. The signature served as proof that the military hostilities leading up to the solemn AGRC memorial ceremony we had just attended in Luxembourg, and others like it in Europe, had mercifully ended.

Upon entering the modest-sized room, I first noticed the slightly battered oak table where the surrender was signed. Then I saw that the walls surrounding the room were covered with several large maps and charts, showing the strategic locations of items such as ports. Statistics noted on the charts indicated movements of troops and supplies.

One map seemed relevant to my father's job in Washington during the war, and he was glad to explain it to my mother and me: "The small cardboard flags that dot this map indicate the supply depots in Belgium, Luxembourg, and northern France. These flags," he said, pointing to a different series, "show the locations of pipelines for supplying gasoline to cities in France." When he pointed at another area on the map, he said, "As you can see here, reserve tanks for fuel and oil are also indicated." Without his explanation, I would not have known these facts.

From Reims, we returned to Paris. On the way home I said to my father, "Thanks for showing Mother and me where so many significant events of World War II took place." I should have also thanked him for giving us insider information based on his own personal knowledge and experience. I felt privileged, inasmuch as such information was inaccessible to the average tourist.

Soon after we returned to Paris from Luxembourg, I had another opportunity to see the effects of World War II. Dad was scheduled to meet with the officer in charge of AGRC activities in Normandy near the end of March, so Mother and I decided to join him. Our driver was Sergeant Cochran, a quiet Colorado native with a small, reddish mustache. He was consistently good at his job. During our years in France, he drove us often in Paris and on many trips out of the city.

On this particular journey, we motored north of Paris for several hours, past diminutive farmhouses with thatched roofs and very quaint villages. In some areas, the flowers of early spring had already started poking their heads through the softening ground. It was a pretty drive.

Eventually, we arrived at a small town in Normandy west of Le Havre, where Colonel Stevenson, an AGRC officer, met us and drove us to his seaside villa, where we would be staying. We lunched with the colonel and his wife on delicious *coq au vin*, accompanied by welcome glasses of cold Perrier water. Then the colonel took my mother and me down to see Omaha Beach, where the D-Day landing had taken place fewer than four years earlier.

"Omaha" was the code name for the six-thousand-yard beach between Vierville and Colleville, the main landing area for the American forces. The view was unbelievably sad, considering the loss of life that occurred on the beach, but it appropriately mirrored Ohio Governor John Bricker's statement that D-Day was "the beginning of the end of the forces of evil and destruction." Barges and military vehicles, strewn at various angles on the broad beach, now stood in empty silence. Foxholes on the sandy banks were as empty as air, and machine-gun nests that once rattled with German gunfire now sat quietly.

That night, while I was asleep in one of the guest rooms at the Stevensons' home, the sound of a dog's plaintive barking suddenly awakened me. It was an eerie bark, and it seemed to come from far away. I wondered whether the dog sensed what had happened in that area of Normandy during World War II, or if he had even been a witness to it. I finally got back to sleep, but that sound stayed with me for a long time.

St. Laurent Cemetery, located on a bluff overlooking Omaha Beach, came into existence only twenty-four hours after that first grim D-Day assault on June 6.

Immediately after they disembarked from the landing craft, many soldiers were gunned down by enemy machine-gun fire and were later buried at St. Laurent Cemetery. Several others buried there had participated in an airborne assault near Sainte-Mère-Église, "where the American flag was first raised over French soil on D-Day." *(U.S. News and World Report, September 27, 1993)*

Brigadier General Teddy Roosevelt, son of former President Theodore Roosevelt and a cousin of Franklin Roosevelt, is among those buried at that cemetery. In the 1960s movie *The Longest Day*, he is portrayed by Henry Fonda. After seeing the movie I wrote my father to ask what happened to the general after D-Day. He explained that Teddy Roosevelt wasn't hurt in the landing, but died of a heart attack soon thereafter. Dad also wrote, "He is buried in the St. Laurent Military Cemetery, and I selected his gravesite—in a plot nearest to the steep bluff which rises from the shore of the English Channel."

On March 31, my parents and I stopped briefly at St. Laurent, after saying goodbye to the Stevensons. Before we arrived, Dad carefully examined the cemetery's final layout plan, which had been completed in February by an architectural firm selected by the ABMC. (Selecting architects for the layout of permanent cemeteries was the ABMC's job, not the army's.)

AGRC personnel would soon start the grading work and construction, a subject that both my father and Colonel Stevenson had discussed at length. Because of St. Laurent's proximity to the English Channel, that work was difficult. "AGRC engineers often had to trudge through thick mud, and workmen frequently had to move their heavy equipment along in clay-like soil," my father explained to us later. Subsequently, reinterments proceeded at a slow pace. Considering its D-Day significance, the results were well worth the painstaking efforts made by AGRC personnel.

Near the beaches where the Allied forces landed more than fifty years ago and where the Rangers climbed the steep cliffs with ladders and grappling hooks, there is now a memorial, the Caen Memorial and Museum for Peace. It is significant that a memorial for peace is located so close to the location of the D-Day landing, the dramatic event that preceded the liberation of Europe in 1944. After paying silent homage to those who lost their lives in the invasion, we continued onward to our next destination in Normandy: Cherbourg, a seaport city that lies along the English Channel on the northwestern coast of France.

During the war, construction of the Major Pipeline was started at this city, a system that eventually ran overland across France to Germany and was the backbone of gasoline supply on the Continent. At his desk in Washington, Dad had been kept apprised of the progress of its construction. Now, however, Cherbourg was important to him for another reason. It was a major port of embarkation for ships carrying the caskets of American war dead to the United States (smaller ports were also used, such as Cardiff in Wales). It had been badly bombed during the war, but the port was serviceable because of repairs made to it since then. Trucks and rail cars brought the caskets to the port.

While the cemeteries were being rebuilt, caskets containing the war dead to be reinterred in Europe were kept in temporary above-ground buildings at their respective cemetery sites.

Because of our desolate feelings, my mother and I couldn't bear to stay very long in the large warehouse to which an official in charge of port functions escorted us. It was here that the deceased were processed before being placed in repatriation caskets. From a respectful distance, we quietly watched my father as he leaned over and looked briefly inside a temporary coffin that was pulled out and opened for his inspection. Out of the corner of my eye, I caught a glimpse of the dead American who lay inside. I couldn't see his face, because he was completely covered with an olive-drab army blanket, in which he had been securely wrapped and on which his identification tag had been neatly placed.

At this point, I recalled the tears my mother had shed on V-J Day because of the many American soldiers who wouldn't be coming home. This soldier and others like him in Cherbourg would be coming home, but not in the joyful way their families would have wanted. Instead, feelings of grief would fall on the hearts of those who would greet them, sorrowfully reminiscent of the pieces of lead that had fallen on the bodies of their loved ones in battle. It would be an understatement to say that the port was a reminder of the terrible tragedy of war.

After we drove away from Cherbourg, silence enveloped my parents, Sergeant Cochran, and me. It stayed with us on our long journey south. When we finally moved across the mile-long causeway that led us to our next destination, the rocky islet of Mont-Saint-Michel, our moods lifted. The ancient abbey sitting atop the mountain seemed to send out an aura of strength as we drove towards it. We would be spending one night in this isolated spot before heading back to Paris.

Early the following morning, after a light breakfast of strong coffee and jam-covered croissants in our hotel dining room, my parents and I walked up the narrow cobblestone street leading to the abbey. It was soothing to deeply inhale the salty fresh air that blew in from the ocean. We continued on to Paris infused with a renewed freshness of spirit. Later, a quick stop at the cathedral in Chartres enchanted us amidst an atmosphere of hushed peace and serenity.

As my father knew so well, making arrangements for the return home of the recovered dead from World War II was an enormous task. More than half the fatal casualties of the war lost their lives in the European Theater, the theater with which my father's AGRC work was most directly concerned. In *Final Disposition of World War II Dead,* authors Steere and Boardman reiterate the statistics from the European Theater that were known in 1957, when their book was published:

The latest figures indicate that a total of 60,719 Americans sleep in the ten permanent cemeteries of the former AGRC-EA. These statistics also show that almost two-thirds of overseas burials in all theaters (92,983) took place in the European Theater. Since the greatest number of deaths occurred in the campaigns against Nazi Germany, it was perfectly natural that the greatest number of interments should take place in this area.

Dad objected firmly to any identification procedure that would interfere with correctly identifying the deceased. This was especially true during the period when repatriation quotas and tight schedules were being met. In a letter to the Memorial Division of the Office of the Quartermaster General, dated February 5, 1948, my father described the four methods (or a combination thereof) that could be used to meet the indicated quotas. The first method would be to expand the workforce. The second would be to increase the proportion of directives calling for repatriation. The third method was selective disinterment, and the fourth was selective processing.

Authors Steere and Boardman discuss Dad's preferences in *Final Disposition*:

> General Peckham emphatically rejected any notion of adopting the latter two courses as utterly impractical and fraught with danger to accurate identification of the deceased....
>
> He recommended a combination of the first and second methods as the best solution to the problem of meeting an admittedly ambitious repatriation deadline the adoption of the first method, i.e., a sharp increase in the working force at the various cemeteries. The OQMG [Office of the Quartermaster General] agreed that selective exhumation and processing would not be undertaken....

The authors also write that the establishment and operation of a central identification point in Europe provided one of the PARAGRAPH FROM highlights of the worldwide operation. They then make this comment, of which the Quartermaster Corps could be very proud: "The successful identification of all but approximately 3 percent of recovered dead [this means worldwide, not just Europe] constituted a great overall achievement."

DAD SPEAKING ABOVE THE SEATED CROWN PRINCE, 1948

LUXEMBOURG SOLDIERS STANDING ATTENTIVELY AT THE HAMM CEREMONY

ACTRESS JUNE TRAVERS STANDING BETWEEN DAD AND COL. KELLOGG (BETTY KRUEGER FAR RIGHT, MRS. KELLOGG FAR LEFT): BACKSTAGE AT THE ST. GERMAIN THEATER, 1948

(L TO R) BOB MATTE, DAD, MOTHER, COL. AND MRS.RAGUSE, AND MRS. MATTE (COL.KRUEGER FAR LEFT): CELTIC HOTEL, 1948

Chapter 11

Effects of the War in Europe

Heroism feels and never reasons and therefore is always right.

--RALPH WALDO EMERSON

FOR INSPECTION TRIPS, meetings, and ceremonies not within a reasonable driving distance, my father had an army plane assigned to him. "You and Jeanie can join me occasionally, if there's enough room on the plane," my father told Mother and me one day about our prospects for traveling with him in Europe. There was also the caveat from my father that my schoolwork not be unduly interrupted. The plane assigned to him was usually a small C-47 with a far-from-glamorous interior. We sat on bucket seats on one trip, I remember.

Our first journey by air started on the morning of May 9, 1948, when our plane roared into the sky from Orly Field and arrived that afternoon in Copenhagen, that day's destination. On this particular trip, a few other AGRC officers and their families joined us. When our group arrived for a late lunch at the Viking Restaurant in Copenhagen, a smiling blond waiter led us to a long wooden table near a picture window. While I was eating a hearty lunch of fresh seafood and fruit, I listened to a colonel at my end of the table describe Denmark's role during the war. "The little country wasn't able to put up much of a fight when the Germans invaded in 1940. It was occupied in just one day." Then he added, "Many people fought back by joining the underground movement, a courageous act on their part." I felt admiration for the people when I heard the colonel's description of their bravery. That feeling intensified when I learned sometime later that the Danes honored our dead airmen who had fallen on their soil. They even built monuments over the burial sites and protested when the AGRC attempted to recover the bodies. Talbot writes about this in *The Story of American Graves Registration Command*:

> In Denmark the natives had buried in their local cemeteries the bodies of all our airmen who fell there. The Danes in practically every case had built substantial monuments over these graves. Naturally when the crews arrived to recover the bodies the native populace very strongly protested. So strongly that the matter got into diplomatic channels. . . .

Our afternoon and night in Copenhagen were followed by an afternoon and night in Stockholm, Sweden, where our plane landed on the morning of May 10. As I mentioned earlier, Sweden stayed neutral during World War II. Neutrality was a historical precedent for that country, but there were additional factors that kept it out of the war. It had strong defense capabilities, so much so that its well-trained army intimidated potential invaders. Sweden's northern location also helped it to maintain neutrality. During dinner that evening, I said to Dad, "Sweden was certainly lucky to avoid German occupation, unlike its neighbors Norway and Denmark. "

"You're right, but the people have helped us recover our fallen airmen and have shown great respect for them," my father said. "Our military attaché in Sweden oversees the search and recovery of American airmen, but he has been greatly assisted by ordinary Swedish citizens," he added.

An example of this aid occurred in 1943, when a fisherman in Sweden's waters found the body of an American. The airman was later identified as Vincent A. White of New Jersey, who was killed in action in October 1943, along with other members of his crew. He was buried in the American cemetery in Malmö, Sweden. The respectful fisherman later made a personal visit to the fallen airman's grieving family in the United States.

Also laid to rest in that cemetery was First Lieutenant Frederick W. Tod from Long Beach, California, a member of the 713th Bomb Squadron, 448th Bomb Group. While on a bombing mission to Germany, enemy aircraft severely damaged his plane, making it impossible for him to return to England. Although he managed to fly his plane along the coast while his crew bailed out, he couldn't stay in the air very long. His B-24 spun into the sea off Falsterbo. He was initially reported as missing in action, until his remains washed up on shore fifty-one days later.

According to an article in his hometown paper, the lieutenant "had completed 24 missions, and he had been decorated with the Air Medal and several Oak Leaf Clusters." He was buried with full military honors in Malmö, but was later permanently interred at Hamm Cemetery in Luxembourg.

When my parents and I left Stockholm early on the morning of Tuesday, May 11, we motored south to Malmö, arriving at around noon. This seaport city on the southern tip of Sweden was only sixteen miles from Copenhagen, so we had come full circle since arriving in Scandinavia. After driving past the historic buildings on Malmö's old main street, we arrived at the small temporary American cemetery. Here we watched helmeted Swedish soldiers stand quietly at attention before bowing our heads while Chaplain Pfeiffer, an AGRC colonel, led us in prayer.

Howard Peckham then delivered a speech describing the heroism of the airmen buried here, whose planes had crash-landed either on Swedish soil or in Swedish waters during World War II. On each grave was a marker, in front of which was a petite bouquet of simple and colorful wildflowers. The decorations mirrored the Scandinavian disdain for ostentatiousness, but the tribute seemed very impressive nevertheless. That ceremony concluded our trip, and we returned to Paris.

We would soon be in a C-47 again, however. Joining Dad on a trip to Germany later in May were Colonel Carl Raguse, his Chief of Staff, and the colonel's wife, Catherine. Dad's aide, Lieutenant

James Murphy, also came along, as did Mother and I. (Jim's wife Jo stayed home to care for their young son, Jimmy.)

The purpose of my father's trip was to attend a conference on May 26 and 27 led by Lieutenant General Clarence R. Huebner, Deputy Commander in Chief of EUCOM. The conference was held on May 26 and 27 at the general's Frankfurt headquarters. Blue-eyed, fair-skinned General Huebner had been commander of the 1st Infantry Division in World War II.

In a 1980 movie about the war, in which General Huebner's name is mentioned, actor Lee Marvin plays the part of a sergeant in the 1st Infantry Division. The movie shows the division's landing in North Africa and subsequent storming through Europe. Its title, *The Big Red One*, is the same as the division's nickname. Its members wear a distinctive shoulder patch on which a large red "1" is emblazoned.

During the conference, my father discussed with Clarence Huebner the effect on the AGRC of the upcoming transfer of General Huebner's headquarters from Frankfurt to Heidelberg. My father also talked with him about the current schedule for AGRC operations. In this regard, he presented to General Huebner the initial plans for phasing out the AGRC's search and recovery operations. This topic is noted in *The Third Year: 1947-1948*:

> The initial phasing-out plans of AGRC-EA were presented to the Deputy Commander, EUCOM, at a conference held in Frankfurt in May 1948.

Although Frankfurt looked dismal and still shattered from wartime bombs, the Huebners lived in an elegant home. We dined there on the evening of May 26, which enabled Mother, Catherine, and me to become acquainted with the general's wife Florence and his daughter Juliet. Brown-haired, twenty-one-year-old Juliet was slender and well mannered, so my parents no doubt saw her as a good role model for me.

In my diary I later wrote, "I sat with his [General Huebner's] daughter and two lieutenants. After dinner, we four went out and walked around the grounds. Very nice!" Officers and enlisted personnel who had their families with them were living well in postwar Germany.

Houses for senior officers, which for the most part the U.S. Army had appropriated from wealthy German executives, were quite attractive. I can recall wondering, as we strolled along the pristine walkways, what the former residents had looked like. Maybe the lady of the house had golden hair and was as slim as the stem of a rose picked from her garden. The man of the house, in my imagination, might have worn a monocle and walked stiffly, as though wearing a suit of armor.

Another topic brought up at the Frankfurt conference was, undoubtedly, the disconcerting behavior of Russia. When the victorious Allies split Germany and its capital Berlin into four zones of occupation, that particular zoning arrangement was not a problem—at least not at first.

But then the Russians began objecting to steps taken in western Germany towards self-government. At the same time, they were highly irritated about the introduction of a new Deutschemark in West Berlin, which they thought would threaten the currency used in eastern Germany. They believed, and hoped, the blockade would force the Western powers to abandon their rights in the city.

On June 24, Russia blocked entry into the three non-Soviet zones of Berlin. Fortunately, sharp-minded General Lucius B. Clay, the military governor of the American zone, found a way to get around this problem. Because Russian occupation forces couldn't block the flight of military planes into the city, General Clay—who graduated in June 1918 from West Point, where my father first met him—ordered an airlift to begin on June 28. Therefore, like heavy, metallic angels of mercy, Allied military planes began flying into Berlin carrying food, medical supplies, fuel, and other necessities to its citizens. General Clay, in the minds of Berliners, was a hero.

A month after our return to Paris from Frankfurt, my parents and I flew to England. Howie, on vacation from West Point, joined us, along with Lieutenant Colonel Frank Marchman and his wife. Colonel Marchman was among the AGRC people stationed in Nancy, in eastern France. To join us, the Marchmans drove from their home in Nancy to Orly Field, an airport then used by the American military.

We arrived in London at five o'clock, in time to do some quick sightseeing before darkness enveloped the places we wanted to see, such as Big Ben, Westminster Abbey, and a few other tourist spots. After we registered at the Cumberland Hotel at Marble Arch, we saw well-known landmarks, at least from the outside. Some bore small craters. "Many London streets and edifices still bear damage from the blitz bombs," my father said. "London was hit severely, especially in 1940 when the raids were just beginning."

Early the next morning, we went back to the airport and into our C-47. Our destination was the small airport at the beautiful college town of Cambridge, fifty-six miles northeast of London. A car and driver met us there. We first motored by the university's stately buildings, and then we continued three miles farther and arrived at the cemetery that bears its name. I got out of the car and surveyed the view spread out before me. The area where I stood was flat and broad, but I saw that beyond the rows of crosses and stars was woodland containing large trees, which framed the cemetery's west and south sides with boughs of green leaves.

"As you can see, our country acquired a fine piece of property," my father remarked as I looked at the scenery around me. Here in this sylvan setting, on land that Cambridge University donated to the United States, he praised the heroism of those Americans buried here. Most of those fatalities had occurred during bombings of northwest Europe or in the Battle of the Atlantic.

Traveling across the Atlantic Ocean had been treacherous for convoys and supplies moving from the United States to Britain, especially in the early years of the war. German U-boats, roaming like hungry sharks, searched for Allied ships to devour. And they often succeeded. During the time that the Battle of the Atlantic was slowing down, the air war in Europe was intensifying. Industrial and military systems were our primary targets in Germany, and before the war ended in 1945, American planes had flown thousands of dangerous sorties into Germany from bases in England.

Even taking off could be dangerous. One of those airmen who suffered a loss of life on take-off was Second Lieutenant Richard K. Angert, a B-24 navigator who died in March 1945. He was laid to rest at Cambridge Cemetery. His crew's target had been the railroad yard at Soest, Germany. Sadly, the crew never left England that day.

After my father's meeting and inspection at Cambridge, we drove to the port of Cardiff, Wales, where he and Colonel Marchman met with officials responsible for the preparations involved in shipping caskets leaving Cardiff on their long voyage to the United States. In the meantime, the rest of us walked around a bit. The typically rainy Welsh weather and a misty fog that smelled like spongy meadows added to the somberness of our visit. Ten days earlier, on June 18, the *USAT Lawrence Victory* left the Cardiff port carrying the first group of deceased from the British Isles to the United States.

An event that occurred in a Mayfair-district restaurant that evening considerably revived our spirits. During dinner at Cunningham's, a fellow patron wearing a well-tailored tweed jacket came to our table and said, "I personally want to thank you Americans for all the help you gave us." He directed his remark primarily to the men at our table, who were wearing their uniforms. My father told the Englishman that he appreciated his graciousness.

Later I asked my father why the man was thanking us. "Mostly because after England asked for our help, President Roosevelt responded by sending arms," he explained, adding, "That was in 1940, so our country got partly involved in the war before Pearl Harbor got us completely into it." The evening at Cunningham's provided a fine conclusion to our visit to England.

In July, as if the summer hadn't been busy enough, my parents and I moved out of our suite in the Hôtel Wagram and into our next Paris home—a three-story corner house on Rue St. James, a quiet street in Neuilly-sur-Seine. This prime residential area in western Paris was adjacent to the Bois de Boulogne, a two-thousand-acre park consisting of winding paths, glistening lakes, colorful gardens, and large trees. The park also had two racetracks. At one of them, Longchamps, we attended the races one day with the Macombers, a prominent American horse-breeding family. Mother wore her fanciest hat for the occasion.

We loved the house and its imposing gated entrance. Its front door opened to a spacious marble foyer, and a winding narrow staircase led from there to three bedrooms and two baths on the second floor. On the third floor was an apartment, which was rarely used. (The landlord did rent it temporarily to an elderly White Russian couple, however, whom we seldom saw.) In addition to a kitchen, living room, and formal dining room, the house had a large, well-furnished library with soft, comfortable sofas and chairs. The piano was here, and the room's tall French windows faced a backyard that looked bright and cheerful on sunny days.

Soon after we moved in, we adopted a mid-size French poodle, named Wagram. I enjoyed taking him for walks in the nearby Bois or the neighborhood marketplace, where he would strain on his leash when some object or person caught his fancy. We all loved him, although my parents didn't appreciate his excitability or the way he barked and pounced on people to welcome them. Wagram was usually banished to the backyard whenever we expected company, especially if they were VIPs.

A hard-working French gardener came with the house. Michel was an expert at gently pulling the weeds that would have entwined themselves around the bushes, and he kept the lush green grass neatly trimmed. His only imperfection was his occasional habit of peering inside the house at us, sometimes while he was standing behind a bush that he probably thought kept him hidden from view. After discarding the idea that he might be a Communist spy—as my mother had believed—my father concluded, "He's definitely the curious type; possibly he's intrigued by seeing real Americans for the first time after only viewing them in movies."

Because my parents expected to entertain more often, now that they lived in a large house in a prime neighborhood and not in a hotel, they decided to hire a cook and a maid in addition to the gardener. Household help was reasonably priced in postwar Paris and was readily available.

The first to be hired was the cook, a stocky, middle-aged man from Indochina (now Vietnam) named Le Van. Our conversations with him involved some French and a lot of sign language. Unfortunately, my parents' arrangement with him didn't work out well. His recipes were too exotic, and, worst of all, we learned he was a thief. My father had to let him go one afternoon after catching him tiptoeing out the door with a bag of stolen groceries.

After Le Van left, my parents hired an elderly French cook, Josette, who wore her gray curly hair piled high on her head—a courtly style that made her look like pictures I had seen of Marie Antoinette. She spoke and understood English well and had been the cook for some "very important people," as she reminded us at times. She was also prim and proper, which was particularly evident one day when she heard the lyrics of a song I was naively playing on my record player.

While vigorously shaking her finger at me, Josette exclaimed, "A nice young girl like you should not leesten to zat naughty song!" The song, *Pigalle*, was sung by one of France's leading artists in the forties, Georges Ulmer. I bought the record because I liked the liveliness of the melody and the smoothness of the artist's voice, but I didn't know enough French to comprehend all the words.

Josette stayed with us the rest of the time we lived in Neuilly, but I selected my records carefully from that day onwards, at least when I knew she was within hearing distance. I shouldn't have been surprised about her dislike of *Pigalle*, however. I had already visited Montmartre's Pigalle district with a group of curious students from the American School. The boys in our group snickered, I recall, when a flashily dressed "lady of the night" strolled by, looking as if she had just stepped out of a Toulouse-Loutrec painting.

Our all-around maid, named Anna, was a husky young Polish displaced person (DP). The DPs who found sanctuary in France for various reasons after the war were afraid of the persecution they would receive if they returned to Poland, where Communist authorities considered them to be traitors. They fervently wanted to stay in France, so they were reputed to be conscientious workers. Anna lived up to that sterling reputation after my father hired her. She didn't hesitate to get down on her hands and knees to scrub the floors, and the fixtures gleamed as brightly as rays of sunlight after she vigorously buffed them.

On July 4 we learned firsthand how Americans living in Paris celebrate Independence Day. On that day, Mother and I watched my father while he participated in a ceremony under the Arc de Triomphe, during which the eternal flame was relighted at the Tomb of the Unknown Soldier. French troops and American Legionnaires stood silently at attention during the ceremony, like a congregation at prayer inside Sacre Coeur.

Following the ceremony, a party was held on the spacious grounds of the American embassy, which gave my parents and me a chance to mix with other members of the American community. Ambassador Jefferson Caffery was the host in 1948, and he affably mingled with the guests. Those guests included tough-guy actor Edward G. Robinson, who, someone told me, would be among the entertainers appearing a few days later at a show at the Eiffel Tower.

Later that month, I had an opportunity to visit Holland when I made a short, solemn visit with my father to Margraten Cemetery. From him, I heard a bit about that area's World War II history. He explained that in the winter of 1944, thousands of troops from the First and Ninth Armies converged on the village of Margraten and its surrounding countryside. They were making their final push towards Germany. Out of necessity, American soldiers took over everything—orchards, homes, barns, attics, and even the town hall. And roads were lined with tanks and trucks. Dad ended his explanation with these words:

> The people of Margraten welcomed the troops and their equipment, because they knew the men were on their way to Aachen. They also knew that Nazi Germany would soon be finished.

Dad also told me that Holland's Queen Wilhelmina attended a Memorial Day ceremony at Margraten Cemetery in 1947. "She was accompanied by Dutch officials and representatives of approximately two-dozen nations," he said. Dad was at Hamm Cemetery at the time, but he had been in charge of Memorial Day ceremonies at all the temporary American cemeteries that year.

During the last two weeks in July and first week of August, I learned more about the effects of World War II on the residents of Normandy. I eagerly accepted when a French family invited me to be a guest at their summer home, located a few miles east of Le Havre—a port city that had been almost completely destroyed by Allied air strikes during the war. The house, formerly an old mill, was picturesque enough to be featured on postcards sold by local souvenir shops and was located near the pretty beach town of Veulettes-sur-Mer. Elianne, the fiancée of Major Dirk ver Hulst, the AGRC provost marshal, had arranged for me to stay there.

"There's a seventeen-year-old girl in the family," Elianne explained about my prospective hosts, "so you'll get to see how French teenagers live and practice your French." Zette was hardly a typical French teenager, though. She was a member of the aristocratic de Courgolay family (to whom Elianne was also related). After I arrived at her house, I spent my days playing tennis, swimming in the sea, and picnicking on the rocky beach with brown-haired, fresh-faced Zette and two of her cousins, Anic and Gelaine. They took me to various local tourist spots, such as the beautiful abbey in the little town of Caudebec. Since they all spoke English, I unfortunately didn't have much of a chance to bone up on my French.

All of the de Courgolay cousins, especially twenty-one-year-old Antoine, were ambitious about improving their English. Antoine lived in an elegant home owned by his family called the Chateau de Cany-Barville. Like Zette's, his home adorned local postcards, but in this case the chateau's immense grounds, trees, and ponds were emphasized on the cards. Zette lived only a short bicycle ride away, so she and I went to his chateau several times. Occasionally when we entered the front door, the dramatic sounds of Beethoven's Fifth Symphony could be heard as they filled the big, sparsely furnished halls. This was a favorite record of Antoine's, and he played it on more than one occasion during my stay in Normandy.

Occasionally when the music stopped and the room was still and quiet, I pictured German army officers walking through the halls. I almost could hear their freshly polished boots making click-click sounds on the wooden floors. During the occupation, Germans had taken over many chateaux temporarily, such as the home of Antoine and his family.

Sometimes he and I would talk about that war. A broad smile would light up his face when he described the American soldiers he had met in Normandy—how friendly they were, and how much they appreciated the fruit, calvados, French bread, and wine he and his friends had given them. His dark brown eyes would flash angrily, however, whenever anyone brought up the subject of Allied bombardments. "There was too much bombing," Antoine once emphatically declared, "especially by the Americans!"

Patriotic American that I was, I felt defensive when he said that, but I tried not to show it. He was, after all, a generous host. Although the invasion had been harrowing for residents of Normandy, I had seen it from a much different perspective than Antoine. I had sadly viewed our rusting vehicles sitting at various angles on Omaha Beach, and I had viewed the swampy, flooded places where our brave paratroopers had landed. And I had watched Dad as he studied the layout of St. Laurent Cemetery, where so many American casualties of the invasion were laid to rest.

In spite of his criticisms, I developed a big crush on the aristocratic Antoine. This was especially true after he twirled me around the room, and we danced like movie stars (in my imagination) to music from his record player. I could tell he liked me, too. When his cousins joined in the dancing, the result was a delightful and lively party atmosphere, with Antoine and me sharing the spotlight.

The romantic magic would soon end, but not at all like a Hollywood musical. On my last day in Normandy, Antoine turned to me and said, "I'd like to show you more of the countryside around here." Then he somewhat shyly asked, "May I take you for a drive this afternoon?"

While I was thinking of what to say, Zette, who was standing nearby, curtly said, "No, she can't do that. She has to pack for her trip back to Paris." The intensity of her words surprised me. Shortly thereafter, she and I got on our bicycles and headed back to her house. Had I gone, it would have been my first time alone with Antoine. During the weeks that followed, my vivid imagination conjured up scenes of him and me touring the countryside in his car and occasionally parking in order to smooch. I never had an occasion to see him again, though.

When I went downstairs for breakfast on August 14, the day after I returned home from Normandy, I saw Mother feverishly preparing for some important dinner guests. The congenial deputy EUCOM commander, General Huebner, would be coming that evening with his wife, Florence, and daughter, Juliet.

Mother's preparations were not in vain. The general and his family were welcomed into our clean marble foyer, which was as bright as the sun shining on the Mediterranean. (Wagram had been taken to the backyard.) First we had drinks in the library, where my father and the general discussed EUCOM issues at one end of the room while Mother and I talked to Florence and Juliet at the other end. During dinner, my father initiated a lively conversation about living in Europe. My diary doesn't mention whether anyone else was present, other than my father's and the general's ubiquitous aides.

After dinner, our group attended the operetta *Violettes Impériales* at the Theatre Mogador, where we heard actress Claudette Noelle, who was playing the part of a flower merchant, plaintively ask *"Qui veut mon bouquet de violettes?"* as she faced the audience. She and the other members of the cast put on a wonderful show. Dad was pleased to see that General Huebner clapped enthusiastically afterwards, as did the rest of the audience.

Whenever General Huebner and my father met, either in France or Germany, the general was updated about the AGRC, in which he showed much interest. On Memorial Day 1947, while my father and General Clay were participating in a ceremony at Hamm Cemetery in Luxembourg, Clarence Huebner was paying his respects at Omaha Beach. *The Stars and Stripes* of May 31, 1947 describes his presence:

> ST.LAURENT SUR MER, France, May 30—The rattle of M1 fire was heard over Omaha Beach today in honor of the men of the Big Red One and the other outfits that stormed this bloody Normandy beachhead. In a simple Memorial Day ceremony, Lt. Gen. Clarence R. Huebner, EUCOM deputy commander, laid a wreath at the U.S. Military Cemetery here in a tribute to men of the 1st Inf. Div., which he commanded on D-Day, June 6, 1944.

Soon he and my father would meet again. On the bright fall morning of September 22, which dawned cool and crisp in Paris, the three Peckhams, the two Raguses, and Lieutenant Murphy were driven to Orly Field. Soon thereafter we were flying away in a small C-47 to Heidelberg, where General Huebner's home and office had been relocated. My parents and I would be spending the night at their lovely villa.

During the dinner party that evening, my parents, the Raguses, and the Huebners sat at a large table in the dining room, while Juliet, Lieutenant Murphy, and I were seated at a small table with Captain Jones (the general's aide) and a Lieutenant Pagnatti (another aide, I believe).

Afterwards, we young people moved to a small sitting room, where the conversation became quite lively. When one of the officers brought both Juliet and me a cup of coffee, another one teased him by saying, "American women are so spoiled. They should be bringing us the coffee." According to my diary, Juliet gave him a hard time about that comment.

The following morning, while Dad, Carl Raguse, and Jim Murphy attended a meeting, Catherine, Mother, and I were taken on a tour of Heidelberg. At the University, the oldest in Germany, I could almost sense the presence of carefree students from prewar, pre-Nazi days, singing a verse of their favorite song:

> Old Heidelberg, dear city,
> With honors crowned, and rare,
> O'er Rhine and Neckar rising,
> None can with thee compare.

At the conclusion of my father's meeting the next day, our C-47 carried our group south to Berchtesgaden. As we approached the Bavarian Alps, Dad suddenly rose from his seat and leaned over my shoulder. "Look out the window, Jeanie," he said as he pointed to the mountains below. "We'll be going over the Eagle's Nest anytime now." And there it was, sitting on top of a mountain peak, the headquarters where Adolf Hitler had planned his devious campaigns.

We saw it up close the following afternoon. After walking through the dingy headquarters, we stepped outside and looked at the beautiful scenery around us. "I'll bet Hitler admired this view while daydreaming about his indestructible Third Reich," my father surmised sarcastically. The view was superb.

Because we arrived and left in topless command cars—those high, awkward-looking vehicles copied by the U.S. Army from the Germans—we got a good look at the scenery on our way down the mountain. When we passed the Berghof, Hitler's official home, echoes of his shrill voice seemed to haunt the atmosphere surrounding it, even though it had been razed by retreating SS men in 1945 and was now in ruins. Undoubtedly, Hitler had frequently ranted angrily about his subordinates' inadequacies. His beloved Third Reich, in the meantime, was falling into pieces like shattered Meissen dinner plates.

A thrilling ride by cable car the next morning to the top of Kreuzeck Mountain concluded our visit to southern Germany. An army car waiting at the bottom of the mountain took us to Munich, where we boarded our C-47 and flew home to Paris.

Summer vacation officially ended for me the day after we returned. Thus far, my education in Europe had consisted of singing lessons given by a former opera singer, Monsieur Vigneau, and French classes at the Alliance Francaise, a school attended by students of many different ages and nationalities. Now the time had come for me to return to high school, and I looked forward to it. Soon after enrolling at the American school in late September, I memorized the school song:

> We'll stand united with our own country
> And to our colors we'll ever be loyal
> Whenever our flag we see
> We will raise our song ever loud and strong
> To our Alma Mater dear
> To the work and fun we had this year
> Evermore we'll give a cheer
> To our friendships we'll ever be faithful
> Though the years may pass away
> To our American School in Paris
> We raise our song today.

The headmaster of the American Community School of Paris, where I began my junior year, was a thin-faced, elegant Harvard graduate named Paul G. de Rosay. The school was closed during World War II, but reopened its doors in a new location in 1946. Mr. de Rosay returned as headmaster, where he took charge of a student body comprised of grades 1 through 12.

Like me, several students were the dependents of AGRC personnel. Quite a few others were the sons and daughters of diplomats. One of those was Barry Bingham Jr., a sophomore when I was a senior. As I have already mentioned, his father, Barry Sr., headed the ECA during its mission in France. (Barry Jr. later became a well-respected newspaper publisher in Louisville, Kentucky.

Some students were children of international businessmen, and one—pert, dark-haired Katie Thalberg—was the daughter of two famous show-business people. Katie's deceased father had been a well-known Hollywood producer; her remarried mother, Norma Shearer, was an academy-award-winning actress who spent much of her time in Switzerland. Although that country had good international schools, they weren't Katie's cup of tea. "I prefer living in Paris," she told some of us one day. Like Barry Bingham, she was a sophomore when I was a senior.

The entire student body benefited from being surrounded by history, but in October a few students personally felt the drama of the Berlin blockade. That's when Cecily Robertson, a tall, brown-haired history teacher, led a group of senior-class students to a meeting of the United Nations Security Council at the Palais de Chaillot.

After the group learned where to get their translating devices and how to use them, they watched unbelievably when Andrei Vischinsky, the delegate from Russia, employed vivid expressions and wild gestures in defense of his country's position. At one point he was engulfed in paroxysms of anger. "We gasped when he temporarily stormed out of the room," one of the students said later.

Even though the atmosphere was often tense at the Palais de Chaillot, attendees of United Nations meetings were entertained at various relaxed social gatherings in Paris. When Ambassador and Mrs. Jefferson Caffery sent an invitation to my parents for one of those events, I was invited to come along with them.

The invitation noted "short dress and hat for the ladies," so Mother and I dressed accordingly. Then I found myself joining other guests at the big reception, held on October 8 at the American Embassy at 2 Avenue D'Iéna.

The distinguished guests of honor were Secretary of State George C. Marshall and his wife, Katherine, who were living temporarily in Paris while Secretary Marshall attended United Nations General Assembly meetings.

At the reception, I joined a long line of guests, primarily members of the local American community, as we moved steadily towards George Marshall. In the receiving line, the folds of flesh beneath his chin gently spilled on his collar whenever he leaned over to talk to someone shorter than he. This gave him a rather grandfatherly appearance. When we shook hands, I don't recall saying anything other than, "How do you do?" or a similar brief greeting. I know I felt privileged to meet him.

Eleanor Roosevelt, widow of President Franklin D. Roosevelt, was also in Paris attending meetings that fall. A compassionate humanitarian, she was serving as a delegate to the United Nations. In this capacity, she expressed much concern for the innocent victims of World War II and made frequent trips throughout postwar Europe to discern how best to help them. One of those trips occurred on October 23, 1948, and the person who accompanied her and her traveling companions to the airport that day was Howard Peckham.

A few days later she wrote about it in her *My Day* column: "Brig. Gen. Howard Peckham called for us at our hotel and took us to Orly Airport, where we boarded a plane for Stuttgart, Germany." No doubt they were glad to have my father accompany them to the airport for that important information-gathering trip. Dad found Eleanor Roosevelt to be gracious and charming, and he was pleased that the General Assembly adopted a Universal Declaration of Human Rights in December of that year. The adoption was primarily due to her efforts.

At the end of that busy October, my father, along with other EUCOM commanders, was asked by the *Stars and Stripes* newspaper to submit a message for publication in its Armistice Day edition of November 11.

These are his words, which were published in that special edition:

On this fourth Armistice Day since World War II and the 30th since World War I, the personnel of the American Graves Registration pause to pay solemn tribute to those Americans who gave their lives so that we may realize victory in those two wars. . . .

Our tasks of establishing 10 permanent U.S. cemeteries, and of returning to the United States those war dead requested by the next of kin, are a constant reminder of the supreme sacrifice of those soldiers, sailors, and airmen who gave their lives in Western Europe during World War II.

Another occasion of interest, especially to Mother and me, took place on November 13. On that day, Dad was awarded the medal of the Legion of Honor, a French order of distinction. During the imposing ceremony, held in a historic location, the Court of Les Invalides, a French band played lively music as its members marched throughout the wide cobblestone court. The event provided a great way for Dad to cement his relationship with French army officers stationed in and around Paris.

A few weeks later, at an AGRC New Year's Day reception in the Hôtel Wagram, quite a few guests congratulated my father for having received the medal. While my parents stood in the receiving line that afternoon, they shook hands with about three hundred invitees (AGRC officers and civilians as well as their wives and older offspring). An orchestra played soothing music in the background as the guests mingled with each other. Large potted palms, set against walls bordered by ornate molding, added to the event's formality. Colonel Carl Raguse and his wife Catherine joined my parents in the receiving line, as did my father's new aide and his wife, Bob and Beverly Matte.

Several offspring who attended the reception were friends of mine, so we had a good time giggling and chatting together. One of those was Tori Lilly, a bubbly girl with twinkling brown eyes who played the piano beautifully and often entertained guests at her parents' social gatherings. Since those days I've never heard anyone play Debussy's *Cakewalk* with such flair.

Like Tori and most of my other teenage friends, I loved going to the movies. Whenever new American films came to Paris, I was among the first to get in line for tickets. I never expected to meet one of Hollywood's current heartthrobs in Paris, however, so I was thrilled when an invitation, in the form of a letter addressed to "Miss Peckham," came to me in November 1948 from the Paris office of Paramount films. It was signed by a Mr. J. Plunkett, Publicity Manager. He wrote that I was invited to a party to be held on December 3 at the Hôtel George V in honor of Mr. and Mrs. Alan Ladd, who would be in Paris for a few days. My parents received a similar invitation. We accepted, and during our drive to the party my father asked me, "Is he a cowboy star?"

(LEFT) OUR HOUSE AS SEEN THROUGH THE FRONT GATE *(RIGHT)* JEAN AND WAGRAM AT THE MARKETPLACE: NEUILLY, 1948

Dad was definitely not a big movie fan and didn't know that Mr. Ladd had starred in a variety of roles, not just cowboy films. He was pleased when I told him that the actor had honorably served as a sergeant in the Army Air Force during the war. After we arrived at the designated room, an executive from Paramount greeted us and introduced us to Mr. Ladd. "This reminds me of home," the actor said while shaking my hand, undoubtedly referring to his teenage fans in California. He wore his trademark bow tie and informal sweater vest under a dark suit. My parents talked to him for a while, and a photographer took their picture.

AGRC PASSENGERS AND CREW POSING BEFORE FLIGHT TO SCANDINAVIA (DAD IN THE MIDDLE WITH JEAN AND MOTHER ON EITHER SIDE OF HIM): PARIS, 1948

SWEDISH SOLDIERS PREPARING TO HONOR AMERICAN DEAD IN SWEDEN, 1948

Many other American stars entertained at bases in Europe, where they lifted the morale of homesick soldiers. In Paris these shows were held in an auditorium at the Isle St. Germain AGRC depot. My parents and I often went backstage to meet the stars after their performances, and Dad once had his picture taken with actress June Travers. Rita Hayworth was indisposed the night she was supposed to appear, but we saw other stars perform, such as operatic star Jeanette MacDonald and "red hot Mama" Sophie Tucker. When Celeste Holm sang *I Cain't Say No*, she got a big ovation from the mostly GI audience. These soldiers are fortunate to be stationed in Paris instead of Germany, I thought to myself..

HITLER"S RUINED HOME

AT A SCENIC LOOKOUT ON THE WAY DOWN FROM THE EAGLE'S NEST (L to R) MOTHER, JEAN, CATHERINE RAGUSE, COL. RAGUSE, AND LT. JIM MURPHY): BAVARIA, 1948

In Germany, American GIs were living in a land that was hard to forgive because of the havoc it had wrought during World War

II Nevertheless, the need for a strong and economically stable Germany was becoming more and more obvious.

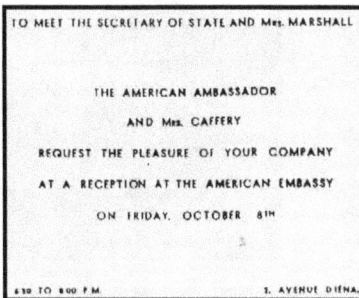

(LEFT) JEAN'S FRENCH FRIENDS ZETTE, ANIC, AND GELAINE: NORMANDY, 1948
(RIGHT) INVITATION TO THE RECEPTION HONORING SECRETARY OF STATE MARSHALL

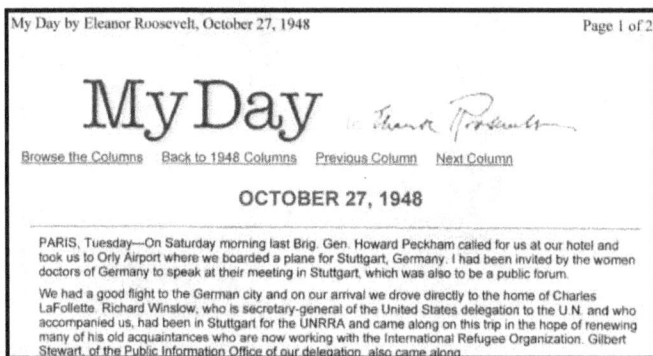

(ABOVE) THE PART OF MRS. ROOSEVELT'S *MY DAY* COLUMN THAT MENTIONS DAD, 1948
(BELOW) MY PARENTS AND THE MACOMBERS (FATHER AND SON) AT LONGCHAMPS

BRITISH SOLDIERS HONORING THE FIRST SHIPMENT OF AMERICAN WAR DEAD FROM THE BRITISH ISLES TO THE UNITED STATES: CARDIFF, 1948 (U.S. Army Photo)

(LEFT) DAD SINGING THE NATIONAL ANTHEM WITH A FRENCH OFFICER: LES INVALIDES
(RIGHT) KATIE THALBERG, JEAN, AND OUR DATES AT SCHOOL DANCE
(BELOW) MY PARENTS AND ALAN LADD AT A PARTY IN THE ACTOR'S HONOR, 1948

Chapter 12

Meetings in France, Germany, and Italy

Economic distress can and must be avoided if Germany is not to return to political apathy.

--LUCIUS D. CLAY

NEAR THE END OF FEBRUARY 1949, my father traveled to Heidelberg, where he was scheduled to attend another meeting with General Clarence Huebner. He was joined by Mother and me. During our drive through eastern France, we made a short detour, at Dad's request.

"You can stop here, Sergeant," he said to our driver after we had motored about fifty miles east of Paris. The site at which we stopped was one that my father had visited before, but he was eager to show it to Mother and me.

We trotted right behind him after Dad left the car and strode with him to a lookout point. When we got there, he quietly said, "This brings back old memories."

My eyes then swept across the sprawling scene before us—a wide view of the Marne River Valley, which Dad first saw when he visited the battlefields in France in 1919. Located on the high hill where we were standing was the Château-Thierry American Monument, which honors American soldiers and marines who fought and died in that region of France during World War I.

"It's inspiring to see our military men honored in such a scenic location," my father said. Nevertheless, the monument reminded us that America got involved in an even more tragic world war soon after the first one. We returned slowly to the car and continued towards Nancy, a city in eastern France, to spend the night.

According to its organizational chart, the AGRC was divided into four zones, which my father often visited. Commanders of those zones, in addition to overseeing reinterment and return activities, gave information to officials who had come to see them, assisted relatives of the deceased, and performed other tasks. Those are some of the topics my father planned to discuss with Colonel Marchman, who commanded the Third Zone. That zone consisted of Luxembourg and the area surrounding Nancy. The other zones were First Zone, consisting of Belgium and Holland; Second Zone, which included southern France, Brittany, and Normandy; and Fourth Zone, the area surrounding Cambridge, England. Each zone had an office, a commander, and personnel. One office was located in Germany, at Bad Kissingen, but instead of "zone" it was called First Field Command.

For my mother and me, the highlight of our stay in Nancy was attending a dinner-dance in the ballroom of our hotel, the Excelsior, which was being used by the U.S. Army. "It's scheduled to be returned to the French by 1951," my father told us later. AGRC people stationed in that zone hosted the dinner, attended by American and French officers and their guests. I wore a long formal dress that I had brought for the trip, and I danced with my father, portly Frank Marchman, and a handsome young French officer who sat with my parents and me during dinner.

After my father's last conference with Colonel Marchman the next morning, we left Nancy bound for Germany. Not long after we crossed the German border, we drove through a lilliputian town where we saw a charming sight. Lined up along the road were several young children dressed in Mardi Gras costumes, who smiled beguilingly at us. Their cherubic faces reminded us of the Hummel figurines that U.S. Army wives liked to buy in

Germany. At my request, my father asked the driver to stop, and I leaped out of the car to take pictures. Mother joined me. *"Guten tag. Bitte...eine photographie?"* I asked slowly asked in heavily accented German, as I pointed to my camera. I got the children to pose nicely, mostly because my mother was holding a few Mars Bars, which she placed in their eager, small hands. *"Danke,"* I said as I returned to the car.

Upon our arrival in Heidelberg, we drove up a winding road to the Schloss Hotel, situated on elevated ground overlooking the city. We would be spending four nights at that beautiful hotel. As soon as I got unpacked in my attractive room, I pulled back the heavy curtains covering my window and peered outside. I could see many small lights twinkling in the downtown windows, as if stars from the late-winter sky had fallen inside the houses and were putting on a dazzling show.

The next morning, I noticed that glistening snowflakes were silently falling on my balcony, so I dressed warmly. My father was scheduled to attend EUCOM meetings, but my diary doesn't mention what my mother did that day. I do know that my day was quite enjoyable and that it began at Juliet Huebner's home, where I had lunch. Afterwards, she and I walked downtown to watch a Mardi Gras parade. The air was wintry, and many branches on the trees were as bare as stones on the shores of the Baltic. I was glad I had worn a woolen scarf around my neck.

It was unusual for me to see German people having a good time, so I wrote enthusiastic words about the Mardi Gras in my diary later. These citizens lived in a historic city with stunning vistas reminiscent of picture postcards, so they were not typical residents of occupied Germany. Allied bombs had flattened cities in more strategic locations, such as Bremerhaven and Frankfurt, but this university city had sustained only light damage.

My father visited with several of his friends when we were in Heidelberg, both officially and socially. One of those was Brigadier General Donald Shingler, a West Point classmate of his. I joined my parents at the dinner party he and his wife, Bea, hosted at their home. Later, I wrote this entry in my diary: "The dinner was marvelous, and afterwards we all sang in the living room while Mrs. Shingler played the accordion."

Like my father, Donald Shingler had been an instructor at West Point in the 1920s. He was later hailed as an expert in Middle Eastern politics. The editors of *Command Decisions* note his service during World War II, when he was a colonel: "During that month [April 1942] General Wheeler himself was transferred to India to become head of the Services of Supply there and was succeeded as head of the Iran mission by Colonel Don G. Shingler."

In regard to Germany's postwar recovery, we noticed with each visit that the towns and villages were becoming more and more habitable, greatly due to the efforts of the Marshall Plan. Before the plan was implemented, a widely held view in Washington was that economic advancement and political stability in defeated Germany were important for the stability of Europe. A nation of impoverished citizens would be ripe for Communist penetration. Besides, America being the charitable country that it is, it seemed like the humanitarian thing for our government to do.

Howard Peckham felt no animosity towards the innocent civilians of Germany, or for young German soldiers who had served their country in the war. He was also genuinely pleased to see that fewer unsightly dumps of concrete and bricks sat where buildings used to be. He knew that when people were cleaning up the ruins and rebuilding their homes, stores, and warehouses at a fast rate, it was a good sign for the future of Europe. "The industriousness of the German people is certainly admirable," he said more than once. The way he felt about the Nazis and their terrible atrocities is a different story, of course.

On our way back to Paris on March 3, we drove through Mannheim, a city on the Rhine renowned for its cultural heritage. We then motored past green meadows and pine-covered hills, until we crossed the French border. When we were about twenty-eight miles from the city of Metz, our driver slowly pulled into the grounds of St. Avold. Here at this large military cemetery were the graves of Americans who lost their lives during World War II in this area of France, so close to Germany. "The German dead temporarily laid to rest in St. Avold were buried in a segregated area, at least a hundred yards away from our fallen soldiers," my father said while I was looking at our surroundings. "They were later taken back to their homeland," he added, as a sober expression clouded his face.

Unlike the other nine permanent cemeteries, which were formerly temporary sites, St. Avold was built on new ground. Many of the deceased, such as Private First Class Wesley W. Daw, were reinterred at St. Avold from a temporary cemetery elsewhere in France. A native of Divide, Colorado, and a member of the 80th Infantry Division, he lost his life in September 1944, after suffering from gunshot wounds.

Another story about St. Avold is as unusual as it is sad, so my father's office gave details about it to *The Stars and Stripes*, which published them on February 25, 1948.

The story is that during the war, a German priest buried seven American fliers in a graveyard in the southern Bavarian city of Straubing. They were crew members of a B-24 shot down over Germany in 1945. The men included three lieutenants and four sergeants—William B. Lyon, William D. Wine, Leslie B. Turner, Charles A. Magan, Raymond J. Collins, David L. Busch, and Herbert M. Catling. The clergyman had undoubtedly given the Americans a proper burial, but the next of kin had the final say. Per their request, in 1948 their loved ones were reinterred at St. Avold, after being positively identified. One aspect of the story that makes it especially noteworthy is that the German priest risked arrest for performing his noble deed of burying the Americans, since it was in violation of a Nazi order.

Visiting St. Avold and seeing other places of interest in France and Germany had been highly educational for me. While Dad was participating in meetings with AGRC people in eastern France and EUCOM officers in Heidelberg, my mother socialized with other army wives, so the trip was enjoyable for her, too. Nevertheless, we were glad to head home to cosmopolitan Paris.

Not all of the American army personnel stationed in the city were under EUCOM. For example, military attachés were attached to the American Embassy in Paris by way of the State Department in Washington, DC. The air force, navy, and army all had attachés in Paris, along with their assistants.

Brigadier Generals Foster J. Tate and his successor, Joseph J. O'Hare, were the two senior army attachés attached to the Embassy when we lived in Paris, and my father knew them well. Part of their job was serving as information-gathering scouts. They were expected to learn critical information about conditions in France and report it to the American Ambassador. This was particularly important as the Cold War began to pick up speed.

They were also required to have strong diplomatic skills and be familiar with the French language and culture. Like my father's aides, they wore a distinctive decoration on their left shoulders, a gold and crimson cord called an *aiguillette*.

Before Foster Tate left for the United States, he stopped by our house in Neuilly to present us with an unusual gift—a pair of green parakeets, named Pierro and Pierrette. He and his wife didn't want to take their pets to his new station, so we were delighted to adopt them. We placed them a new cage that stood about six feet above the hallway floor. When we left Paris, the winged transients were placed in yet another home. In the meantime, they were pleasant additions to our household.

Joseph "Red" O'Hare was a husky man whose red hair and wry sense of humor were palpable evidences of his Irish ancestry. During the war, when he was a colonel, General Omar Bradley chose him to be G-1 (engaged in administrative issues) of First Army. He was "as valuable an officer as I had on my staff," General Bradley writes in *A Soldier's Story*. The two men had played football together when they were cadets at West Point. Later, Joseph O'Hare returned to the Academy to teach French and serve as part-time football coach.

His thorough knowledge of French was a valuable asset in his current job in Paris. When my parents and I attended a party that he and his wife hosted at 39 Rue Franklin in February 1949, he spoke in perfect French to his staff. "He seems to have no trace of an American accent," Mother whispered to me after hearing him speak to one of them. Later I wrote in my diary that embassy personnel and military attachés from all over Europe had attended the party. Each country in Western Europe had its own postwar adjustment problems and concerns, so attending a social event such as this one gave the attachés a chance to compare notes in a relaxed, congenial atmosphere. The fact that the party was given in one of Europe's loveliest cities helped to ensure a large turnout.

A later invitation my parents received from the O'Hares—this time to a party at the Hôtel Crillon—was written in French, with evident diplomatic formality. The hotel, located near the American Embassy on the Place de la Concorde, had been official German headquarters during the occupation of France, those tense days during which Parisians felt as if their city were imprisoned in a tightly laced corset. Now they could breathe easily and be once again embraced by freedom.

In March 1949, Mary Horkan, the wife of EUCOM's Chief Quartermaster, Major General George A. Horkan, came to Paris on a short visit from her home in Heidelberg, joined by daughter Katherine. A pretty girl with short blonde hair, Katherine was a couple of years older than I. She obviously adored Paris. One evening during their visit she and her mother joined my parents and me for dinner at the Petrograd, where we ate small Russian-style potato pancakes, called bleenies, in addition to the meat entrée. During dinner we listened to an orchestra play gypsy-like music, led by a man with the unusual surname of ter Abranoff.

"The food and music remind me of the Balalaika Restaurant in Washington," I told Katherine (or Kay, as she was usually called). She was furtively apartment hunting in more glamorous Paris, however, so when the subject of cities came up, her face wore the enigmatic smile of the *Mona Lisa* I had seen in the Louvre. Understandably, Mrs. Horkan was concerned when Kay announced that she planned to get her own apartment in Paris and live there by herself.

I don't know what her father thought about the idea. Round-faced, blue-eyed George Horkan, a genial Georgetown University graduate, served as Chief Quartermaster of EUCOM until the summer of 1951, when he became Quartermaster General of the U.S, Army and moved with his family to Washington, DC. Kay stayed in Europe, at least for a few more months after her parents left. She enjoyed Paris nightlife, especially the restaurants.

Dining in moderately priced restaurants such as the Petrograd was a favorite pastime of AGRC personnel in Paris and EUCOM visitors from Germany. Once in a while, my parents splurged and ate at fancy restaurants. I often joined them. *Votre canard est 185,552,* a note near my plate informed me one spring evening. Dad, Mother, and I were eating at the plush Tour d'Argent, overlooking the Seine, where each roasted duck—the restaurant's specialty—got a number. Even from 1948 to 1950, when the American dollar went reasonably far, eating there was expensive.

The same was true of Maxim's, where we were given big, stiff menus with the restaurant's name written in wavy red letters. For a teenager like me, it was quite a treat to eat at least once in those famous establishments.

In April 1949 an event occurred that was of great interest to Howard Peckham, George Horkan, and other senior military officers in Europe—the formation of NATO. My father's officer friends agreed with him that an organization made up of friendly and cooperative nations could prevent Russia, with its troops and tanks firmly entrenched in both Eastern and Central Europe, from using military aggression in Western Europe.

After NATO was formed, its twelve charter nations linked arms like compatriots and vowed that an aggressive move by Russia on one member would be like an attack on all of them. The Russians abhorred NATO, for the same reason they disliked the Marshall Plan. They didn't want other countries in Europe to gain strength.

Much to my father's dismay, the Russians didn't seem to like the AGRC either, as evidenced by their lack of cooperation. For example, they insisted that an escort officer accompany every AGRC recovery team that traveled through the Russian zone of Germany. This created delays, because an escort often wasn't available. Also causing delays to the work of the AGRC were the many Russian holidays, when work literally came to a halt. Russia's precipitation of the Berlin airlift even created delays for the mortuary rail cars that traveled through the Soviet zone, as noted in *The Third Year: 1947-1948*:

> Soviet restrictions on truck and rail travel through the Soviet zone of occupation immobilized the two mortuary rail cars normally used by the Berlin detachment [of the AGRC].

Therefore, planes had to be used to carry the deceased during a period when those planes were badly needed to transport supplies into isolated Berlin. The lack of mortuary rail cars and Russia's general lack of cooperation had a negative impact on the AGRC's schedule. My father knew that General Huebner, who had set up a timetable for the end of recovery and return operations performed by the AGRC, was bound to be disappointed by the delays.

In view of EUCOM's increased tensions with Russia, and undoubtedly for other reasons, General Huebner called for acceleration in military preparedness. As a result, during the period April 18 through 24, extensive combat-style maneuvers were held in which thousands of U.S. Army troops took part. They converged north of Frankfurt from all over Europe, and Dad was among the officers participating. Mother and I decided to tag along, at least for part of the way.

On the morning of April 14, the three of us left Paris in a convoy of six army cars, headed in the direction of Metz. (Coincidentally, this was the same day that saw the end of the infamous Nuremberg war crimes trials.) It was a lovely drive and I later wrote these words in my diary: "All the fruit trees are in full bloom, and the leaves on the trees are a light green color." After a night in Metz, we continued to Frankfurt, where we stayed overnight. The next morning we parted company with my father, who went off to the maneuvers.

My mother and I had other plans. A husky, dark-haired AGRC officer, Captain Beaver, picked us up in Frankfurt that morning. From there, he drove us about sixty miles east of Frankfurt to our destination, a quaint hotel in the center of the spa town of Bad Kissingen, where we were to spend ten days with AGRC personnel who were living there. The pretty town was also a recreational center for military personnel stationed in Germany, who took advantage of its restful atmosphere and healing waters.

Our stay in Bad Kissingen included golf for my mother and sightseeing for me, and it provided an enjoyable interlude— especially the night my mother and I danced the hoky-poky at the officers' club. (Dad came from Wetzlar to spend that night with us and joined in the dancing.)

Because Bad Kissingen was situated in the American zone of Germany, cooperation with AGRC search and recovery was of course excellent. Authorities in the British zone were also helpful and cooperative when AGRC search and recovery teams entered that zone, as was the case when they entered the French zone. This is noted in *The Third Year: 1947-1948*: "French civil and military authorities continued to show interest and cooperation in the return program."

Nevertheless, the work of the AGRC in Germany was difficult, even in the friendly American, French, and British zones. There was danger in certain areas because of imbedded mines left over from the war, which I mentioned earlier. Geography was also a problem. Germany's many thick forests, deep lakes, and often-murky rivers created a variety of geographical challenges for search teams. In one case, AGRC workers looked for weeks in the dark waters of the Rhine River to recover a plane and pilot lost there. As noted in *Passing in Review,* he was located elsewhere:

> The pilot, who was later located, was buried under a German marker and positively identified by the numbers on his machine gun, which was retained at the site.

The fact that the pilot was eventually found elsewhere highlights the unique skills of AGRC search teams. It also is an indication of their determination to look everywhere possible for a lost American.

When our stay at Bad Kissingen ended, Mother and I were driven to the army's Victory Guest House, a mansion set aside for VIPs and located in the Taunus Mountains near Frankfurt. After my mother and I ate dinner in the dining room that evening, I joined other guests in another room to watch *Flight Squadron*, a World War II movie about the air war in Europe. A group of waiters in the back of the room were watching the movie intently. "I wonder what they were thinking," I later wrote in my diary. Probably thoughts crossed their minds about "what might have been" had Germany not lost the war.

My father, along with a car and driver, picked us up at the Victory Guest House the next morning. Then we headed home. On our drive to Paris, Dad talked to us about the maneuvers and implied that they had been successful. Nevertheless, it seemed to him as if the Russians had thrown a big sheet of Siberian ice over Europe.

Fortunately, the satellite nations did not entirely succumb to Russian domination, and therefore much unrest existed among non-Communists in those nations. Russian control in religious matters, for example, had become increasingly bitter. This was especially true when the Communists engaged in disputes with the Catholic Church in Poland, a conflict that became more and more hostile in 1949. Several Polish DPs worked for my father at the AGRC, and he sympathized with those whose families still lived in their conflicted homeland.

A battalion of DPs also worked at the AGRC Fontainebleau Depot, about thirty miles south of Paris. Equipment such as forklifts and bulldozers used by AGRC workers was stored and repaired here. A number of DPs were present on Army Day, April 6, when Mother and I went to Fontainebleau to hear my father's speech and watch the soldiers march. My father explained to the assembled crowd that Army Day was established to make people aware of U.S. Army activities and to draw attention to the need for America to have strong defense capabilities. The Poles who worked for my father respected him as a man and a leader, and he in return appreciated their hard work.

In Germany, a long-awaited event occurred in May 1949 that heightened the morale of Berlin's blockade-weary citizens and gave encouragement to U.S. Army personnel. Even though the Berlin airlift would continue until September, the blockade was officially lifted on May 12. General Lucius Clay felt ready to retire, so he left Berlin soon afterwards.

When the idea of an airlift was conceived, dark-eyed General Lucius Clay was both military governor of the American zone and commander-in-chief of United States forces in Europe. Because the AGRC was under EUCOM, General Clay was at the top of Dad's chain of command—and one step above General Huebner. In 1918, General Clay graduated from West Point into the Corps of Engineers, so he and Dad had known each other since that time. His deft handling of the blockade ensured that Germans would fondly remember him, and on the day of his departure they held a big parade in his honor. Later that same day, May 15, my parents, the Mattes, and I went to Orly Field, where his plane stopped for refueling. My diary notes that my parents and I greeted him and his wife Marjorie on the plane and then took them to the officers' club on the field for refreshments.

He had been a formidable commander in postwar Europe, so I felt both ill at ease and awed when the general's piercing, dark eyes observed me sharply while my father introduced us. "His looks are deceiving," my father told me later. "He's not as stern as you think." In comparison, Mrs. Clay greeted me with a gentle smile, and I thought she looked beautiful.

A few days after that official farewell to General Clay, my father received information from the Memorial Division in Washington that would profoundly affect our future. He learned that on May 14 President Truman had signed a document at the White House authorizing the transfer of the fourteen American military cemeteries on foreign soil to the ABMC. In item 1 of that document, the order stated that all administrative functions, supplies, and records of the ten cemeteries in Western Europe (under my father's command), as well as the two in Italy, the one in North Africa, and the one in the Philippines, would be turned over to ABMC "in no instance later than December 31, 1951" or "at such earlier date as may be determined by the president or the Congress." In items 2 and 3 it stated:

> 2. The Department of the Army shall have the right to re-enter any of such cemeteries subsequent to the effective date of the transfer of functions with respect thereto for the purpose of making exhumations or reinterments should any such action become necessary. 3. There shall be transferred to the American Battle Monuments Commission so much of the unexpended balances of appropriations now, or which may become, available to the Department of the Army for the performance of the functions transferred by the provisions of this order as the Director of the Bureau of the Budget may deem necessary for use prior to July 1, 1949, in connection with such functions.

HARRY S. TRUMAN
THE WHITE HOUSE,
May 14, 1949

For me, the document signified that my days in Paris were unfortunately drawing to a close. Howard Peckham, on the other hand, had been expecting to receive word about the President's signature, and he was pleased. The hard work of the AGRC would soon be done, and he would be in a good position to transfer all of the cemeteries to the ABMC. Status letters sent to the next of kin from the Quartermaster General's office in Washington advised them about the upcoming transfer.

The following excerpt from a letter dated April 15, 1949, and signed by then-Quartermaster General Herman Feldman, lets the next of kin know that permanent interment had been completed.

It also lets them know what to expect next:

> This is to inform you that the remains of your loved one have been permanently interred, as recorded above, side by side with comrades who also gave their lives for their country. Customary military funeral services were conducted over the grave at the time of burial. . . . After the Department of the Army has completed all final interments, the cemetery will be transferred, as authorized by the Congress, to the care and supervision of the American Battle Monuments Commission. The Commission also will have the responsibility for permanent construction and beautification of the cemetery, including erection of the permanent headstones. . . .

The ABMC performed its work with finesse. When it replaced the army's wooden markers with headstones made of marble and added other structures, it made the cemeteries the beautiful tourist attractions they are today.

On June 9, my brother arrived in Paris on vacation from West Point. His social life got off to a lively start two nights later when he joined Mother, Dad, and me at a ball that lasted from ten o'clock at night until six o'clock in the morning. Georges Choumitzky, a student at the Beaux Arts Academy and an occasional date of mine, had invited us to join him and his parents at the annual Beaux Arts Ball.

In my diary I later wrote:

> Most of the students were decked out in elaborate costumes, and they wandered around the halls and gardens of the school singing and playing pranks. On arrival, we were greeted by students in costumes, spotlights, a brass band, and a hallway lined with Guard Republicaine. Quite something! From there Georges led us to a small reception room where we met some of the other honored guests. Had champagne, then a bunch of us went out to the big courtyard filled with mobs of people, where we watched the wonderful skits put on by the students and the marvelous fireworks. I then went off with Georges to dance in one of the big

ballrooms, after which we went into another room to eat. Left at 5:30.

It had been a gala occasion, thus adding to my displeasure about leaving Paris within a year. It meant that some magical moments would be over. The Beaux Arts Ball had been an exceptional event, but I knew that I would even miss evenings spent at Monseigneur, an elegant café on Rue d'Amsterdam and a favorite haunt of the American community in postwar Paris. I always jumped at the chance to go there, especially because amiable violinists would slowly wander among the tables and honor song requests.

I particularly remember spending a summer evening at Monseigneur with my parents and some of their AGRC friends. My diary states that the date was June 18, 1949. Ambassador David Bruce, who succeeded Jefferson Caffery as American Ambassador to France, was there too that evening, seated at a table near ours. Joining him was visiting Secretary of State Dean Acheson, who was easily recognizable because of his bushy eyebrows and distinctively large mustache.

Glamorous brunette actress Joan Bennett was also seated at that table. My diary doesn't mention their spouses, but I believe they were present, too. When the musicians serenaded her table and ours with *God Bless America*, she and the rest of us stood up. After the song was sung, Mr. Acheson raised his glass and gave a patriotic toast, causing some of us to have tears in our eyes. The men at our table wore their uniforms—including Howie, who was dressed in cadet gray.

It had been only five years since another June day: D-Day, June 6, 1944, when so many American casualties were laid to rest at St. Laurent.

The first transfer of an American cemetery in Europe from the AGRC to the ABMC was not St. Laurent, however. It was the American cemetery in England. On July 1, 1949, the ABMC assumed control of Cambridge, one of the most beautiful of the ten cemeteries built under my father's command.

A simple ceremony in honor of the event took place on the tenth of the month, when my father presented the keys of the cemetery to Brigadier General Thomas North of the ABMC. Army chaplains of the Catholic, Protestants, and Jewish faiths were present to consecrate the site. (Army chaplains of the three major faiths also performed benediction ceremonies when temporary cemeteries were closed.)

Later that month, a similar ceremony was held at Épinal Cemetery in northeast France. The authors of *Final Disposition of World War II Dead* describe it as follows:

> On 31 July, a simple religious ceremony was held at Épinal to solemnize the recent transfer of responsibility to the ABMC, by General Peckham, Commanding General, AGRC-EA. Épinal thus became, along with Cambridge in England, one of the first two permanent cemeteries transferred to ABMC—an event which had occurred on 1 July 1949.

Among the many young infantrymen who lie at rest in Épinal are two privates whose stories are especially heart wrenching: their names are Ralph E. Adams and Joseph L. Bale III.

Private Adams, from Alhambra, California, died in February 1945. While scouting at the front lines near Saarbrucken, he was killed by shrapnel wounds to his right side and head. He had been at the front lines for only a short time when he died.

Private Bale was from Detroit. For his extraordinary heroism, he was posthumously awarded a Distinguished Service Cross (DSC). On January 30, 1945, while fighting in France, he attacked an enemy tank with his rocket launcher, causing the frustrated Germans to retreat. Later that day, he braved shell fire while trying to destroy another German tank. This single-handed maneuver resulted in his death.

Another particularly sad story concerned the arrival of caskets of three sons of a widower in Kansas. They had been returned to the United States in November 1948. One son had been killed in the Battle of the Bulge; another had died in a

German prison camp; and the third was killed in 1945 in Germany. Like blades of grass regularly cut down on the Kansas plains, the scythe of worldwide conflict had cut down this Midwestern family in an extremely cruel fashion. My father learned that well-attended services in tribute to the sacrifices of the brothers were held, and that they were buried in a cemetery near their father's home.

The father and his five surviving children had the consolation of knowing they could visit the nearby site whenever they wanted to, particularly on special occasions. To some next of kin, the proximity of their home to the gravesite was an important consideration when they made the difficult decision whether to have the deceased returned home or laid to rest in Europe.

As his days in France were drawing to a close, Dad expressed more and more his appreciation to the French for having cooperated well with the AGRC. He personally thanked many people who had visited cemeteries, such as Épinal. French people often honored fallen Americans by reciting prayers in churches near the cemeteries and by placing bouquets of flowers near American gravesites.

The French of course admired their own military heroes, those presently serving in their army and those lost in battle. This pride seemed most evident on Bastille Day, which commemorates the storming of the Bastille prison by livid French citizens and the start of the French Revolution.

The biggest Bastille Day celebration since the beginning of World War II was held on July 14, 1949, and it bounded into the city like a jolly traveling circus. On the preceding evening, people already started celebrating. Beginning at around six o'clock, Paris took on the atmosphere of a country festival. Lanterns and flags hung gaily on apartment balconies and from windows. On the outside of nearly all the corner cafés, orchestra stands seemed to jump onto the pavement. At seven o'clock, the city fathers marched—along with columns of Paris police and Republican Guards—to the Arc de Triomphe, where they laid a wreath on the Tomb of the Unknown Soldier. By nine o'clock, tables at cafés that provided live music were fully occupied. Street dancing went on until dawn.

I didn't dance until dawn, but I did watch the parade as it traveled down the Champs Élysées the following day. These are only a few of the words I wrote in my diary: "The parade was really spectacular. I especially liked the Moroccan troops who, dressed in white turbans and capes, rode by on horseback, blowing trumpets." The fountains and edifices were beautifully lighted that night, and the fireworks cascaded magnificently across the summer sky with rainbow-hued streaks of light.

I remember skipping and dancing on the cobblestone streets of the Left Bank until two o'clock in the morning with a group of American college students. Hundreds of Parisians were doing the same thing, perhaps for the second night in a row. They wanted to enjoy every minute of this day, the biggest and happiest Bastille Day since the end of the war.

The French people joyfully welcomed this long-anticipated celebration partly because their defeat in World War II had been so humiliating. A teacher of mine at the American School, Madame Marguerite Dubus, didn't let her class forget how well trained her country's soldiers were, in spite of their capitulation. "Our soldiers got good training and fought well. They didn't have all the good equipment the Americans had," she reminded us. She was basically correct about that.

France didn't have the economic advantages of the United States, which placed that country in a defensive rather than offensive position at the beginning of the war. Later, the Germans destroyed much of their best equipment.

Even if they sometimes envied American military might and economic prosperity, the French people my parents met seemed eager to maintain a good relationship with the Americans who lived in France and with American citizens in the United States who had sent them food, clothing, and other gifts after the war.

Their appreciation was visibly demonstrated in Paris on January 7, 1949, when a train composed of forty-nine small boxcars left the city. The cars were filled with such items as cheeses, fruits, vases, works of art, books, and various items that the French people themselves had made.

After a lively band played *The Star-Spangled Banner* and the *Marseillaise*, a young girl blew the departure whistle, and the train went on its way. As reported by *The Stars and Stripes* on January 8, my father was one of the officials who gave the train, called the Merci Train, a big send-off that day. The boxcars were shipped from Le Havre to the United States, where they were greeted happily by the states through which they traveled.

On August 10, my parents and I visited Italy, another country gradually benefiting from the Marshall Plan. Accompanying us was Dad's new aide Lieutenant Woody Tomaw and wife Jackie, a Belgian woman Woody had met in Belgium during the war.

Before our plane took off, my father told me that many Americans who died in Italy during World War II fought bitterly in Sicily and southern Italy. When we flew over those locations, I looked at them intently through my semi-shaded window and thought about Uncle Bob Shaw and his World War II service. I knew he had traveled with the 3rd Infantry Division from North Africa to Sicily and southern Italy, via Salerno and Anzio, and then to France.

I didn't know until years later, when I read his fine memoir *Clan Shaw,* that my uncle had been awarded numerous medals during his thirty-year military career, including Distinguished Flying Cross, Distinguished Service Medal, Combat Infantry Badge with star, Master Parachutist's Badge, Silver Star, Legion of Merit with three oak leaf clusters, Bronze Star with two oak clusters, and seven awards of the Air Medal. (An oak leaf cluster is equal to an additional award of the same medal.) After the war, he was stationed all over the world, including India. He and Bunny lived in Florida during his retirement, until he succumbed to cancer in 1990.

The purpose of Dad's twelve-day trip was partly to enjoy a vacation, but mainly to inspect graves registration activities in Italy and North Africa and attend meetings with Quartermaster Corps officers involved in these activities. Back in the summer of

1947, he joined some officials, who had arrived from Washington, to discuss and inspect permanent military burial sites in those two areas. Because fatalities in Italy and North Africa occurred in the Mediterranean and North Africa Theaters, respectively, and not in the European Theater, return of the war dead from those locations was under the Quartermaster Corps but not directly under the AGRC-EA.

Upon our arrival in Rome, a Quartermaster Corps officer, Major Townsend C. Anderson, met our plane and took us to the apartment he shared with his wife. We then enjoyed drinks on their terrace, from which we could see pointed church steeples and the red-shingled rooftops of several old houses. The subdued darkness of evening was just beginning to creep over them, thus adding to their antiquated appearance.

The Andersons then drove us to an outdoor restaurant in the outskirts of Rome. While we were dining on melon, ham, and spaghetti, which were merely the first courses of a seven-course dinner, we admired the bright moonbeams reflected on nearby Lake Albano and the lights of Rome twinkling in the distance. When the major described various sights that the city offers its visitors, my father said, "Jean would especially like to visit the Colosseum."

My wish soon came true. "It's a great time to see it," the major said enthusiastically when we arrived at our after-dinner destination. He was right. The soft glow cast by the moon on the historic Colosseum walls, near which the first Christian martyrs gave their lives so many years ago, provided a perfect conclusion to our day.

The magical atmosphere of Rome continued the following day when Mother, Jackie, and I toured famous tourist spots with Vincent, our Italian guide and driver, whom Major Anderson had arranged for us. In addition to being knowledgeable, Vincent was a careful driver and could speak English reasonably well.

My father, meanwhile, attended a meeting with the major and Colonel Whitfield W. Watson, the Quartermaster Corps officer in charge of graves registration activities in Italy.

Rome was bright and summery the following morning when Vincent drove my parents, the Tomaws, and me through its busy streets. We were bound for Naples, where my father's work would continue. Here he planned to meet with AGRC personnel and go with them to the American cemetery at nearby Nettuno, the burial place of those soldiers who bravely fought at Sicily, Anzio, and other places in Italy. On our way there, we spent one night in Sorrento and also visited Capri. We even squeezed in a quick tour of the ruins in Pompeii.

The next day, while the Tomaws and I loafed at the beach and my mother rested in the hotel, Dad boarded an American military plane for an early flight to Tunis, where he would be inspecting the American cemetery and meeting with graves registration officials.

"Getting an appropriate site for a permanent cemetery in Tunisia wasn't easy," he had told us before he left. For various reasons, the sites of the former temporary cemeteries were found to be inappropriate. Therefore, excavation was done in 1947 at a proposed location that was on high ground and had beautiful views of the Mediterranean Sea. It was revealed, however, that the location contained ancient ruins. My father knew that to use such a site would antagonize both the French and Tunisian governments. Another one was therefore chosen. As reported by the *Final Disposition of World War II Dead*, he helped to expedite approval of the site:

> Nevertheless, on clearance of the site by the French Antiquities Service, Gen. H. L. Peckham, CG, Hq, AGRC-EA, requested the American Ambassador in France to open formal negotiations for its acquisition. On 10 January 1948, The Quartermaster General urged quick French approval in order that work might begin.

The work began quickly thereafter; in fact, the cemetery was established that same year, 1948. The ABMC had selected the architectural firm that would do the layout, and they did an outstanding job. The cemetery consists of twenty-seven acres and is situated ten miles northeast of Tunis. As my father told us later, it is particularly interesting to see from the air because it lies on a plateau and is divided into nine rectangular plots.

American casualties near Tunis and Carthage had been sustained during heavy fighting in the North Africa Theater. The army officer in charge of graves registration activities there was Colonel Earl B. Wadsworth. After attending meetings with Colonel Wadsworth and his personnel, my father checked into a Tunis hotel for the night. The Tomaws, my mother, and I meanwhile spent another night in Naples.

Early the next day we began our trip by car to Rome, where my father would fly from North Africa to join us. Vincent knew the route by heart. Best of all, he was adept at swerving away from donkey carts that moved too far into vehicle traffic and from women who confidently walked along the roads' edges while balancing gigantic bundles on their heads.

In the afternoon, Vincent stopped at Monte Cassino and parked the car, per Woody's request. We all then got out to view the abbey, which was founded in the ninth century by Saint Benedict. Somberness overtook us as we looked up from the bottom of the hill towards the abbey, which was surrounded by damaged, crumbling walls. "The fighting here in 1944 between the Allied forces and Germans was intense because the location was so important strategically," Woody explained. Allied bombing had unfortunately torn the abbey apart swiftly, and practically the entire nearby town was destroyed as well during subsequent fighting.

Many other war-torn towns in Italy had already benefited greatly from the Marshall Plan. New housing in several parts of the country was constructed with the Marshall Plan funds, and employment in small towns was increasing as well. In the long run, economic recovery was an effective weapon against the spread of communism in Italy.

Dad greeted us at our Rome hotel when we arrived. That evening, we all attended a dinner party in the Quirinale Hotel, at which Colonel Watson was the host. In my diary I wrote later that I had worn the "dainty silver bracelet and earring set" my father had brought me from Tunisia and "the silk print dress" I had carefully packed before leaving Paris.

Although the combined total of casualties suffered in the Mediterranean and North Africa Theaters had been far fewer than in the European Theater, the terrain involved in search and recovery of our war dead covered thousands of miles. Searches involved traveling all around that vast territory, through which search teams traveled along miles of parched terrain and areas thick with cactus plants.

We left Rome on the sixteenth, arriving in Florence about six o'clock. Captain Thomas, a heavy-set, jovial Quartermaster officer, joined us for dinner in our hotel. The next day, he took us on a short sightseeing and shopping trip. When we stopped briefly at an outdoor marketplace, Jackie and I enthusiastically bought floppy straw hats, while my parents strolled among the wares. Captain Thomas, a bachelor who was obviously fascinated by the vivacious (and buxom) Jackie, then drove us to the station. Right after we boarded the train, it inched its way slowly from Florence, taking us north to Venice.

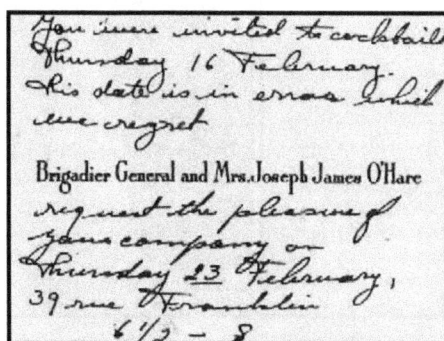

A PARTY INVITATION FROM BRIG. GEN. AND MRS. O'HARE, 1949: PARIS

We spent two days in this beautiful city, which included the obligatory but enjoyable gondola ride down the Grand Canal.

Early on August 21, we returned to Florence, where Vincent and his car greeted us at the railroad station. *"Buòn giorno!"* we exclaimed when we saw him, a greeting we used many times on our trip. He then drove us to Leghorn, a military depot on the west coast of Italy and a half-hour drive from Pisa (where we had made a dizzying climb up the stairway to the top of the Leaning Tower). Leghorn was then a popular vacation spot for American army personnel in Europe. We could understand why when we saw our palatial hotel, facing the sea.

"Welcome to Leghorn," square-faced Major Duncan said upon our arrival. Before shaking our hands, he removed the green-lensed designer sunglasses he was wearing, and I saw that he had a fabulous suntan. He and Dad toured the depot that afternoon, while the rest of us relaxed on the beach. The suave major was a perfect host. That evening, he took us out for dinner in town; the next morning, he breakfasted with us at the depot, and then accompanied us to the airport in a car driven by Vincent.

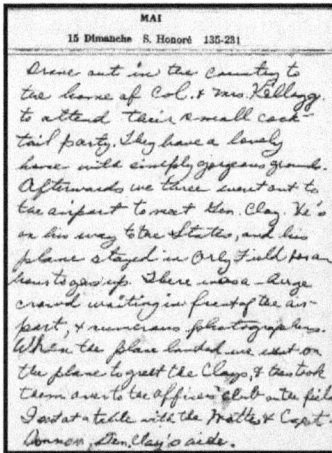

(LEFT) JEAN'S DIARY ENTRY ABOUT GEN. CLAY'S STOPOVER: PARIS *(RIGHT)* JEAN DANCING WITH COL. MARCHMAN IN NANCY: 1949

"Grazie," I said to Vincent when we arrived at Pisa Airport. While shaking his hand, I mumbled *"Arrivederci."* Then I jumped

into the plane quickly, afraid that the tears in my eyes would overly expose my sentimental feelings about leaving Italy. I felt the way Browning must have felt when he wrote: "Open my heart, and you will see, carved inside of it *Italy.*"

(L TO R) JEAN, FRENCH OFFICER, AND MY PARENTS WATCHING A FLOORSHOW
AFTER DINNER: NANCY, 1949

MOTHER AND DAD DOING THE HOKY-POKY NEXT TO A LADY IN A FLOWERED
DRESS: BAD KISSINGEN, 1949

(LEFT) (L TO R) CAPT. BEAVER, JEAN, LT. MAYER, AND DAN: BAD KISSINGEN, 1949
(RIGHT) JACKIE, DAD, AND CAPT. THOMAS AT THE MARKETPLACE IN FLORENCE

(LEFT) JACKIE, MY PARENTS, AND WOODY IN A GONDOLA: VENICE
(RIGHT) AIRPLANE VIEW OF THE U.S. CEMETERY IN TUNIS

MAJOR DUNCAN, MOTHER, JEAN, VINCENT, AND THE TOMAWS: PISA AIRPORT

Chapter 13

Preparing to Leave the Old World

All the millions who have gone before, who have lived in the city and loved it, have left something of themselves to be still a part of it.

--WILLIS THORNTON

WHILE RETURNING TO PARIS in August 1949 from our visit to Italy, our C-47 encountered unexpected turbulence, about which I wrote in my diary: "The going was a bit rough at times. Anyway, we started making a lunch from the bread and cheese we bought in Italy. Slicing the bread was a challenge." Mother looked quite tense during the bumpy periods, but when we flew over the lofty Italian Alps, a crewmember invited her to come to the cockpit and admire the scenery. Soon afterwards, she timidly peered over his shoulder, fascinated by the view and taking it all in. The Alps looked majestic from our height of fifteen thousand feet.

In September, Paris newspapers shouted the news that the Federal Republic of Germany was being established that month, thus ending American, French, and British occupation of that country's western sector. For some worried French citizens, it was much too soon after World War II for the establishment of a German republic. They were reassured somewhat, however, by news that the Allies would continue to have ultimate authority over military security, foreign trade, and several other crucial issues. Bonn was to be the headquarters of the new republic.

Fortunately, thousands of Allied troops were to remain in West Germany, thus being able to maintain a stabilizing effect there. Nevertheless, the news was controversial.

In contrast to that news, which stirred up controversy, the *International Herald Tribune* didn't neglect to publicize Armistice Day on November 11. It published a short article describing Dad's attendance at a special Mass at the Church of Notre Dames des Victoires in honor of Allied forces. Also on Armistice Day, my father watched as an AGRC platoon took part in a ceremony at Fontainebleau, where a French-donated plaque was unveiled honoring Allied airmen.

Not many weeks thereafter, my parents and I started on our last car trip related to my father's job with the AGRC. A blanket of cold air hovered over the Seine when Sergeant Cochran began driving us through Paris on our way south. We were headed to Draguignan in southern France, where my father was scheduled to participate in a memorial ceremony.

We spent our first night in the ancient town of Vienne, south of Lyons, arriving just as the hush of evening was falling like a cape over the cobblestone streets.

Right after breakfast the next morning, we journeyed to Aix-en-Provence, one of France's most famous spas, where we lunched. We then went past sun-splattered vineyards and rows of citrus trees until we reached St. Raphael, where we had our first full view of the Mediterranean Sea.

The sun was just starting to set when we arrived at the Ruhl, our hotel in Nice. My father tipped the porter who had brought our bags to our suite and then went for a half-hour walk in the environs surrounding the hotel. "It'll be a relief to breathe the clear sea air," he had said cheerfully on his way out the door. Paris had been quite smoggy for the two weeks before our departure. As I mentioned, my father was a fast walker, so my mother and I didn't want to gallop along behind him in an unfamiliar area. Instead we unpacked.

At ten o'clock the next morning, Sergeant Cochran drove us to Cannes, where we briefly stopped to look at the boats anchored in the harbor. Some had huge sails that flapped noisily in the breeze. Others were more modestly appointed.

Sergeant Cochran then drove us on a winding road until we reached Draguignan American Cemetery, twenty-eight miles west of Cannes. Here, at the foot of a hill, lay the fallen Americans who lost their lives in the invasion of southern France. Years later I wondered how many carefree boat owners at Cannes knew about the cemetery. I also wondered how many tourists would tear themselves away from the blackjack tables at Monte Carlo or the beaches of St. Tropez to visit that solemn place.

In the 1980s, an article appeared in the *Los Angeles Times* that gave a somewhat encouraging answer:

> Like the battles themselves, most of the war cemeteries and monuments scattered across Europe are off the beaten track, yet collectively they are one of Europe's most popular and enduring tourist attractions. European tourists are particularly interested in visiting the sites because the cemeteries are placed in historic battle sites. The battles are conveniently mapped and summarized on the walls of the memorials. On the headstones of those victims who could not be identified, the tourists see this explanatory sentence: "Here rests in honored glory a comrade in arms known only to God."

When my mother and I walked down the winding path towards the reviewing stand, we passed several crosses and occasional Stars of David. Before taking our seats, we shook hands with some of the French dignitaries and American officers seated near us. We then listened while my father spoke to the crowd about our soldiers who arrived during the invasion. Most had come directly from battle areas of Italy. Before they arrived, American planes fortunately bombed and destroyed vital enemy installations and defenses in southern France, thereby enabling our troops to advance rapidly. Nevertheless, it was not without a high price. More than eight hundred American dead were laid to rest in the permanent American Cemetery at Draguignan.

After hearing my father's speech, I watched the disciplined footwork of French Army troops as they marched by me. The flag bearers wore snug caps and dark overcoats, which sharply contrasted with their white belts and white spats. When the band played *La Marseillaise* and *The Star Spangled Banner*, a lump rose up in my throat. When the ceremony ended, we walked slowly to the car and drove to Nice, where we spent the night.

At about eight o'clock the next morning, Sergeant Cochran drove us along the coast to Toulon, where we lunched. We then traveled west into Marseilles to gas up the car. "The city was badly damaged in World War II," my father said during our drive through town, and I saw several gutted buildings and disheveled warehouses. Unexpectedly, our drive turned dramatic after we got gas and headed towards the waterfront. Usually the sight of my father's army car—with its general's star displayed on the bumper plates—evoked smiles or at least curious stares from the people we passed on rural roads or city streets.

Here we received unfriendly glares, and we saw the words *"Vive Stalin"* scrawled in big red letters on a few walls. These markings clearly revealed the Communist affiliation of many Marseilles citizens. Then a bearded, scraggly young man raised his clenched fist and shook it threateningly at us as he walked towards the car. My father ignored him and told Mother and me to do the same. To our driver, he said, "Sergeant, keep an eye on that guy, but let's get out of this area right away." It was a relief to leave unfriendly Marseilles.

We then drove north to Arles, where we stayed in a big, drafty hotel. Fortunately, the hotel provided foot warmers, a small but bulky item that allows one's feet to become as warm as croquettes.

The next morning, December 31, we walked around for a short while to admire some of the old Roman ruins for which Arles is known and then drove through Avignon, the walled city with its famous arched bridge. Finally, after winding for several miles over a narrow road, we arrived at the mountain town of Le Puy, where we checked into a hotel. All of us, especially Sergeant

Cochran, were tired after the long drive, and we fully expected to have a quiet New Year's Eve. We were wrong about that.

When my parents and I came down for dinner, we were surprised to see that a party was in full swing in the dining room and that most of the tables, which were decorated with horns, confetti, and other New Year's Eve decorations, were occupied. A jolly waiter, who seemed as effervescent as a geyser, soon came over to greet Dad with a *"Bonsoir, Monsieur Général."*

The waiter then led us to a tableful of celebrants, who smiled widely while pulling out chairs for us. *"Merci, mesdames et messieurs,"* my father said before taking a seat and speaking a few more polite greetings. Even if they may have felt uneasy at first about our presence, Dad's engaging smile and ability to speak French (albeit with an American accent) put them at ease. They could probably tell he wasn't a "stuffed shirt," and a joyous atmosphere prevailed throughout the evening.

When the band played *The Stars and Stripes Forever*, our tablemates, as well as most of the patrons in the dining room, stood up to toast us with their wine-filled glasses. Except for Sergeant Cochran, who sat a few tables away from us with some young people he had met, we were the only guests who weren't French. That friendly and unusual New Year event provided an excellent end to 1949.

Early in 1950, my father had another opportunity to enhance his Franco-American ties. On the morning of January 29, 1950, our army sedan, again driven by Sergeant Cochran, took my parents and me past frost-covered lawns in the northern part of Paris and then onto a highway running northeast of the city. The purpose of this trip was not directly related to AGRC work. My father had been invited to serve as the main participant in a cornerstone-laying ceremony at Berck Plage, a town on the northeast coast of France. We arrived there at about noon.

A well-dressed host of the event welcomed us. *"Bonjour, mon général,"* he said enthusiastically, while looking in my father's direction. He then invited us to go with him to a reception a short distance away, where we were introduced to the architects and engineers participating in a plan to rebuild the town. It had been badly destroyed by Allied bombs during the war. He then took us on a tour of what remained of the town, which sadly wasn't much. Its gutted buildings looked ragged and inhabitable.

The local hospital was functioning adequately, however, thanks in part to ECA funds. There we learned about the methods its doctors were using to treat patients, particularly children who were suffering from crippling bone diseases. It was heartwarming to see appreciative glances in response to my father's words of encouragement and to hear people express their thanks by saying *"Merci beaucoup"* so frequently. Some interesting events followed the tour.

The first event was an outdoor ceremony near the beach, where my father laid a cornerstone symbolizing construction of five new buildings in the town. During the event, a priest faced the crowd and offered a prayer, while the chilly breeze created ripples in his long, black ecclesiastical robe.

Next on the agenda was a luncheon at the Hôtel Villa Maritime, where we were seated at a big U-shaped table. Many of the invited dignitaries stood up, one after the other, and raised their champagne glasses high in the air. They toasted to the success of the project and then shouted *"Vive l'Amerique!"* My parents, Sergeant Cochran, and I were the only non-French guests at this French-sponsored event. "The English Channel is at its narrowest point in the area of Pas de Calais, not far from here," one of the English-speaking dignitaries told me during lunch. From him I learned that Hitler mistakenly believed Allied forces would cross at that narrow point of the Channel to launch their invasion of Normandy.

My father was pleased whenever French people expressed gratitude for American assistance received through the Marshall Plan (by way of the ECA), and this had been quite evident at Berck Plage. A crowd of townspeople waited near the hotel entrance as we made our exit after the luncheon, and they waved goodbye when we got into our car. *"Au revoir!"* they kept shouting, until the car disappeared from their viewing range. Sergeant Cochran then drove us out to the main highway and to Paris, where we arrived at about ten-thirty that evening. We were gratified to read in the February 7 edition of *The Stars and Stripes* a description of the day's event and my father's participation in it:

> PARIS, Feb. 6 (Special)—Brig Gen Howard L. Peckham, CG, 7966th EUCOM Det, laid a cornerstone during a ceremony symbolizing construction of five new buildings at Berck Plage, in the Pas de Calais region of northern France. Prior to the ceremony, Peckham, in company with French military and civilian dignitaries, visited the Franco-American Hospital in Berck Plage. The village was badly damaged by Allied bombing during World War II and is a medical center for treatment of bone tubercular patients. Reconstruction is being partly financed by ECA funds.

In February, my father welcomed into his Astoria office a visiting U.S. Army major general who was also an ordained Southern Baptist minister. His name was Roy H. Parker, and he was the newly appointed Chief of Chaplains for the Department of the Army. Accompanying him was a party of officials from Washington. On his agenda were meetings with AGRC chaplains and participation in ceremonies relating to the transfer of AGRC records and functions to the ABMC.

This congenial clergyman knew firsthand what it was like to be in combat. He had served in World War II as chief chaplain of the North Africa Theater and then theater chaplain at the headquarters of the Far East Command, under General Douglas MacArthur. When he and his party were ready to leave Paris, my father invited me to come with him to the railroad station to see them off. They were scheduled to go from northern France to London and then to the American cemetery in Cambridge for an official ceremony.

The following month brought a day that was extremely sentimental for my parents and me. On March 12, 1950, members of the AGRC officers' club bade their official farewells to the three of us at a large reception at the club. One by one, people shook our hands or embraced us. We had gathered with those people at New Year's Eve celebrations and other functions at the club, and those people would be missed.

Also in March, Dad said an official goodbye to the Polish AGRC workers. To show their appreciation for his kindness in enabling them to work for him and for other kindnesses he had shown, a unit of DPs led by their liaison officer presented him with a commemorative badge. A picture and explanation of this event appeared on March 22, 1950, in *The Stars and Stripes*:

> The honorary and commemorative badge of Polish Labor Service Units is presented in Paris to Brig Gen Howard L. Peckham, CG, 7966th EUCOM Det, by Maj Henry S. Zdrodowski, liaison officer for the Polish units attached to the 7966th Det.

A few days after that article appeared, I suddenly heard the strains of *The Harry Lime Theme* drifting from a radio in a café on the Champs Élysées, where I had gone for *café au lait* with Tori Lilly. The somewhat gloomy movie from which the music came, *The Third Man*, was an enormous hit in Paris that month. The provocative film reflected a Europe worn out from World War II and fearful of "the bomb" and the Cold War.

I would have preferred to hear the Gallic singing voices of Charles Trenet or Edith Piaf instead of zither music from a film set in postwar Vienna, especially since my time in Paris was ending. The city would always be a part of me, as the words of Willis Thornton at the beginning of this chapter imply. For one thing, where else but in "the City of Light" would I be invited to parties given by royalty, such as Count and Countess Xavier Rostan D'Ancezune and Countess de Uribarren, who had graciously entertained my parents and me?

Saying goodbye to my boyfriend Jim and other schoolmates at the American School was also difficult for me. Many of them, at least the sons and daughters of AGRC personnel, would be leaving soon, too. Unfortunately, I lost touch with most of my school friends over the years, as we became scattered around the globe.

Dad's work was done, however, and the time for him to move on had come. In spite of delays, such as those caused by problems in the Russian zone of Germany, bad weather during interments at Normandy Cemetery, and heavy rains in other areas—especially in the spring—the AGRC accomplished its goals. *Final Disposition* provides this assessment of the work done under Dad's command: "The permanent burial of over 60,000 American servicemen in ten selected cemeteries represented a great overall achievement."

After the AGRC turned over the ten permanent cemeteries to the ABMC, that agency changed some of their names. Margraten is now Netherlands Cemetery, and Hamm is Luxembourg Cemetery. Neuville-en-Condroz is now called Ardennes Cemetery. One of the Americans who rest at Ardennes is Second Lieutenant Everett H. Weise, a co-pilot aboard a B-24 that caught fire. Although he successfully jumped from the plane, he was strangled by his parachute lines, in which he became entangled. It was a tragic end for a veteran of twenty missions with the 579th Bomb Squadron.

In France, the ABMC has also changed some names, thus making it easier for visitors to locate them. St. James is now called Brittany Cemetery. St. Avold is now Lorraine Cemetery and has 10,489 graves, more than any of the other nine. St. Laurent is now Normandy Cemetery.

In June 1994, near the crosses and occasional Stars of David at Normandy Cemetery, the ABMC commemorated the fiftieth anniversary of D-Day. President Bill Clinton attended the commemoration along with President François Mitterrand, Queen Elizabeth II, and other Allied leaders. They were joined by thousands of World War II veterans who came and listened intently when President Clinton spoke about the sacrifices of those gallant men who died during the invasion.

A weekly magazine noted that the "hand of Providence" seemed to touch the President at that moment: "Just as he began to speak the sun came out, etching in breathtaking brilliance the white crosses against the tender green landscape" (*Time,* June 20, 1994).

As far as the cemetery in Normandy and the other American cemeteries in Europe were concerned, my father was satisfied with the work he had done as head of the AGRC and was ready to take on another challenging assignment. He didn't have to wait very long. In February 1950, he was ordered to command the Quartermaster Procurement Agency in New York City.

Our upcoming departure didn't go unnoticed by the news media. A picture of Dad and an accompanying article appeared on March 18 in *The Stars and Stripes*. The wide headline was followed by a description of his AGRC work and of our plans to vacation in Switzerland and Germany before sailing to New York. The vacation about which the paper wrote was superb.

In Switzerland, we admired the beauty of St. Moritz. Then, during a train ride to Lucerne, Mother and Dad socialized with other passengers. My outgoing father really liked that aspect of our trip. In our small compartment were two middle-aged Italians from Florence, who could speak English. One of the men had a wide, slim mustache, coal-black hair, and olive-colored skin as glossy as marble. Dad, in an animated fashion that echoed theirs, talked with them primarily about the pleasures of travel. He seemed relaxed—he was now having a real vacation, not a trip related to AGRC work.

On March 21, we caught a train from Zurich to the railroad station in Stuttgart, where the ever-punctual Sergeant Cochran was waiting for us with an army car. Soon thereafter, we were dashing along on the autobahn (the German highway system that had no speed limit) to our hotel in Garmisch. Woody and Jackie greeted us at the picturesque hotel, which was nestled at the foot of the Zugspitze, Germany's hlghest mountain. During dinner that evening, Woody told us about the history of Garmisch, which in those years was a popular recreational area for the U.S. Army:

> Fortunately the war didn't touch Garmisch. In April 1945 the 10th Armored Division entered it from the direction of Oberammergau. The division stayed there until the war ended, and remodeling of the sports center then began. Existing hotels in the

area were converted into billets and clubs for officers and enlisted men.

The lively nightlife in the area helped members of the armed forces forget about Hitler and the misery he had brought to the world. The nightclub scene also helped them forget about their homesickness. Here, at the Casa Carioca club, they could dance to excellent band music and watch an extravagant floorshow. Ice shows were especially popular in this recreation spot, built with German labor under U.S. Army supervision. The night we were there a new fantasy on ice, *Alice in Wonderland*, was being presented.

We also re-visited the nearby town of Berchtesgaden. Our one night there included dinner in our hotel's luxurious dining room, once a favorite haunt of high Nazi officials. "Look! The napkins still have swastikas embroidered on them," I exclaimed after unfolding mine. The symbols were small and dainty, but menacing reminders of Hitler, nonetheless.

When our stay in southern Bavaria ended, Sergeant Cochran drove us to the residence of Major General and Mrs. George Horkan in Heidelberg, where we would be houseguests for four days. Lieutenant Gilbert, the general's aide, greeted us when we arrived at the family's large home. A German servant wearing a spotless white jacket and black bow tie assisted us with our suitcases and took them to our rooms, but not before the loquacious Mrs. Horkan asked my mother and me to join her for tea in the sitting room to discuss our schedule. While sitting on a plushly cushioned chair, I listened intently.

Kay had left the nest and gotten her own apartment in Paris, so her mother treated me as if I were a surrogate daughter. She even arranged an escort for me (a lieutenant named Al Wedemeyer, Jr.) for a supper party to be held that evening at the Macogen Club, a club for majors, colonels, and generals and their guests.

During the time that my father was conferring with EUCOM officers and saying his goodbyes in the days to follow, their wives and daughters were entertaining my mother and me. On April 1, Mrs. Horkan gave a farewell luncheon in my honor at the Schloss Hotel, attended by several daughters of EUCOM officers.

On April 3, I lunched there again, this time with my father, the Tomaws, and a petite lady whom my father first met at Fort Benning in 1940—Mrs. George S. Patton. She had just visited her husband's grave in Luxembourg and was on her way home.

General Patton had been laid to rest temporarily at Hamm because it was one of Third Army's largest cemeteries. Although it was a temporary location at first, Talbot writes in *The Story of American Graves Registration Command* why Hamm Cemetery became General Patton's final resting site:

> He was buried there on 24 December 1945 in the next open grave in a regular plot. It was here that Mrs. Patton told General Littlejohn that it was her wish that General Patton remain permanently in Hamm Cemetery together with those of his army who would remain there.

Mrs. Patton spoke in a quietly firm voice that belied her small stature, assuring my father she was satisfied with the decision made back in 1945. He agreed and said he was convinced that someone with her husband's prominence, now lying at rest in a beautiful site in Europe, gave encouragement to other families. Many had wanted to leave their loved ones in overseas cemeteries but were hesitant to do so. As Howard Peckham knew so well, however, the ABMC would beautifully maintain them in the future. It had already done so with the World War I cemeteries in Europe, which Dad had personally visited.

That afternoon we feverishly packed our suitcases and prepared to depart. Time seemed to fly by much too quickly. The Tomaws drove us to the train station, where Jackie gave Mother a beautiful bouquet of flowers. On my father's cheek, she planted a great big kiss. Among the other people who saw us off was my father's friend Brigadier General Everett Busch (who would later be a neighbor of mine in San Francisco), the Deputy Chief of the

Quartermaster Division in Heidelberg. After we boarded the boat train, my mother put the flowers in a vase and surveyed our surroundings. "It's more room than we'll ever be able to use." That was quite an understatement. Our private car consisted of a sitting room, two bathrooms, and three bedrooms. The events of the past few days had been so prodigious that I didn't sleep well that night, in spite of the excellent accommodations.

When I awoke the next morning, I noticed that our train, which had sometimes clacked like castanets during the night, was strangely quiet. I looked out the window and noticed that we had arrived at the port of Bremerhaven. I could even see the *USS General Maurice Rose,* our transport, anchored in the distance. The U.S. Army was using this large navy ship, named in honor of Major General Maurice Rose, who had been killed in action near the end of World War II. As I said earlier, he and my father served on General Willis Crittenberger's staff at Fort Benning.

At two o'clock in the afternoon, we boarded the ship and were directed to our staterooms. Before we sailed, I stood on the deck and listened to the U.S. Army band play *Auld Lang Syne*, a Robert Burns poem that became one of the most sentimental songs ever written. I felt like crying but stoically held back my tears. The band members sat in a covered shed-like structure that was open on the side facing the ship. When the music stopped, a voice over the loudspeaker shouted "All ashore that's going ashore!" Then the gangplank was raised, and we headed towards New York.

By the time we left Europe in April 1950, all of the reburials in Western Europe and return of the war dead to the United States had been completed, except for about six thousand of the deceased who were being held for further investigation or for information from next of kin. The responsibility for maintaining the ten permanent cemeteries was completely transferred from the AGRC to the ABMC by the end of 1951.

Our ship rocked peacefully in the North Sea that night, but the fact that we were on a military ship was obvious early the next morning. Again a voice bellowed over the loudspeaker, aimed primarily at the troops on board: "Rise and shine!"After breakfast, my parents and I strolled along the deck and watched the White Cliffs of Dover, standing as straight and tall as banks of salt, gradually fade out of sight. The ship soon moved into the open seas of the Atlantic Ocean and sailed uneventfully homeward.

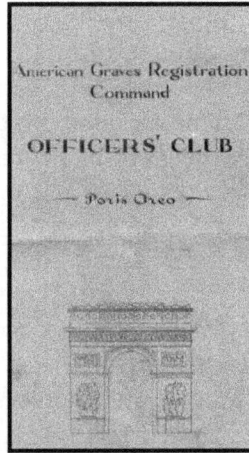

(LEFT) JEAN AND CLASSMATE JIM ON THE CHAMPS ÉLYSÉES
(RIGHT) AGRC OFFICERS' CLUB BROCHURE, 1949

1949: Armistice Day

International Herald Tribune

Thursday, November 11, 1999

PARIS — United States Army troops will take part in three Armistice Day ceremonies today [Nov. 11] in France, the American Graves Registration Command announced. At Paris, Brigadier General H.L. Peckham, AGRC commander in Europe, will attend a special mass at the Church of Notre-Dame-des-Victoires. An AGRC platoon will participate in a ceremony at Fontainebleau, where a plaque donated by France to honor Allied airmen killed in combat over the Fontainebleau area will be unveiled. At Cherbourg, AGRC troops will stage a review.

INTERNATIONAL HERALD TRIBUNE ARTICLE ABOUT DAD'S PARTICIPATION IN THE ARMISTICE DAY OBSERVANCE, 1949

(LEFT) INVITATION FROM COUNTESS DE URIBARREN (RIGHT) SCHOOLMATES PEGGY CULBERTSON, TORI LILLY, AND JEAN PECKHAM IN FRONT OF OUR SCHOOL, 1949

(CENTER) DAD IN TAN OVERCOAT PREPARING TO SPEAK: DRAGUIGNAN CEREMONY, 1949
(BELOW) FRENCH SOLDIERS SALUTING WHILE THEIR BAND PERFORMS: DRAGUIGNAN

STARS AND STRIPES ARTICLE ABOUT DAD'S WORK: PARIS, 1950

LUNCH AT HOTEL MARITIME (DAD IN THE MIDDLE, SGT. COCHRAN ON THE FAR RIGHT, JEAN FOURTH FROM THE LEFT): BERCK PLAGE, 1950

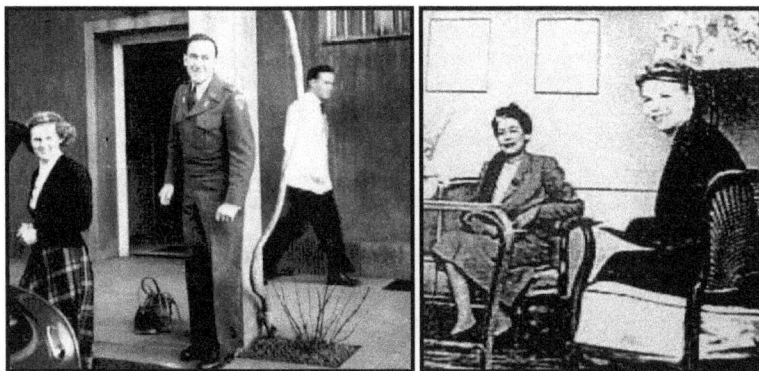

(LEFT) ARRIVAL AT THE HORKAN HOME (L TO R) JACKIE, LT. GILBERT, GERMAN BUTLER
(RIGHT) MOTHER AND MRS. HORKAN IN THE HORKAN SITTING ROOM:HEIDELBERG, 1950

(CENTER) DAD, WOODY, AND SGT. COCHRAN WITH A BRONZE GERMAN MAIDEN
(BELOW LEFT) U.S. ARMY BAND AS SEEN FROM THE SHIP
(BELOW RIGHT) MOTHER, JEAN, AND THE WHITE CLIFFS OF DOVER" 1950

AVRIL

3. LUNDI S. Richard   93-272

4. MARDI S. Ambroise   94-271

GENERAL PECKHAM AND FAMILY RETURN
TO NEW YORK

Brig Gen., Howard L. Peckham and his
wife and daughter, Jean, are returning to New York, after having lived
three years in Paris where General
Peckham commanded the American Graves
Registration Command, European Area.

General Peckham directed the disposition of 147,000 World War II
victims who died in Western Europe
and who were originally buried in
37 different temporary cemeteries,
scattered throughout Ireland, England, Sweden, Switzerland, Holland,
Belgium, Luxemburg and France. Under
his command, 83,000 were shipped back
to be re-buried in the States and 58,-
000 were buried in 10 permanent
American cemeteries in Europe. Six
thousand are still to be taken care of.

Crossing the Atlantic is no new
experience for General Peckham. In
the spring of 1945 he flew to the Malta
Conference and back, aside from that
he made two other round trips by air
as well as a sea voyage which was the
beginning of his recent European tour.

His next command will be with the
New York Quartermaster Procurement
Agency at 111, 16th St., New York City.

(TOP) JEAN'S DIARY ENTRY ABOUT LUNCH WITH MRS. PATTON (BELOW) ARTICLE IN THE SHIP'S PAPER ABOUT DAD, 1950

Chapter 14

New York and Fort Lee

East side, west side, all around the town
The kids sing ring around Rosie, London Bridge is falling down
Boys and girls together, me and Mamie O'Rourke
We tripped the light fantastic on the sidewalks of New York

--JAMES BLAKE & CHARLES LAWLOR

OUR VOYAGE TO NEW YORK IN APRIL 1950 was a lot smoother than the one Mother and I made from New York to Europe in the stormy month of February 1948. Now the sea was as calm as a lake, and because Howard Peckham was with us, everything seemed so much easier. He made sure that our passports, baggage tickets, and other papers were in order and in their proper places. We had at least one fire drill, but my father, with his usual knack for efficiency, made sure that we got to our correct stations swiftly.

Mother and Dad made friends with several passengers on board and were often invited to other staterooms for before-dinner drinks. My days were filled with movie going, card playing, and lots of eating. I talked to people occasionally, especially when lounging in a chair to gaze at the ocean or strolling on the deck to get needed exercise. Nonetheless, the days seemed much too long.

Finally, sometime early on April 13, our ship dropped anchor at a New York harbor. It was about ten o'clock in the morning when my parents and I walked slowly down the gangplank to the pier, where we received an unexpected and enthusiastic welcome.

Half a dozen army officers from the Quartermaster Corps and their wives had come to greet us. One of the women gave both Mother and me a gardenia corsage, and then another member of their group took pictures of us.

Because of all this attention and diversion, we overlooked Granddad Peckham, who was also there to meet us. It took quite a while before we saw him waving his arms in an effort to attract our attention. After we hugged him, the four of us were driven to a ferry that took us over to Fort Jay, an army post on Governors Island. We would be staying for two weeks in a comfortable guesthouse there. It was conveniently near the historic officers' club, where we would be having our meals.

As is the case in so many parts of the country today, there is no longer a military base on Governors Island. Located in the middle of New York Harbor and surrounded by outstanding views of the Statue of Liberty and the New York skyline, Fort Jay was in those days off limits to the general public. Several lucky army families lived in its oasis of big, red-brick officers' quarters, where, offshore, sea gulls and foghorns made beautiful music together. For several years, lovely Fort Jay was the headquarters of First Army.

Howie arrived at the island early Saturday afternoon from West Point. He had to return to classes, however, so he could only spend one night with us. After making small talk about Europe during dinner that evening in the club, my father and brother discussed the possibility of another war. My mother and I listened to their words, but we didn't want to believe what we were hearing. We learned that Communist-controlled North Korea was trying to cause non-Communist South Korea to collapse by way of propaganda and acts of terrorism. "Their main objective is to bring the whole country under communism, and then reduce our influence throughout all of Asia," my father said. Howie agreed with him.

After World War II, the United States and the Soviet Union agreed to divide Korea, a former colony of Japan, in half at the 38th parallel. North Korea would be under Soviet control. Control of

South Korea would be under the United States. Each country's army left Korea at the end of World War II, but continued to administer its own region.

When my father asked Howie about his studies and life at the Academy in general, my brother answered, "It's all going well, but several cadets graduating this June will be heading out to Asia soon." He wouldn't be among them, since he was in the class of 1951, but still Mother looked alarmed. It was hard to believe that another war might be starting so soon after World War II.

It did begin, however. On June 25, 1950, North Korea brazenly crossed the 38th parallel and massively attacked South Korea. The United Nations Security Council was determined to defend South Korea, so President Harry Truman immediately committed American land, naval, and air forces to the cause of protecting non-Communist South Korea and preventing the spread of communism within Asia. Many young lieutenants from the West Point class of 1950 participated in the escalating war soon after they graduated, and it wasn't too long before casualties became heavy among that group. The first casualty from the class of 1950 was Teddy Lilly. It's ironic that my father's friend Colonel Edmund J. Lilly survived grim life as a prisoner of the Japanese during World War II only to suffer the loss of his son in Korea.

While I lived in Paris, my schoolmate Tori Lilly once showed me a framed picture of her brother, who looked so handsome in his cadet uniform. I doubt that Edmund and his wife Victoria ever recovered from the blow of losing their son.

During the period when the Hot War was steaming in Korea, Cold War tensions were escalating worldwide. As a defense measure, the State Department saw the need for a big military organization within NATO, comprised of military units from NATO nations. The member countries agreed that such a force was necessary and complied with the request to send their units where required. The military organization that evolved was called the Supreme Headquarters, Allied Powers Europe (SHAPE). General Dwight Eisenhower was its first commander. In spring 1951, General Eisenhower's personnel moved into SHAPE's first headquarters, located in Paris at the Hotel Astoria. Only a year earlier that hotel had housed the busy offices of the AGRC. More and more personnel came to work for SHAPE, so its headquarters moved in July 1951 to a much larger space in the Paris suburbs. The AGRC, which had dominated the American military scene in Paris from 1946 through the first half of 1950, would soon fall into the strong, solid arms of history.

Right after my brother returned to West Point after visiting us at Fort Jay, my parents and I scouted around in my father's new grey Chevrolet (in which he had patiently given me a few driving lessons) for a school where I could finish my senior year of high school. They intended to move to New York City after my graduation, but we all felt it would be better for me to attend a public school in the suburbs. The school we picked was A.B. Davis (nicknamed "Hilltop") located in the town of Mount Vernon, a few blocks from the apartment into which we moved.

When not in classes, I spent most of my free time studying assiduously for the comprehensive regents examinations that were required of seniors who expected to graduate from New York high schools, and I wanted to do well on the tests. My studying paid off, and I passed with flying colors. A.B. Davis was considered a very good school, but I wasn't there long enough to become sentimentally attached to it, even when a nice article about me appeared in the school paper. I was very glad when graduation day rolled around in June.

My first weeks at the University of Maryland in September were exciting but hectic, mainly because I decided to go through "rushing" and had to attend several formal sorority teas. At the same time, I was going to orientation meetings and freshman classes, which were located in several different colonial-style buildings throughout the campus. It took me some time to learn my way up, down, and around the lovely rolling hills.

One of the first letters I received in September came from my father. The letter contained a lot of impersonal information, such as letting me know that he had mailed a tuition check to the university and that my large black trunk would soon be delivered to me. In the last paragraph, he gave me some sage advice, but he also hinted at his loneliness:

> I am happy and proud that you are now enrolled at the University of Maryland. Your future lies before you and will be largely determined, in my opinion, by your years at college. Study decently hard but do not be a grind. Take part in University activities, athletics, etc. and have a healthy, cheerful, happy life. Naturally, I hope you will not completely neglect me, and to that end if you would write me just a few lines at least once a week it would be very nice. . . .
>
> With all my love and best wishes, Dad.

He was adapting well to life in the United States, and he really enjoyed his job. He didn't like being alone, though. My mother's problem with alcohol was hardly noticeable in Europe, but it worsened considerably after we returned to the United States. She was temporarily away at a treatment center when my father wrote that letter. He meant well and had always tried to be a good father. Obviously, he missed me, and I regret that I didn't write him as often as he would have liked.

In December, my parents moved to Peter Cooper Village, an apartment complex in New York City near the East River. A taxi deposited me there when I came home on Christmas vacation. After I found their building and got off the elevator on their floor, my parents came out to embrace me.

"Welcome home!" my father said before kissing me on the cheek. Then I suddenly felt at home in this unfamiliar apartment, because everything inside was recognizable: the refinished mahogany tables and lovely Oriental rugs, the hassock my father had bought in Tunis, and souvenirs from Europe displayed in bookcases. During the Christmas Eve service a few nights later at St. George's Church on Stuyvesant Square, my parents, Howie, and I joined in the singing. My father loved to sing Christmas carols and, as usual, his voice was hearty. After the service, we stepped into a New York night that was as frigid as ice, but the warmth of our reunion made it seem less that way. The four of us had not been together as a family since the preceding April at Fort Jay, and I was happy to see that my mother seemed to be doing well.

Dad immersed himself in his work while my brother and I were away at school during the next few months, but he took time out in June 1951 when he and my mother attended a very special occasion for our family: Howie's graduation from West Point. When the ceremony ended, my father and his brother-in-law Richard Lawrence, who had also pursued a military career, posed for pictures with him. Howie, a new second lieutenant of the U.S. Air Force, would soon begin flight training.

For him, it was a dream come true.

In the autumn of 1951, my father received the dividends of his hard work and was ordered to Washington to serve as Acting Deputy Quartermaster General. The assignment didn't include a promotion in rank, but it did provide my father with a big increase in responsibility. He would be working under George Horkan, a good friend. General Horkan, in whose Heidelberg home we had once been guests, now held the prestigious job of Quartermaster General. (His wife Mary also became a good friend of my mother's over the years.)

My parents found a nice apartment they liked in historic Alexandria, Virginia, from which my father made a relatively easy commute into Washington each day. On my weekend visits to their apartment from College Park, the three of us laughed and joked a lot, and my father made some plays on words that I hadn't heard for a long time.

For example, one Saturday afternoon I listened while he talked on the telephone to a clerk in the local photo shop, where he had taken a roll of film to be developed. "They're not ready yet?" he asked in a plaintive tone of voice. After hanging up the receiver, he sang in a falsetto voice to a tune from *Snow White and the Seven Dwarfs*: "Sooome day my prints will cooome."

The imitation of Snow White was corny, but we all chuckled anyway. It felt good to enjoy a family joke again and to see Dad lean his head way back as he laughed heartily at one of his own jokes. He had another reason to feel in a happy mood, though. In April 1952 he was promoted to major general.

Just a couple of months after his promotion, my father was called to testify before Congress on behalf of the army, as he had done during World War II. Only this time, the subject was wool for military clothing, not a pipeline in Canada for transmitting petroleum or a discussion of postwar petroleum needs.

He spoke on June 21, 1952, before a subcommittee chaired by Senator Joseph O'Mahoney of Wyoming, the senator before whom he had testified during World War II.

Again, the venue was the Senate Office Building, but the topic now was defense appropriations for the year 1953. Obviously, the senators were concerned in one way or another with the President's budget. Homer Ferguson, before whom my father had testified during the war, questioned him:

SENATOR FERGUSON: General, is that your understanding? Does the Army ever stock any raw wool?

GENERAL PECKHAM: We have done that in one instance, Senator.

Further testimony at the hearing revealed the fact that the Quartermaster Corps had traditionally granted preference to domestically produced wool for the manufacture of fabrics needed by the military forces, but that a certain amount of its goods were manufactured in foreign countries.

When Senator Ferguson asked whether any conflicting policy was involved, my father deferred to Harold Pearson, Deputy Assistant Secretary of the Army, who then testified that off-shore procurement was being done in several NATO countries "for the mutual defense of our country and our allies."

As Acting Deputy Quartermaster General, Dad needed to satisfy many different factions when it came to the acquisition of supplies for American troops: the U.S. Army, which required quality goods for its soldiers; Congress, which was concerned about the President's budget; and manufacturers in the United States, who were worried that the jobs of their workers might be sent overseas, where workers' wages were much lower. For Howard Peckham, it was often a delicate balancing act.

Most notorious among the subcommittee members was Joseph McCarthy of Wisconsin, whose postwar investigations of alleged Communists during other hearings had earned him the unflattering nickname of "witch hunter."

The other senators were Carl Hayden, Dennis Chavez, Pat McCarran, William Knowland, Richard Russell, Burnet Maybank, Lester Hill, and Leverett Saltonstall. Senator Saltonstall, who hailed from Massachusetts, completed the term of Henry Cabot Lodge Jr. after the latter joined the army, but he was reelected three times on his own. My father felt particular sympathy for Senator Saltonstall upon learning that his son Peter had been killed in action during World War II.

Soon my father learned that his own son would be heading off to war. In May 1953, my brother left for Korea. It turned out to be only a six-month assignment, however. In December he was ordered to report to Tokyo, where he would be serving as aide-de-camp to General Otto P. Weyland.

My family seemed blessed. My brother was transferred from Korea safe and sound, and my father was pleased that his son had a chance to serve as a general's aide, as he himself had done early in his U.S. Army career.

What we didn't know at the time was that my brother had flown very dangerous missions over North Korea and China from his base in South Korea, Kimpo Air Force Base. The missions were so "top secret" that the U.S. Air Force didn't declassify them until decades later.

While my brother was serving in Korea, my father was busily working in his new assignment: Commanding General, Fort Lee, Virginia. This army post, located near the town of Petersburg, was the headquarters of the Quartermaster Training Command, and it trained thousands of men in preparation for Quartermaster Corps duty throughout the world. Fort Lee was also the Women's Army

Corps (WAC) Training Center; however, those activities were transferred to Fort McClellan, Alabama, in 1954. In fact, the entire women's corps was discontinued two decades later, when there no longer was a need for a separate force made up of women soldiers.

The commanding general's quarters at Fort Lee bore little resemblance to the ones I saw during my childhood. Those were always large homes with spacious lawns, on which magnolia trees or ancient elms elegantly grew.

This one was a rather small, wood-frame house, although a more permanent and larger home had been on the drawing boards for some time. Its tiny front yard faced the busy road leading to the officers' club, and cars passed by frequently. Dad welcomed unexpected guests who stopped by, however, and one evening a young private dared to ring our doorbell.

After Dad opened the door, I could hear the man voicing some complaints about the army. My father listened patiently to what he had to say, and then offered some words of advice. When their conversation ended, I heard my father say, "Good luck, soldier." The private walked away after expressing his thanks, his facial expression noticeably upbeat. This episode showed me what I had heard other people say—that Dad had a way of charming people of all ranks.

Sometimes I would bring home friends from school for the weekend, mostly my Alpha Xi Delta sorority sisters. My father charmed them, too. Occasionally he would tell them one of his famous (but often corny) jokes, which they thought were cute and funny. I don't recall taking any weekend guests to the colorful reviews on the Fort Lee parade ground, which I occasionally attended on Saturdays.

I do recall that whenever the band played *Hail to the Chief*, I knew that my father had arrived on the vast grounds to review the troops. I also knew that it was time for me to rise from my spectator seat and stand at attention, along with everyone else.

One sunny day I watched him pass through the color guard at a retirement review for Major General Joseph P. Sullivan, who had been the quartermaster of Fifth Army during World War II. Because of all the "brass" that was present for the event, the Public Information Office took a picture.

On another day, that same office took a picture of my parents standing with the Deputy Quartermaster General, Major General Kester L. Hastings, who was on a visit from Washington with his wife Ruth. He and Dad were classmates at West Point, but whereas my father went into the Corps of Engineers, Kester Hastings chose the Infantry. He transferred to the Quartermaster Corps in 1934.

Like my father, Kester Hastings spent most of World War II in Washington, DC, where he performed important work for the Quartermaster Corps. While serving in the Korean War, he expedited supplies to combat troops and went into the forward area to gauge firsthand any supply problems, in spite of possible enemy attack. He was awarded a Silver Star for gallantry in that war. In 1954, he was promoted to Quartermaster General and ordered to Washington, the job he held at retirement. As is the case with so many of my father's friends, General Hastings and his wife Ruth now rest at Arlington Cemetery.

Dad always looked good on the Fort Lee parade ground and in official photographs, but especially so before he set off for his job at post headquarters in the mornings. I noticed that his bearing was as straight as a board and that his uniform, with its perfectly pressed trousers, looked spotless. I also saw that the two silver stars on each shoulder were shining brightly and that the ribbons on his chest added just the right dash of color.

My parents' years in the glaring spotlight of Fort Lee ended in the summer of 1954, however, when Dad received new orders. From then on, the parades, cannons, bugle sounds, receptions at the officers' club, and various other military trappings would just be memories. We never had the opportunity to live on an army post again.

My life was changing dramatically in other ways, too. The warm day of June 5, 1954, was memorable for my parents, but even more so for me. Accompanied by the Coronation March from

La Propheta, played by an air force band, my classmates and I steadily approached the area where university officials sat and where we were to be awarded our bachelor's degrees.

After returning to my seat, I looked back on my four years at the University of Maryland. Some events stood out in my mind as having been especially enjoyable—English and sociology classes (those subjects were my major and minor, respectively), prom dates, sorority activities, and a short but sweet romance with Donald Jones, a lieutenant I had met at a party in Washington.

Not long after that happy June graduation day at College Park, I went on a two-week vacation to Newport, Rhode Island, where I stayed with Aunt Mary and her daughter Diane. We spent pleasant days swimming in the ocean and sightseeing, such as viewing some of the enormous mansions of the rich and famous, at least from the outside. I then lived temporarily with my parents. *Who's Who in America, 1954-1955* listed Dad's address as Fort Lee, but effective July 1, he became Chief of the Army and Air Force Exchange Service (AAFES), whose headquarters were in New York City.

My parents rented an apartment in the same complex, Peter Cooper Village, in which they had lived previously. This one had an even better view of the East River than the one they had rented in 1950; it was also more spacious. Dad brought with him his natural gregariousness, so he enjoyed having visitors. For buffet suppers, my parents' usual mode of entertaining in the city, Dad would unfold the large drop-leaf mahogany table at one end of the living room before the guests arrived and then cover it with a white linen cloth. He would also inspect the drinking glasses to ensure that no lint was on them, which he had done ever since my childhood. I can still see him holding up tall glasses to the light, carefully examining them one by one.

Dad seemed to like his job. The AAFES ran thousands of facilities where American military personnel could buy retail-store goods, fast food, and various other items. These facilities, called post exchanges (PXs) or base exchanges (BXs), are located both in the United States and in many other parts of the world.

From time to time my father made trips within the United States or to other countries, where he would inspect the exchange operations and attend meetings with exchange personnel.

During the American Revolution, soldiers bought items such as soap and tobacco from roving peddlers, who followed them from one army camp to another. After 1895, small independent stores replaced these "traveling salesmen." In 1941, the War Department established the Army Exchange Service (AES), which provided unified and consistent guidelines worldwide for army personnel. After the United States Air Force became a separate force in 1947, the AAFES evolved into a joint-service organization and received its current title.

Friends from other places my parents had been stationed would often drop by, which is one reason I wanted to live with them after graduation. It gave me a chance to maintain my army ties and friendships. One of those visitors was Paul Smith, my father's former aide. After a quick dinner that my mother prepared, he took me to Nick's in Greenwich Village, where we listened to a jazz band and reminisced about life in postwar Paris. Another visitor from our Paris days was Jackie Tomaw, who came by to give us the unexpected news that she and Woody were now divorced. Jackie was feeling distraught about the matter, even though the two of them, she said, had become very incompatible. She sought consolation from my parents. Occasionally my aunts, uncles, or other relatives would visit.

One guest of whom all of us were especially fond was Granddad Shaw, who made a four-day visit in 1955. After he retired from the U.S. Army, he and Bell settled down in the Washington area, where Granddad enjoyed playing bridge at the Army-Navy Club. He continued to play bridge at the Club until he was eighty. Someone would drive him there from his home and then pick him up later. For many years he had been a good player, and other members of his bridge group had enjoyed the challenge of playing with him.

When he appeared to be overly forgetful, however, one player whispered to another: "Maybe it's time for Fred to leave the group." He got the subtle hint, and he did give up bridge. Persuading him to give up the aromatic cigars he loved was much more difficult, his devoted and patient second wife Winnie learned. She would often dash to retrieve one from his hand just before it would have burned his fingers. My parents were understandably concerned about his increasing symptoms of senility during that visit to their apartment. One day, before they knew what was happening, he turned a knob that he thought would lead him into his guest bedroom. In fact, he had turned the faucet in the shower. After he walked out of the bathroom towards my parents, he looked down in disbelief. "One million damns" he softly muttered. His business suit was soaking wet.

In April 1956, Granddad received a blow from which he never recovered—the death of his youngest son Dan at Sloan-Kettering in New York. Even the amputation of one arm didn't stop Uncle Dan's cancer from spreading uncontrollably, as I mentioned earlier. After losing his son, Granddad's senile dementia degenerated to the extent that Winnie was not able to handle him at home. A nursing home arrangement didn't work out well, either. Therefore, he entered St. Elizabeth's Hospital in Washington as an incompetent veteran. He died there in March 1957 and was buried at Arlington near Bell, his first wife.

My father was enormously grateful for the friendship he had developed with his father-in-law over the years, beginning at Fort Hayes, where they first met. He had received so much firsthand information from General Shaw about the Spanish-American War, the Philippine Insurrection, and the early days of the army's history. Upon Granddad's death these memories filled my father with nostalgia.

Dad's retirement on November 30, 1956, was also extremely nostalgic. I watched a military review take place that crisp, late-fall afternoon on Fort Jay's green parade ground. Troops marched, a band played, and speeches were given in his honor. The retirement dinner at the officers' club that evening was filled with tributes. As described in the *Daily News Record* newspaper, a tray was presented to my parents.

It had this inscription:

> Maj. Gen. and Mrs. Howard L. Peckham, from their many friends of the Quartermaster Association, New York Chapter, Dec. 1, 1956.

The article also notes that Dad sang a song in honor of my mother. It is based on a poem by Robert Burns, whose poetry both he and Mother liked a lot. Here is the first verse:

> My love is like a red, red rose
> that's newly sprung in June:
> My love is like the melody
> that's sweetly played in tune.

He was obviously very devoted to my mother. When Dad finished singing, everyone clapped and then turned to smile at her. She looked very happy while returning their smiles.

The New York Times stated on November 4 that Howard Peckham had taken "one of the most progressive steps in post exchange history by introducing worldwide fiscal integration into the exchange system." The *Exchange Post*, in an article dated November 1, 1956, noted that this integration "assured a high standard of service. "

I had been to Governors Island fairly frequently over the years, sometimes for Thanksgiving dinner or another occasion, but not for an event as sentimental as my father's retirement. Mother felt sentimental, too. She had been associated with the U.S. Army most of her life, and now her association with it was officially ending. In spite of the hardships brought to her by that way of life—the frequent moves, the uncertainty, and the pressures—she dearly loved it. Best of all, my parents had made many loyal army friends over the years.

Retirement, however, was not realistically a word in my father's vocabulary. He still had important work to do for his country.

Jean Peckham, Globe Trotter,
Comes to Hilltop from Paris

By Nancy Block

A stranger in our midst; and a well traveled one at
that! A newcomer to Davis is attractive, blonde, blue-
eyed Jean Peckham, a senior, who is an accomplished
globe trotter.

PORTION OF AN ARTICLE FROM JEAN'S SCHOOL PAPER: MT. VERNON, NEW YORK, 1950

(LEFT) FATHER AND SON AT HOWIE'S WEST POINT GRADUATION *(RIGHT)* UNCLE DICK
LAWRENCE WHILE VISITING HOWIE: WEST POINT, 1951

HOWIE PECKHAM IN FLIGHT TRAINING, 1951

HOWIE PREPARING TO TAKE OFF IN A TA-181 PLANE, 1951

LT. HOWIE PECKHAM: KOREA, 1953

DAD AND MOTHER WITH RUTH AND KESTER HASTINGS

RETIREMENT REVIEW FOR GENERAL SULLIVAN (FAR LEFT, NEXT TO DAD): FT. LEE, 1953

(LEFT) JEAN IN WASHINGTON ON SPRING BREAK FROM UNIVERSITY CLASSES
(RIGHT) MY PARENTS WITH THEIR DOG SHEBA AND A WAC OFFICER: FT. LEE, 1954

N. Y. QM Assn. Honors Peckham at Dinner

(DAILY NEWS RECORD Photo)

Daily News Record,
New York,
December 1956.

Excerpt from an
article in the
Exchange Post,
November 1, 1956.

Maj. Gen. and Mrs. Howard L. Peckham were honored by the New York Chapter of the Quartermaster Association at a buffet dinner and dance at the Governors Island Officers Club. General Peckham, who retired Nov. 30, was chief of the Army-Air Force Exchange Service and previously commander of the N. Y. QM Procurement Agency.

Seated at the head table in the above photo are, left to right, Mrs. Stanley B. Finch; Mr. Finch, Pabst Brewing Co., president of the N. Y. QM Chapter; Mrs. Howard L. Peckham; Gen. Peckham; Col. James V. Demarest, chairman of the board of managers of the QM Association, and Mrs. Demarest. Standing, left to right, are Lt. Col. Paul C. Turner, secretary-treasurer of the QM Association; John Farinacci of the N. Y. QM Market Center, vice-president of the QM Association

and Mrs. Farinacci; Edward Fox of the "Quartermaster Review"; Col. Harold R. Schaller, A-AF Exchange Service, and Mrs. Schaller; and Col. Jewell H. Cook, quartermaster of the First Army.

Colonel Demarest presented Gen. and Mrs. Peckham with a silver tray engraved with the QM insignia and the inscription "Maj. Gen. and Mrs. Howard L. Peckham, from their many friends of the Quartermaster Association, New York Chapter, Dec. 1, 1956."

General Peckham, who was once a member of the West Point choir, was asked to sing by Mr. Fox. His rendition of "My Love Is Like a Red, Red Rose" in honor of Mrs. Peckham brought forth much warm applause.

Progressive Step Taken

During General Peckham's tour, one of the most progressive steps in exchange history was taken with the introduction, in May 1956, of exchange world wide fiscal integration which will do much to assure a uni-

New York Times,
November 4, 1956.

Maj. Gen. H. L. Peckham

The retirement of Maj. Gen. H. L. Peckham chief of the

NEWSPAPER ARTICLES REGARDING DAD'S RETIREMENT, 1956

Chapter 15

Helping to Fight Communism

Only if the American people convince themselves and convince the world that they believe in liberty can we hope to meet the aggressive ideology of Communism.

--ROBERT A. TAFT

IT WOULD BE AN UNDERSTATEMENT to say that my father was restless after only a few months of not working, and he was glad when two good consulting offers came along. The only problem was that both arrived at the same time, and both were tempting. Both jobs required adapting to foreign countries, which was nothing new to him, and he was highly proficient at dealing with people from other cultures.

The first offer required that he spend eighteen months in charge of a highway construction program in Laos. It would tie in well with his engineering background, WPA work, and strong skills as a project director. The second offer, twelve months as a consultant with the Free Europe Committee (FEC), of which Radio Free Europe (RFE) was a division, would incorporate his many years of experience as a manager. In addition, it required that he meet with European diplomats, which would fit perfectly with his extroverted personality and work in postwar Europe as head of the AGRC.

Not surprisingly, he chose the latter offer. Another asset in its favor was that it was in agreement with the focus of President

Dwight D. Eisenhower's Republican administration. Howard Peckham completely agreed with the goals delineated in the President's second inaugural address of January 21, 1957, especially these words:

> In the heart of Europe, Germany still stands tragically divided. So is the whole continent divided. And so, too, is all the world. The divisive force is international communism and the power that it controls. The designs of that power, dark in purpose, are clear in practice. It strives to seal forever the fate of those it has enslaved. It strives to break the ties that unite the free. And it strives to capture—to exploit for its own greater power—all force of change in the world, especially the needs of the hungry and the hopes of the oppressed. . . .
>
> We honor the aspirations of those nations which, now captive, long for freedom. We seek neither their military alliance nor any artificial imitation of our society. And they can know the warmth of the welcome that awaits them when, as must be, they join again the ranks of freedom.

Strongly relating to the message of President Eisenhower, whose election my father had supported (now that he was retired and free to become involved in politics), were these words my father wrote me in a letter in March:

> The Russians have succeeded in sealing off the nations held captive behind the Iron Curtain. Most of the captive people are strongly anti-Communist, so radio programs such as those transmitted by Radio Free Europe, which proclaim democratic ideals, supply a means to lift the morale of those people.

Dad was enthusiastic about becoming a part of the FEC's agenda. "I'll work first in New York City, then in France," he added in his letter. Another bonus for him was that he would again be serving under General Willis Crittenberger, on whose staff he had served at Fort Benning early in World War II. The general, who had since retired from the U.S. Army, was then-president of the FEC. He was no doubt pleased when my father accepted his offer of employment, since he knew first hand that Howard Peckham was conscientious, ethical, and diplomatic.

On the morning of March 16, 1957, Dad introduced me to General Crittenberger in the lobby of the Waldorf Astoria, where the general was staying. My father had flown to New York the previous day from my parents' apartment in Florida to attend a West Point Board of Trustees meeting that weekend. In those days I lived in a women's residence club, Katharine House, on West 13th Street, where I had moved after living for nearly a year with my parents in New York.

Shortly after my father picked me up at my residence, we had a notoriously fast taxi ride to the Waldorf, where he and I walked quickly into the hotel's elegant lobby. A distinguished-looking, square-jawed man was waiting for us. "Critt, this is my daughter, Jean," Dad said as he put his arm around my shoulder and guided me towards the general, whose light-colored eyes sparkled as he reached towards me to shake my hand.

After the introduction, the three of us made small talk over drinks in the lounge. They then went to the Waldorf's Peacock Alley for a business lunch, and I headed towards nearby Fifth Avenue to do some window-shopping. During the week, I worked at Church World Service, near Union Square. Later, my father recorded the morning's events in his diary:

> Breakfast in the Coffee House. Called Adicks [my parents' former neighbors in Peter Cooper Village], Critt, and Jean. Went to Katharine House to see Jean and take her box of candy. She came back to Waldorf with me for a cocktail and to meet Gen. Crittenberger, who took me to lunch in the Peacock Alley.

Over their vegetarian lunch, Howard Peckham and Willis Crittenberger talked about the work of the FEC, whose primary mission was helping nations held captive behind the Iron Curtain become free and independent. Dad strongly believed in this mission. It was also the main goal of the radio division, RFE, and of the publishing division, Free Europe Press (FEP). Among its other tasks, the FEP for many years printed millions of leaflets. These messages of hope were carried by balloons from Germany and dropped into countries behind the Iron Curtain, like feathers drifting down from the wings of eagles.

A peaceful end to the Communist regimes in that part of Europe, my father believed, would be good for America's national security and for the security of the non-Communist world as a whole.

The FEC and its FEP and RFE divisions recruited émigrés from Communist-controlled nations to write or speak in their native languages, or to serve in other significant ways. Those who worked at RFE's New York office often created uplifting tapes about the American scene and other topics, which they sent to Munich for transmission to the captive nations. At the end of their busy workday, the émigrés would join their countrymen in small, out-of-the-way restaurants that served such delicacies as Polish sausages, Hungarian goulash, and Czech Kolácky (prune biscuits). These tasty morsels made them feel more at home in their new environment.

During the time that Howard Peckham worked for the FEC, a prominent member of the immigrant population in New York served as its senior vice president. Bernard (Bernie) Yarrow, a Columbia Law School graduate and former practicing attorney, had been in the United States ever since the 1920s. During World War II, the Russian-born Mr. Yarrow worked for the Office of Strategic Services (OSS), predecessor of the CIA. Bernie Yarrow was a skilled intelligence officer, and in a few months, he and Dad would become traveling companions on some important information-gathering trips for the FEC.

In the meantime, Dad's meetings with General Crittenberger continued. On June 5, 1957, they met with each other in the general's office at 2 Park Avenue. Here the general briefed my father on the FEC's operations, a five-hour briefing that was temporarily interrupted, according to my father's diary, by their excellent lunch at Rockefeller Center's 65th floor luncheon-club restaurant. One of the items they discussed was the FEC's history.

Its remarkable story began when American diplomat George Kennan of the State Department made an interesting proposal to the National Security Council (NSC). Why not form an anti-Communist organization to help restore democracy in Central and Eastern Europe? To ensure the effectiveness of this plan, shouldn't the assistance of talented émigrés from those lands, as well as prominent American citizens, be secured? George Kennan's idea caught fire, and in the following year (1949), the Free Europe Committee, originally called the National Committee for a Free Europe, was created.

Covert funding for the FEC, through the CIA, was approved by the administration of President Truman and later by the Eisenhower administration. Among the eminent FEC members in 1957 were former director of the OSS, William J. Donovan; Ambassador Joseph Grew; General Lucius Clay (retired); Laird Bell, esq.; State Department official W. J. Convery Egan; and C. D. Jackson, publisher of *Fortune* magazine.

After that initial briefing in June, my father moved into the Astor Hotel, where, in the weeks that followed, he studied reams of material on FEC policies and procedures and attended several crucial meetings. Mother joined him about a month later, after leaving the Florida apartment in which they had briefly lived.

Informative sessions conducted by General Crittenberger continued, and other staff members briefed my father on the political situations in the various satellite countries. Out of curiosity, Dad asked one employee what he liked best about working for the FEC. The man told him, "People are getting the truth about what's happening in the world, the kind of news the Communists don't allow them to get." My father appreciated his answer.

Hopeful messages from the RFE division were beamed to the captive people like rays from the sun, exposing the fallacies of communism but reminding people to resist it nonviolently. In lands where vacant country churches wore the heavy cloaks of atheism, RFE encouraged parents to teach their children religious values. It also let workers know the ways in which communism was exploiting them.

In July, at the 52nd Street offices of CBS, my father met with James Seward, the Radio Division's executive vice president, to determine how much time he would need to spend being briefed on radio transmission and antenna systems. On August 16, he "learned some fundamentals," according to his diary. On a later day, he was escorted to the master control room to view its operations.

A welcome respite from my father's formation program at FEC occurred in the fall, when he attended a West Point Board of Trustees meeting and football game at the Academy. On this day, October 19, my father was joined by Generals Anthony McAuliffe, Jacob L. Devers, and Willis Crittenberger. An official car came from the Academy to pick them up in New York City. That night, my father wrote these words in his diary: "Critt, Jake Devers, Tony McAuliffe and I rode to W.P. in an official car from U.S.M.A.; attended meeting of Board of Trustees; went to parade; had lunch."

My father ended his diary entry by noting that he "saw Army lick Pitt 29-13" and that there had been a "big crowd." He also noted that he saw "beautiful fall foliage." While growing up on a farm in Connecticut, he had learned to appreciate the wonders of beautiful trees, shrubs, and flowers. He never outgrew that appreciation. During my childhood, he often pointed out various trees, bushes, and flowers to me as we strolled by them. I was impressed that he knew most of their names. He also could name the birds we saw, especially after he joined the Audubon Society in his later years.

Only four days after Dad's visit to West Point, formalities related to his work began in earnest. On October 23, 1957, two men from the McClellan Committee, which had formerly been known as the McCarthy Committee, interviewed him. Joseph McCarthy died in May 1957, but that's not why the Committee no longer bore his name.

When the Republicans lost control of the Senate in the election of November 1954, a Democrat from Arkansas, Senator John McClellan, was appointed to replace Joseph McCarthy as head of the former McCarthy Committee. He, too, was a staunch anti-Communist, but he didn't like or approve of the aggressive interrogative tactics his predecessor had used. My father felt the same way about McCarthy's abrupt methods.

On November 21, after walking briskly from the Astor Hotel to Penn Station and catching an early train to Washington, Dad lunched at the University Club with Emmons Brown and the articulate Cord Meyer, a top CIA officer. As noted in his diary, he then made a courtesy call on CIA Director Allen W. Dulles:

> Went to University Club, near Statler on 16th St., for lunch with Cord Meyer and Emmons Brown. Then the latter took me to CIA to call on Mr. Allen W. Dulles.

Cord Meyer had the responsibility within the Agency to oversee its relationship with RFE. He fully describes this bond in his 1980 book *Facing Reality: From World Federalism to the CIA*, in an interesting chapter entitled "The Radios." (Sadly, Cord Meyer's life took a tragic turn two years later when his nine-year-old son, Michael, was struck and killed by a car. He and his wife, the former Mary Pinchot, were divorced not long afterwards.)

On the morning of December 18, my father and Bernard boarded an 8:30 a.m. American Airlines flight from New York to Washington, where they checked into the Hay Adams Hotel at 1 Lafayette Square. About two hours later, they held a luncheon meeting in their room.

It's an understatement to say that the meeting was small. According to my father's diary entry, the only attendees besides my father and Bernard were Cord Meyer and Emmons Brown. FEC-related meetings were often brief and secretive, but there is no mention anywhere in my father's diary that the FEC was being covertly funded by the CIA.

I wouldn't learn that until many years later.

At 3:00 p.m. that same day, Howard Peckham attended a meeting at the CIA office with Stanley Grogan and "others," and again called on A.W.D. (Allen Dulles). In his diary my father wrote:

> Cord Meyer and Emmons Brown of CIA for lunch in our room. Attended meeting at 3:00 p.m. at CIA with Stanley Grogan and others, and saw A.W.D. at about 5:15 p.m.

The visit with Allen Dulles was the last meeting of a long day. Afterwards, my father invited Bernard for dinner at the Army-Navy Club, followed by a taxi ride to the airport and a flight through ink-black sky to La Guardia Airport. "Home at about 11:30," my father noted in his diary.

Not clandestine at all were several events my parents attended in New York sponsored by satellite nations. One of the most interesting was a party on October 22 at the 74th Street apartment of Bernard Yarrow and his wife Sylvia. Sylvia was known to be a charming hostess and astute businesswoman. In fact, Bernard often invited her to sit in on FEC meetings. My father was a bit surprised by her presence at these meetings—until he learned firsthand that she was quite smart and well informed about Cold War politics.

It was no accident that the party was held on the eve of the first anniversary of the revolt in Hungary. Among the guests were Mayor and Mrs. Koevago (mayor of Budapest during the revolt); Doctor Masems, President of the Assembly of Captive European Nations (ACEN), and his wife; and Major General Béla Király, commander of the Hungarian Freedom Fighters. After the party, the guests went to a poignant rally at Carnegie Hall put on by the general's brave fighters.

As an Immigration Assistant with Church World Service, a division of the National Council of Churches, my job was also concerned to a great extent with the sad circumstances of Europeans who had fled from their Iron Curtain homelands, although the organization gave assistance to other refugees as well—Dutch colonialists, for example, who had been forced to leave Indonesia but had not been welcomed to the Netherlands, where many of them had never lived.

The organization had a penchant for hiring Europeans, but it also hired young American-born people who, like me, had traveled widely. I had already worked at Church World Service for nearly two years before my father became a consultant with the FEC.

A primary function of mine was to correspond with various churches and individuals throughout the United States related to securing jobs and housing for the refugees. I also corresponded with Church World Service field offices located abroad about progress made in regard to refugee relocations.

My most vivid memories of the job concern the escapees from Hungary. At the conclusion of the Hungarian Revolution, which began on October 23, 1956, and ended nearly a month later, Hungarian escapees arrived in droves at Camp Kilmer, a then-inactive army post located about two miles east of New Brunswick, New Jersey. The first arrivals came in November 1956, followed by thousands more in the months to come. Some people arrived in New York by ship; others by plane. Army buses brought them to Camp Kilmer, where they were billeted in wooden barracks until jobs and housing could be found for them throughout the United States.

My organization set up a temporary office at the camp, where several other employees and I worked for a few months at the end of 1956 and during the early months of 1957. The acronym CWS was sewn on our armbands to differentiate us from employees of other agencies who were temporarily at the camp, such as the International Rescue Committee (IRC) and the Catholic Relief Services (CRS).

Stacks of dossiers on my desk described the job experience of the hopeful candidates, many of whom sought professional jobs. As they sat in straight-back chairs waiting to be interviewed, frustration swept like a chilly breeze over their faces. When they were told that a good job and housing had been found for them, their faces lit up with bright smiles.

Church World Service fortunately received good publicity for its humanitarian efforts on behalf of the Hungarian refugees. The role of RFE, on the other hand, evoked a certain amount of media controversy in the months following the brutal crushing of the revolt by the Russians. Respected CIA guru Cord Meyer admits this fact in his book *Facing Reality*, but he also writes:

> After the Hungarian revolt was crushed, my office in the Agency, with the help of two Hungarian-speaking analysts, did a careful review of the taped broadcasts that had been made in the weeks before the revolution. We could not find evidence that in this period RFE had violated the standing instruction against inciting to violence or promising external assistance. . . .
>
> From my own exposure to these events and from the findings of the working group within the Agency that reviewed the taped RFE broadcasts, I am satisfied that RFE did not plan, direct, or attempt to provoke the Hungarian rebellion. . . .

Many factors entered into the failure of the revolution. Arch Puddington, in his excellent book *Broadcasting Freedom*, speaks of the confusion that erupted at RFE "and presumably, the American government as the revolution collapsed under volley after volley of Soviet tank fire." One can imagine those few staff members with knowledge of the Hungarian language rushing to assemble scripts, like marathon runners charging towards the finish line. After noting that it was RFE's first and last major public scandal, Puddington writes:

> This is an enviable record by any reasonable standard, all the more so given the sensitive issues that RFE dealt with on a daily basis, the microscopic scrutiny devoted to its broadcasts by Communist officials, and the intense emotions of the radio staff.

In regard to the Hungarian controversy, there are two truths that cannot reasonably be disputed by anyone. It was tragic that thousands of Hungarians died while fighting for their freedom. It was also tragic that the West could not come to their aid. Nevertheless, it was rewarding for employees of Church World Service to know that so many Hungarian escapees were settling down in good housing and were working at jobs our organization had secured for them.

Also it's important to note that their countrymen didn't die in vain, as pointed out in *Voices Through the Iron Curtain: The Radio Free Europe Story* by Allan A. Michie: "The image of communism as the system of the working people was shattered: a worker's state had coldly shot down the workers who rose against it." The author also states that "RFE often became a scapegoat for the revolt's failure," when, in fact, the radio broadcasts helped so much in defeating communism.

Early on the snowy morning of January 16, 1958, my parents went by taxi to Pier 86, at the foot of West 46th Street. Here they boarded the SS *United States* for France, their first voyage on a big luxury liner. My boyfriend Bob Kavale (who later became my husband) and I saw them off. On their five-day trip they had mostly overcast skies and couldn't sit on the deck very often, but they had plenty to do indoors. "We especially liked listening to Meyer Davis's orchestra in the ballroom," Dad wrote me.

In Paris, a suite at the Hôtel Celtic awaited them, where the manager, Mr. Percepied, heartily welcomed them and their twenty pieces of luggage. It was a nostalgic reunion. "The Celtic cuisine is excellent," Dad wrote in his diary. "Many employees now here were here in 1947–50, and they have greeted us cordially." He and my mother had six relaxing days in Paris before his diplomatic work for the FEC began in earnest.

Howard Peckham's diplomatic missions on behalf of the FEC in Europe officially started on January 30. On that day, he was supposed to fly from Paris to London, where several prominent émigrés from the beleaguered captive nations lived. The trip didn't go as planned, however.

When he arrived at Orly Field at 10:45 a.m., the Air France desk clerk said, "Because of heavy London fog, your flight is delayed and will be cancelled." He was never one to give up in the face of unexpected inconveniences, so he went on a frantic taxi ride from Orly to the Gare du Nord.

From there, he boarded the train for London, which left at 12:24 p.m. At 7:30 p.m. it arrived at Victoria Station, where he took a taxi to his hotel. Bernard Yarrow, who had flown directly from New York to London, met up with him there. One of the reasons for their trip to Europe is alluded to in General Willis Crittenberger's *President's Report for the Year 1957*:

> The uprising [Hungarian Revolt] in Eastern Europe brought into focus the activities of exile organizations and highlighted their increased potentialities in fighting Communism.

In accord with General Crittenberger's desire to strengthen exile groups and to broaden the effect of émigrés on the battle against communism, Dad and Bernard were directed to meet with several Central and Eastern Europeans.

Their first visits were to those men who made London their home. The most interesting of these was General Wladyslaw Anders, a retired general who had completed a long military career in the Polish Army. When my father and Bernard arrived on the morning of February 3 to meet him at the Polish historical institute and museum, located at 20 Princes Gate, he greeted them amiably.

He had been a young cavalryman when he led his regiment against the Russians in 1919 during the Polish-Soviet War. The retired officer's competence and bravery were renowned, and by the time the Germans invaded Poland in 1939, he had attained the rank of general and was the commander of a cavalry brigade.

Unfortunately, his brigade and others like it couldn't defeat the motorized forces and modern tactics of the German army. He had no choice but to flee eastward, where he was arrested—not by the Germans, ironically, but by the Russians. He then spent several dreary months in a Moscow prison, from which the Soviets released him after Poland was invaded by the Germans. Fortunately, General Anders was able to make his way to Britain, as was the case with several other Polish military men and civilians. Like General Anders, many Poles stayed in Britain permanently after the war to avoid returning to a Communist country. Overall, they were treated quite well in their adopted land. This treatment is due in part to the help Polish airmen had given to the British in World War II, when experienced Polish pilots joined the RAF. At that time, even Winston Churchill publicly praised their gallantry.

After the war the émigrés proved to be good citizens, even when, like General Anders, they chose not to officially accept British citizenship. Their attachments to their Polish homeland would always be strong and sentimental.

The general was especially proud of the Sikorski Institute. It was named after another Polish hero, General Wladyslaw Sikorski, who was killed in a plane crash in 1943 after serving valiantly in World War II. While showing my father and Bernard around the property, General Anders pointed out the museum's interesting exhibits that depict the wartime history of the Polish army.

"Nice property, which they now own," my father wrote later in his diary. (*Nice* was one of my father's favorite words, and he used it often, especially when writing or speaking about people.) He was obviously pleased about their success. My father knew all about General Anders' service in World War II, but he appreciated the opportunity to become acquainted with this modest national hero and to enlist his assistance in the mission of the FEC.

Not only was the general personable and amenable to the idea of assisting the FEC in its fight against communism, but he was also calm when being driven through the hectic streets of London. My father discovered this quality later when he, the general, and Bernard were driven to the Polish Hearth at 55 Exhibition Road, a club for Polish civilians and military officers. The car narrowly managed to avoid double-decker buses, boxy taxicabs, and occasional horse-drawn wagons.

The Polish Hearth was another source of Polish pride. It was attractively decorated, and my father wrote in his diary that he was served "a nice lunch." After introductory remarks by the hosts, he and Bernard were each presented with a sealed and packaged bottle of Zubrowka, a yellow-colored vodka. "It has been seasoned with a sprig of bison grass from a forest in Poland," my father was told.

Another change at the FEC that came about as a result of the Hungarian Revolt—aside from the need to increase the effectiveness of exile groups and émigrés—was the realization that prominent Western Europeans should be more involved in its future operations. In this regard, the Committee's *President's Report for the Year 1957* states:

> Early in the year, the Board considered the advisability of expanding the base of the Free Europe Committee to include a more understanding support by the people of Western Europe. In exploring the possibilities of such a plan, representatives of the Council of Europe visited our activities in Munich, and were later invited to the United States for consultation. As the year drew to a close the desirability of such an accord had become more evident, and plans were made to send Committee representatives [Dad and Bernard] to Europe in the first weeks of 1958, to ascertain the feeling of prominent Europeans in the matter.

The above reference to sending "Committee representatives to Europe in the first weeks of 1958 to ascertain the feeling of prominent Europeans" points to another important mission the FEC was embarking upon in Europe, besides enlisting the aid of prominent exiles. The organization recognized more and more the need to help strengthen the bonds between Western Europe and the United States in their fight again communism, which was a matter of concern to people on both sides of the Atlantic.

The first prominent Western European on whom my father and Bernard called in London was a member of parliament (M.P.) and a Royal Navy veteran who favored the goals and purposes of NATO. Peter Smithers was also a Conservative Party member and, like other staunch British conservatives, was strongly opposed to communism. He had been a British spy during World War II, later causing a rumor to spread that he had been an inspiration for the fictional "James Bond, Agent 007." During their visit to his attractive home, the politician apparently charmed both Dad and Bernard. Even more important, he was amenable to their proposals, as reflected in these words my father wrote in his diary later that day: "He was very charming and sympathetic to our mission." Sir Peter Smithers obviously favored the idea of involving Western Europeans in future FEC endeavors.

My father returned to Paris feeling satisfied with the success of his meetings in England. Whenever he called on prominent Europeans or attended business meetings, he wore a business suit and tie. Otherwise, he would dress informally, most often in a sport jacket and slacks. He didn't want to be incorrectly labeled as a "rich American," especially in Paris.

Back in the 1940s, when he wore his uniform in Paris, he was the recipient of admiring glances while he walked down the wide sidewalk next to the Champs Élysées. At that time, Dad would occasionally hear *"Vive L'Amérique"* from a flower vendor or shopkeeper and *"Bon soir, mon général"* from a headwaiter, who would smilingly lead him to a good table. In those days, Parisians' memories of the occupation years were still fresh in their minds, and restaurant waiters remembered the humiliation of having to lead pompous, stern-faced Nazi officers to their tables.

Although Dad dressed casually and stayed as inconspicuous as possible during his current stay in Paris, one day he was treated rudely. It happened while he was walking down the same Champs Élysées sidewalk where he had once been treated as a hero, and he was chagrined at the difference. Mother and Dad were discussing their luncheon plans when a pedestrian turned to them and said, in a rather loud voice, *"Les Americains. Bah!"* Dad wrote me these words about the unfortunate incident:

> I realize that American economic domination is resented in France, which is suffering from a high cost of living and soaring inflation. However, I am disappointed that so much could change in

seven short years. In my view, American help during the war [World War II] and right after [Marshall Plan] is not being remembered and appreciated enough by the average Frenchman.

In his dealings with French diplomats, however, my father received mostly courtesy and cooperation. The four Frenchmen he met with were of varying political persuasions, but all had experience in handling themselves well in tense situations and responsible jobs. All were pleasant.

On February 11, joined by Bernard and Sylvia Yarrow, my father visited André Francois-Poncet, who had been the French ambassador to Germany in the period 1931-1938. It was during those years that Hitler was becoming powerful and increasingly dangerous. Like a growing cancerous tumor, Hitler's growth in power created a stressful atmosphere for international diplomats who, like Francois-Poncet, were stationed in Germany. In 1956 he became the president of the French Red Cross, his job at the time of his meeting with Dad.

Later that day, my father wrote these enthusiastic words in his diary:

> The Yarrows came for me at 5:15 p.m., and we went to the office of the French Red Cross to call on M. André Francois-Poncet, its president, a former French ambassador to Germany. He is in entire accord with the proposal that we have Western European consultants, and he would serve. . . .

Obtaining a commitment from such a prominent statesman such as André Francois-Poncet was a big feather in Bernard's cap as well as Dad's.

On February 13, according to my father's diary, they met with a seemingly unusual contact for the anti-Communist FEC. Guy Mollet, the bespectacled son of a textile worker, was a former teacher who joined the French Resistance during World War II. The Gestapo, a tough German police force, arrested him at least once and also interrogated him. Politically, Mollet leaned much further to the left than Francois-Poncet, and, in 1946 he became Secretary-General of the French Socialist Party. He continued to support left-wing causes during the 1950s and beyond.

Nevertheless, information that was freely given by a left-wing politician could be useful to the FEC, which is no doubt one of the main reasons that the meeting was arranged. When it ended, my father wrote the following discreet entry in his diary, making no mention of Mr. Mollet's words or possible service to the FEC: "We went to see former Premier Guy Mollet at his office in the Hq. of the Socialist Party."

The next day, they visited Robert Schuman, a prominent statesman with a long, kind face whom my father described in his diary as "very nice." Like Guy Mollet, he served in the French Resistance during World War II and was arrested by the Gestapo, from which he eventually escaped.

After the war, Mr. Schuman served France as Minister of Finance and Prime Minister. He was also the author of the Schuman Plan, a plan involving the international sharing of coal and steel. Politically, he was a Christian Democrat. A pious Roman Catholic, Schuman was known for his modesty and lay religious apostolate. Because he had a history of supporting international causes, he undoubtedly agreed with my father and Bernard that Western Europeans should support the goals of the FEC.

On February 15, my father and Bernard made their final visits to prominent French diplomats, Henri Bonnet and Paul Reynaud. In his diary, my father wrote: "He [Bernard] and I called on former ambassador (for 10+ years) to the U.S. Henri Bonnet, and at 12:00 noon on former President Paul Reynaud."

Henri Bonnet began his tenure as ambassador to the United States in 1944, when he represented the provisional government of Charles de Gaulle. His tenure ended in 1955, more than a decade later. During that period, the popular ambassador and his stylish wife Helle made friends with many Americans, both in France and the United States.

In contrast, Paul Reynaud's life and career were much more traumatic than Bonnet's. He abhorred the Nazis and refused to sign the document created in 1940 that would have put France in the hands of Germany.

Reynaud left that humiliating task to his successor, Philippe Pétain, and instead chose to resign from his job as prime minister. After Pétain became leader of the Vichy government, he had Paul Reynaud arrested and handed over to the Germans, who kept him a prisoner until the end of the war. For Reynaud, it was a dreadful four years.

When the war ended, he served in several political offices and was a member of the Alliance Democratique Party. At the time of his meeting with Dad and Bernard Yarrow, Reynaud was seventy-nine years old. Because of his wisdom and experience, they knew that he could advise them on beneficial ways to get Western Europeans involved in the work of the FEC.

Overall, my father's meetings with diplomats had been highly productive, particularly in the matter of ascertaining Western European support. The FEC Board was pleased with Bernard Yarrow's and my father's efforts to determine the feelings of prominent Europeans in this regard.

When their three months in Paris ended, my parents moved to Strasbourg, near the German border, where the FEC's European headquarters had been transferred. In this picturesque city, FEC headquarters were being set up in a large chateau converted into offices. Built more than two hundred years ago, the Chateau Pourtales was the home of various wealthy families over the years. Nobility from many places in Europe had been entertained there at one time or another, including Napoleon III. For this assignment, my father received a promotion along with a new title—Representative of the President of the FEC. General Crittenberger would be keeping in touch with him from the head FEC office in New York City, but Dad would be his personal spokesman in Europe.

Obviously, the general was pleased with the way my father had performed as FEC consultant, reminiscent of the general's appreciation of Dad's service as his Assistant Chief of Staff at Fort Benning early in World War II.

Mother and Dad lived six miles from the chateau, in a comfortable suite at the Hotel Maison Rouge, right in the center of the city. Soon after they got settled, my father wrote me a few words about the city's culture and the excellent features of the hotel suite in which they were staying:

> We are living in a bright, sunny suite at the Hotel Maison Rouge on Place Kleber. . . .
>
> This university city on the border of France and Germany reflects a blend of two cultures in both its scenery and people. My chauffeur, for example, is a French-speaking man with a typically German name, Fritz Matz. He picks me up every morning in front of the hotel and takes me to my office in the Chateau. . . .

Mother occasionally joined my father on short work-related jaunts within the Continent, and sometimes the trips were hectic. At 8:00 a.m. on February 18, they took a train from Strasbourg to Bonn. Along with heavy traffic, a snowy squall greeted them when they arrived at the station in Bonn. Nonetheless they managed to keep an important appointment: "Met Ambassador Bruce at 5:00," my father noted later in his diary.

I can just imagine how tired my mother was at the end of that day, particularly since she always felt nervous about riding in fast taxis that wove in and out of traffic. Also, she came down with several bad colds while living in Europe, so the unexpected snowstorm was most unwelcome.

From Bonn they traveled to Munich where, on February 24, my mother was escorted on a tour of RFE headquarters. These sprawling headquarters were located next to the Englischer Garten, a lovely public park. My father in the meantime chatted with RFE's Dutch-born Director, Erik Hazelhoff, who told my father he was glad so many broadcasts were successfully reaching behind the Iron Curtain. The director admitted, however, that there were problems with a lot of the broadcasts.

My father once described the major problems in a letter that he wrote to me:

Unfortunately, the Russians succeeded in electronically jamming many broadcasts that RFE was attempting to transmit to the captive people. As you can imagine, jamming was frustrating to them. It was especially annoying for the many young men and women who patiently waited for a signal from RFE, maybe to hear Western music or listen to a sporting event. Instead, they heard all kinds of noises, sometimes Halloween-like screeches and howls....

Two days after their visit to RFE headquarters, my parents boarded a train from Munich to Strasbourg, where Stetson Holmes, administrator of the FEC's Free Europe University in Exile in Strasbourg, met them on the station platform. His wife Eleanor joined him. After stepping off the train and greeting them, my parents hurriedly transferred their luggage to another train and went with the Holmses to Paris, where the FEC and the Free Europe University had offices. Except for a couple of restful days in Paris, it had been a whirlwind trip.

On March 15, 1958, my father sat at his desk in the Chateau Pourtales and wrote a few words on a small sheet of paper, which he quickly handed to a nearby assistant. The words were then incorporated into a telegram and sent from Strasbourg to General Crittenberger's New York headquarters that same day: "OFFICE OF FREE EUROPE COMMITTEE ESTABLISHED AT CHATEAU PORTALES THIS DATE."

This cryptic message meant that Dad, in addition to having contacted and interviewed prospective western consultants for the FEC, as I described earlier in this chapter, had completed another important task that he had been chosen to perform in Europe—setting up the FEC office in Strasbourg. The next day, as if to celebrate the important event, he walked completely around the grounds of the University of Strasbourg, No doubt there was a spring to his step.

Howard Peckham continued to work in Strasbourg until the end of September 1958, when he and my mother returned to the United States, where they lived first in New York, then in San Francisco, and finally in Washington DC. There they resumed a retirement life that was for the most part restful.

Saturday, October 19, 1957

Critt, Jake Devers, Tony McAuliffe and I rode to W.P. in an official car from U.S.M.A.; attended meeting of Board of Trustees; went to parade; had lunch at W.P.A.M. with other members of the Board; went to the stadium in a bus provided for the Board; saw Army lick Pitt 29-13 (big crowd and beautiful fall foliage); went to the Supers for a big reception (Gen. & Mrs. Taylor

HOWARD L. PECKHAM'S (HLP'S) DIARY ENTRY ABOUT A WEST POINT EVENT HE ATTENDED WITH GENERALS WILLIS CRITTENBERGER, JACOB DEVERS, AND ANTHONY MCAULIFFE: NEW YORK, 1957

Gen. Frederick B. Shaw, Veteran of 1898, Dies

GRANDDAD SHAW'S OBITUARY, 1957

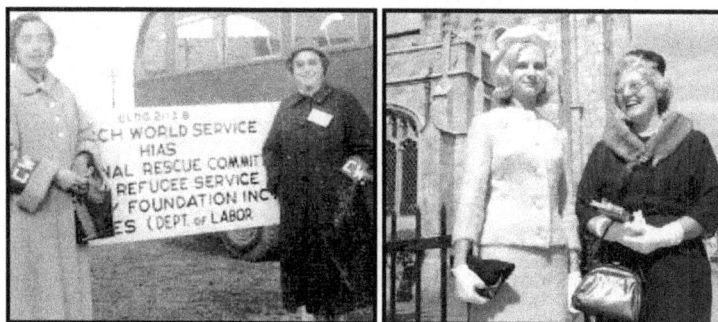

(LEFT) JEAN AND CWS CO-WORKER ANGELA MAVROMARAS: CAMP KILMER, 1957
(RIGHT) AUNT MARY AND HER DAUGHTER DIANE: NEWPORT, CIRCA 1958

ADMINISTRATION

Mr. David K. E. Bruce resigned as a member of the Board of Directors and of the Corporation effective March 18, 1957, by reason of his appointment to the post of United States Ambassador to the Federal Republic of Germany at Bonn.

Mr. C. D. Jackson was again elected a member of the Board of Directors on January 25, 1957.

Mr. W. J. Convery Egan, a Vice President of the Corporation and Director of Radio Free Europe, died on November 16, 1957.

Mr. Stetson S. Holmes, Assistant Secretary from February 1, 1956 to September 1, 1957, resigned to become Administrator of the Free Europe University in Exile at Strasbourg, France.

Major General Howard L. Peckham, U. S. Army (Ret.), who joined the Committee as Consultant to the President on July 24, 1957, was appointed Representative of the President of Free Europe Committee, Inc., with headquarters at Strasbourg, France, to take effect in January 1958.

Mr. Laird Bell resigned effective October 2, 1957, as a member of the Corporation.

At a Special Meeting of the Members of Free Europe Committee, Inc. held on January 8, 1957, the Certificate of Incorporation and the By-Laws were amended to authorize an increase in the maximum number of Directors of the Corporation from fifteen to twenty.

As in previous years, the Corporation's accounts and records for the fiscal year ended June 30, 1957 were audited by Haskins & Sells, Certified Public Accountants. This firm was reappointed, at the Annual Meeting of the Corporation, held on October 2, 1957, as the Corporation's auditors for the fiscal year ending June 30, 1958.

On the basis of a recommendation made by Haskins & Sells, the Board of Directors, at their Annual Meeting on October 4, 1957, approved the establishment of a European Central Accounting Office at Munich, Germany.

FEC PRESIDENT'S REPORT DISCLOSING HOWARD PECKHAM'S APPOINTMENT TO THE COMMITTEE, 1957-1958

Went to University Club, near Statler on 16th St., for lunch with Cord Meyer and Emmons Brown. Then the latter took me to CIA to call on Mr. Allen W. Dulles.

HLP'S DIARY ENTRY ABOUT CIA-RELATED LUNCH: WASHINGTON, 1957

Wednesday, December 18, 1957

up at 6:00 a.m., breakfast at the
Spa on 44th St., took taxi and
picked up Bernie Yarrow at his
home in E. 74th St., took 8:30 a.m.
American Airlines plane to
Washington. Went to the Hay
Adams Hotel, and then took
walk to National Art Gallery,
spent an hour there, walked back
the way I could to the Hay Adams, had
Bud Meyer and Emmons Brown of
C.I.A. to lunch in my room.
Attended meeting at 3:00 p.m. at C.I.A.
with Stanley Grogan and others, and
saw A.W.D. at about 5:15 p.m.

HLP'S DIARY ENTRY ABOUT HIS SECOND CIA-RELATED MEETING, 1957

THE LOCATION OF FEC OFFICES IN STRASBOURG: CHATEAU POURTALES, 1958

Wrote letter to Howie and Jane, and cards to Ed & Mildred, Adicks and Simmons, yesterday.

Monday, February 3, 1958

Historical

Bernie and I took taxi to the Sikorsky Institute, 20 Princes gate, arriving at 10:30 a.m. Gen. Anders and his colleagues greeted us and showed us the museum. Nice property, which they now own.

Took taxi to #1 Grosvenor Square, and consulted with Tracy Barnes and Mr. Cooper, before calling on our Minister, Mr. Walworth Barbour. Discussed our mission with him. Then took car again to 20 Princes gate, where we met Gen. Anders and others who drove us to the Polish Hearth, 55 Exhibition Road, a club for Polish army officers and civilians. Had nice lunch, and they presented Bernie and me each with a bottle of Zubrowka, a Polish vodka seasoned and colored with a sprig of special grass. Embassy car came to take us to the Bank of England for a talk with Mr. Glen Stevens, one of its directors. Then to

At 12:00 noon, we called on Mr. Peter Smithers, a Conservative M.P. at his home. He was very charming and sympathetic to our mission

HLP'S DIARY ENTRIES:
(TOP) DAY-LONG VISIT WITH GEN. WLADYSLAW ANDERS
(BELOW) MEETING WITH SIR PETER SMITHERS: LONDON, 1958

Thursday, February 13, 1958

We went to see former Premier Guy Mollet at his office in the Hq. of the Socialist Party at 11:00 a.m. Thereafter, Marion and I had luncheon together at the Celtic...

Yanov, Hagelhoff, McGargar and I met for breakfast at 9:30 at the Continental Hotel, to bring H. and M. before we saw Goedhart. Then at 11:00 a.m., Bernie and I went to see former Prime Minister Robert Schuman, who was very nice. At 12:00 noon,

Saturday, February 15, 1958

Car came at 10:00 a.m. and I picked up Bernie at a shop on Rue St. Roch. At 10:45 a.m., he and I called on former Ambassador (for 10+ years) to the U.S., Henri Bonnet, and at 12:00 noon on former President Paul Reynaud. Then

HLP'S DIARY ENTRIES:
(TOP) VISIT WITH FORMER PREMIER GUY MOLLET
(CENTER) MEETING WITH FORMER PRIME MINISTER ROBERT SCHUMAN
(BELOW) VISIT WITH HENRI BONNET AND FORMER FRENCH PRESIDENT PAUL REYNAUD

The Janows came for me at
5:15 p.m. And we went to the offices
of the French Red Cross to call on
M. André Francois-Poncet, its
president, a former French ambassador
to Germany. He is in entire accord
with the proposal that we have
Western European consultants, and he
would serve.
The Janows and I went to Ambassador
Houghton's residence to have a cocktail.

(LEFT) HLP'S DIARY ENTRY ABOUT FRANCOIS-PONCET AND AMBASSADOR HOUGHTON
(RIGHT) GENERAL WLADYSLAW ANDERS

(L TO R) SIR PETER SMITHERS, ROBERT SCHUMAN, GUY MOLLET

(L TO R) HENRI BONNET, ANDRÉ FRANCOIS-PONCET, PAUL REYNAUD

Chapter 16

The Era of Kennedy and Johnson

For every generation, there is a destiny. For some, history decides. For this generation, the choice must be our own.

--LYNDON B. JOHNSON

MY FATHER HAD NOTIFIED HENRY LOLLIOT, director of Radio Free Europe (RFE) operations in Portugal, that I would be coming to Lisbon at the end of August 1958, but I was pleasantly surprised when two secretaries from RFE arrived in a limousine to meet my plane. From there, the driver took us to a charming seaside restaurant for lunch. At that time, I was on a two-week vacation from my job, and Lisbon was my first stop.

The weather was perfect—not too hot for a summer day in Portugal—so we ate at an outdoor table on the terrace under a large umbrella, while the sea sparkled like crystal jewelry in the distance. I listened enviously when the two women talked about their glamorous lives in Lisbon, but I detected that one of them (I don't recall whether it was Sue or Betty) sounded a bit homesick.

The next day, the two young women arrived at my hotel with the limousine and a knowledgeable driver, Juan, to escort us to several tourist attractions in the bougainvillea-laden countryside. My favorite spot was the partially ruined Castle of the Moors, which sat like a crumbling crown of stone on a mountaintop overlooking the old town of Sintra. The beauty of Lisbon and its environs, plus the hospitality of Mr. Lolliot's employees, made my two-day stay unforgettable.

Although Portugal's beautiful weather and scenery were a definite plus for RFE employees working in that country, RFE had radio transmitters and offices there mainly for political and technical reasons, as author Arch Puddington notes in his book *Broadcasting Freedom*:

> Several problems confronted the radios as they searched for ways to enhance their signals. One problem was technical: the radios required sites that were ideally situated to beam short-wave broadcasts to the East. An ideal transmitter site was not necessarily located in close proximity to the target country....
>
> The second problem was political. As RFE learned during its search for a country that would play host to its European headquarters, most European democracies were not enthusiastic about permitting the United States to establish an anti-Soviet radio facility on their territory....
>
> Spain and Portugal were perfectly situated from a technical point of view, offering short-wave broadcasters a clear signal to the Eastern bloc. Both were run by conservative dictators who were firmly anti-Communist and generally pro-West....
>
> With the construction of the Gloria transmitters [near Lisbon], and the facilities that already existed in Germany, RFE had its technical facilities in place for the duration of the Cold War.

The author mentions both Spain and Portugal; however, only Radio Liberty (RL) had transmitters in Spain. RL was an entirely separate organization from RFE. Unlike RFE, it sent propaganda broadcasts into Russia and was not incorporated under the National Committee for a Free Europe.

After leaving Lisbon, I spent a few days with my parents in Paris and Strasbourg, where I renewed my fascination with Europe. I then went by myself to the World's Fair in Brussels for a couple of days before flying back to my job at Church World Service.

My parents returned to New York in late fall 1958, but this time they decided to move into a rented home in the country instead of the city. One afternoon during their first Christmas in the country house, my father received an unexpected letter from General Omar Bradley, who was president of the Bulova Watch Company at the time. The general assumed the presidency of that famous company in 1953, after retiring from the U.S. Army as a five-star general. (Only four army men have ever attained that rank.)

That night, my father described the Bradley letter in his diary: "Received a lot of Christmas cards and a letter from General Omar Bradley, asking me if I would accept a position with the Bulova Company." His diary entry a couple of days later states: "Typed and mailed a reply to General Bradley." His diary doesn't mention the contents of his reply, but it appears that the offer from Omar Bradley was declined. My father undoubtedly didn't want to accept a job in the private sector at that stage in his life. He had only recently completed his tiring and demanding work with the FEC.

Furthermore, my parents were now nicely settled in Pound Ridge, New York. I had recently moved to California when my father wrote to let Bob and me know about their plans "to live in a country house on several acres." It was a surprise to me, because I thought they had gotten to like city life. Perhaps my father, who enjoyed reading poetry in his spare time, was swayed by the following words written by seventeenth-century English poet John Dryden:

> How blessed is he who leads a country life, unvexed with anxious cares and void of strife.

The environment in which my parents found themselves was indeed pastoral. The property even had a small pond, where my father would go fishing with his visiting elder grandson, Larry. Dad wrote that he also eagerly pursued his bird-watching hobby, often joined by Granddad Peckham, who stayed with my parents on visits from his nearby Connecticut farmhouse. Dad appreciated the opportunity to visit with his aging father more often now.

There were several other things about the location that he liked, such being able to attend events at West Point, a relatively short drive away, and the opportunity to get together frequently with "Rags" Raguse. A retired colonel, Rags had served as Dad's chief of staff at the AGRC and had now settled near Pound Ridge with his wife and daughter.

I enjoyed my father's rapturous letters about their life in the country and the cute but mischievous coon cat that he and my mother had adopted. Then the tone of my father's letters gradually changed. The somewhat wild coon cat was tearing up the furniture and scaring birds away, so he and my mother agreed to put him up for adoption. (Because of Dad's love for birds, I'm sure that getting a cat was mostly my mother's idea.)

Another problem was that Mother's feelings of isolation intensified. She hadn't driven a car since 1946, when nervousness resulting from surgery and a subsequent early menopause eroded her self-confidence. She had no current driving license and was getting tired of asking other people for rides.

It didn't help matters when she saw a large snake curled up in the corner of their front porch one day, which caused her to run frantically into the house. "It wasn't poisonous," my father wrote, "so I just shooed the creature away with a sturdy broom." The agent who had shown them the house hadn't mentioned the abundance of snakes. Therefore, their year-long experiment with country life ended.

They spent the following year in San Francisco, in an apartment near the Presidio and near my husband, Bob, and me. (We were married in 1959.) Here they looked up army friends who lived on the West Coast and rekindled old friendships. One of those friends was retired Brigadier General Everett Busch. He and his wife Margaret lived in a tall building in Parkmerced, a nice residential community in San Francisco near a golf course. (Bob and I lived near them in a one-bedroom garden apartment.) During dinner at their apartment one evening, Bob, who was born and raised in Czechoslovakia, was kept enthralled by the spry general's description of his 1945 entry into Pilsen. "It was a triumphant entry for Third Army," Everett Busch reminded us. On May 6, 1945, George Patton's Third Army freed Pilsen from German occupation.

Because the Russians freed most of Czechoslovakia from the Nazis, the fact that Americans had anything at all to do with freeing the Czechs of Western Bohemia was kept more or less quiet by the Communist regime that took over the country after the war. After the Iron Curtain was lifted, however, celebrations began being held in Bohemia to commemorate the May 5 event and to welcome back American veterans.

Everett Busch, a well-respected colonel during World War II, had served proudly as George Patton's chief quartermaster in the European Theater. Ross and Romanus, in *Operations in the War Against Germany,* refer to General Busch's concern for proper winter clothing for the troops. "It's getting cold up here," he wrote to the ETO chief quartermaster, urging that something be done quickly about the situation. Fortunately, the clothing that Everett Busch requested arrived as soon as possible, and, much to his credit, an overcoat became as essential combat item.

Incidentally, when he and his wife Margaret were living in Heidelberg, their daughter met and married General George Horkan's aide, Lt. Gilbert, a fun-loving man whom everyone called Gil. When my parents and I visited the Horkan family in 1950, I took a picture of him. (That picture appears earlier in this book.)

Bob and I had some good times with my parents in San Francisco during that year. One highlight was Thanksgiving dinner together at the Presidio Officers' Club, where my father ran into a couple of officers whom he had met at other places he had been stationed. He introduced them to Bob and me along with the announcement that we were current residents of "the

Golden State." We also made several nice trips with them to scenic places such as Lake Tahoe, Carmel, and Point Lobos.

Nevertheless, I could tell that my father missed the East Coast. Also, both he and Mother realized that Washington, where they had so many friends, would be the best place for them to settle down. So Bob and I helped them load their car for their trip to Washington and waved a nostalgic goodbye. About ten days later we got our first postcard from them, a novelty postcard that my mother had bought and then mailed to us from somewhere in Utah. No doubt she thought we would get a kick out of the funny picture of worn-out tourists, which we did. She wrote:

> Your dad wanted to stop at every tourist spot between San Francisco and Salt Lake City, so this trip will probably take much longer than we expected.

I could just picture my father bending over a map spread out on the hood of their car, as he often did during my childhood. He would study the map intensely, as if he were back in Louisiana on pre-war maneuvers, planning a battle campaign against the Germans.

"Now if we stop for a quick lunch at the Frontier Restaurant in Roosevelt," he might have said to my mother, "we'll be able to reach the Dinosaur National Monument by late afternoon." They also planned to visit a few family members and friends, especially West Point classmates, along the way.

The long trip gave them an opportunity to daydream about their upcoming life in Washington. Mother especially looked forward to walking on their Oriental carpets again. (At that time, the carpets were rolled up and lying on a floor in Marshall Storage Company in New York.) They also were eager to enjoy and display their mementos from the many places where my father had been stationed during his long career: for example, the two brass chow pots from the Philippines, the wood-carved statuette from Puerto Rico, and the watercolor scenes of Paris that my father had bought in Montmartre.

Mother particularly missed the items of sentimental value that she had inherited from the Shaw family, such as the small, colorful screen from China and the pair of elaborate silver candelabra, about which she and her sister Barbara had once argued. After they moved into an apartment at the Greenbrier on Massachusetts Avenue, a large truck from Marshall Storage Company unloaded my parents' possessions, and they were happily reunited with their carpets, furniture, silverware, and mementoes.

A busy life then began, especially for my father. In addition to West Point alumni and other military events, he pursued an assortment of interests with vitality in Washington. He served for two years as a consultant to the National Industries for the Blind and another two years as executive secretary of the President's Committee on Purchases of Blind-Made Products. He also worked for a year as treasurer of the Army Distaff Foundation (ADF), an army retirement residence for women located in northwest Washington, and served on its board in other capacities. Serving as vice president of the Audubon Society of the Central Atlantic States gave him an active role in an organization through which he participated in many bird-watching excursions.

My parents readily took part in the army-officer social scene. In June 1962, my mother wrote me enthusiastically about a 2nd Armored Division party she and Dad had recently attended at the Army-Navy Club. The hospitable Willis Crittenbergers, who had also made Washington their home, hosted the party.

"The guest of honor," Mother wrote, "was the urbane Henry Cabot Lodge Jr." Another important social event in 1962 was a dinner party hosted by General Maxwell Taylor and his wife, Lydia. After they attended the dinner, held at the general's Fort Myer quarters, my father described the event to Bob and me in a letter:

> As you know, he [General Taylor] is the Chairman of the Joint Chiefs of Staff, hence the senior military man on active duty under our Department of Defense. It was a seated dinner, 20 places, and a

good time was had by all. Mother and I knew most, if not all, of the other guests. After dinner, part of the Army Chorus, a wonderful group of soldier voices, sang several songs, grouped in one end of the living room.

Lydia Taylor, who married her husband three years after his 1922 graduation from West Point, was a co-founder of the ADF and had therefore attended several meetings with Dad and other ADF officers. On July 10, 1962, my father wrote in his diary about an ADF-related gift she had delivered to him: "A messenger brought to the Greenbrier from Mrs. Maxwell Taylor this pen, with which President Kennedy signed the bill relieving the Army Distaff Foundation from paying D.C. real estate tax, and a picture of him signing it." My parents and the Taylors were glad for this action on behalf of my father's favorite charity and for President Kennedy's signature.

Mother was a big fan of the Kennedys. In her letters to me, she sometimes described news items she had read in the daily papers concerning the glamorous first family. Occasionally she sent me clippings about them. "Jackie Kennedy dresses so beautifully," she wrote. "And don't you just love those pillbox hats?" Unlike my mother, I have never been a "hat person." Nevertheless, I could understand the reason for her fascination with this particular item in the first lady's wardrobe.

My mother apparently had many good times in Washington. Sadly, those good times were coming to an end. During the Christmas season of 1962, only three months after the enjoyable family reunion that she, Dad, Bob, and I attended at my brother's house near Patrick Air Force Base in Florida, her health began to decline. She died in May of a cerebral hemorrhage at the age of sixty.

One quality that everyone admired about my mother was her habit of treating people with kindness, respect, and friendliness, regardless of their station in life. She was never one to pull rank. I noticed how sad the apartment building staff seemed to be when Bob and I arrived at my parents' building upon our arrival in

Washington for the funeral. The elevator operator had tears in her eyes.

At the funeral, to which we had flown the day before, attendees wrote their names in a slim, white Memorial Book. Among the many contributors to the ADF was Dad's classmate Lieutenant General Leslie Groves. Another contributor to that charity was Lieutenant General Willis Crittenberger. His wife, Josephine, had been so kind to my mother over the years, both in New York and Washington. Dad appreciated her consoling words to him. General Taylor and his wife were among those who sent beautiful flowers.

At this melancholic time in his life, my father especially appreciated his "band of brothers." One of the pallbearers at that quiet service in Fort Myer Chapel was my parents' longtime friend Bonner Fellers. Their good friend Colonel Redmond Perry was also a pallbearer, along with a civilian friend from my parents' Bronxville days, John Lee. The other pallbearers were Major General Herman Feldman, Brigadier General William F. Heavey, and Brigadier General Donald G. Shingler, all of whom had distinguished careers before retiring from the army. Their wives had been among my mother's good friends.

Herman Feldman served during World War II as Assistant Chief of Staff, Services of Supply, in both the European Theater and North Africa Theater. For his service in the Pacific Theater, he was awarded a Legion of Merit by Admiral Chester Nimitz, on whose staff he had served. General Feldman was present on the *Missouri* when Admiral Nimitz signed the surrender document. In 1949, he was nominated by President Truman to become the Quartermaster General, the position he held until retirement in 1951.

William F. Heavey, a brilliant engineering graduate of the West Point class of 1917, was the author of *Down Ramp! US Army Amphibian Engineers in World War II*. The book tells the story of engineer brigades that moved landing craft from shore to shore in the Pacific Theater and to the shores of North Africa, Sicily, and Normandy during World War II, a subject with which he was personally very familiar. He arranged to set up an assembly plant first in Australia and then in New Guinea, to which sections of craft were shipped and then assembled. Because of his efforts, the number of landing craft in the Theater was vastly increased.

Earlier I described the career of General Shingler. When I saw him serving as pallbearer that sad day, I thought back to a happier time, the evening when my parents and I attended a party at the beautiful home he shared with his wife Bea in Heidelberg.

Other memories of Heidelberg entered my mind when Mary Horkan came over to speak kindly about my mother's "charm, wit, and sensitivity." Her presence reminded me of the wonderful days in 1950 that my parents and I were her houseguests in Heidelberg. She and her husband, Major General George Horkan, later settled in Washington, where she became active in the Quartermaster Association of Wives. After the service, she spoke sympathetic words to me about my loss, as did Nancy Fellers and her mother, Dorothy. They had all been very fond of my mother.

Another Washington family also grieved deeply in 1963. This family was far more prominent than ours, so much so that millions of people throughout the world mourned the family's loss. The assassination in Dallas of President Kennedy, which occurred only five and a half months after my mother's funeral, sent the whole world into a state of shock.

My father was a Republican, but he admired President Kennedy's eloquence and his support of the ADF. Like Mother, my father was often fascinated by the President's family, especially by his two attractive small children. The citizens of Dallas and Washington were probably the most affected by this national tragedy, which happened so close to Thanksgiving. If Mother had lived until November 23, she would have mourned greatly, along with the rest of Washington's population.

Dad slowly adjusted to being a widower, but he was very lonely and not eating well, according to a letter I received from my step-grandmother, Winnie Shaw. She stopped by to see him several times from her home in Rosslyn, just outside the gate to Fort Myer. Therefore, I shouldn't have been surprised when Dad wrote Bob and me with the news that he planned to remarry in December 1963.

Nonetheless, I was quite surprised, but I knew his decision would be for the best. His intended bride was "a pretty redhead," he wrote, "who is about the same age as I am." Thus my father and the former Evelyn Hemenway, the widow of a West Point classmate of his, were married in December 1963. The ceremony took place at Washington's stately National Cathedral.

I never got to know Evelyn well, but I've always been grateful for the many caring things she did for Dad. She was obviously devoted to him during the nine years they were married. For example, Evelyn carefully took his medals out of a small, musty box and placed them in a nice frame, which she then hung in their front hallway. Their home was in the Greenbrier, a different unit from the one in which my parents had lived together. "I always cook him good dinners," she assured me once when I came on a visit. His days of ordering take-out food were apparently over.

Church activities and religion became very important parts of their lives after my father and Evelyn were married. She encouraged him to become a more committed Episcopalian, so in the spring of 1964 he was confirmed at St. John's Episcopal Church. She wrote me a glowing letter about it, saying how proud she was to see my father kneeling at the altar rail to receive communion. Ironically, I later became a Catholic, my husband's lifelong faith. Dad had no objections. When I told him, he said, "It's wonderful when a husband and wife share the same faith." He was obviously speaking from experience.

After they were married, Dad regularly gave talks at St. John's about its history. "I speak on the third Sunday of each month, following the 11:00 a.m. service," he wrote me. The rector, Father John Harper, was undoubtedly pleased that someone with my father's speechmaking ability and experience had accepted the job as a volunteer.

The first service at St. John's took place in 1816, and every President of the United States since then has attended a service there. The President's pew is number 54. Some have attended more regularly than others, but it has always been known as the church of the presidents. "It's deserving of the title," my father wrote us after he had seen the President and his family there. During the vesper service one Sunday in 1964, he and Evelyn heard some commotion in the aisle behind their pew. My father wrote me about it: "Lo and behold, President Johnson, Mrs. Johnson, and their elder daughter had arrived. Men who were obviously from the Secret Service were sitting in front of, behind, and all around them."

My father and Evelyn (who had the nickname "Jimmie"), a vivacious woman with becomingly dyed red hair, had many army friends in common. She liked to prepare gourmet hors d'oeuvres and serve them when friends dropped by. Once my father wrote Bob and me about their preferred method of entertaining: "Those who have nice gardens like to have their parties in the spring. We, being cliff-dwellers, with only some potted philodendrons in the windows, can't do that, so we give our annual party in the fall, as do many others."

He didn't covet the residences owned by friends and didn't invest in real estate, although he did inherit some farmland from his dad. Many times we lived in lovely government-supplied homes on army posts, but when military housing wasn't available, my father didn't mind being a renter. He just wasn't drawn to home ownership and the problems it often brings. He was a strong believer in stocks and bonds, however, and did well with those kinds of investments.

Howard Peckham wasn't drawn to fancy cars, either. A few times when Evelyn tried to talk him into upgrading to a more luxurious car, my father said, "I'm definitely not interested." He emphatically told her that his Chevrolets had served him well over the years, and he didn't intend to change to another make. (He may have secretly thought that if they were fancy enough for my mother, they were good enough for Evelyn.) He usually traded in his car every three years for the latest model.

As shown by the preceding examples, my father was basically unpretentious and, maybe because of his simple upbringing on a farm and the exposure to traditional values that it gave him, he was basically humble. Those are traits I always admired about him. Another trait I recall with gratitude is the way he employed his considerable influence so that I could enjoy interesting and educational experiences.

For example, in 1964 he arranged a visit for Bob and me to RFE headquarters in Munich. In a letter dated July 11, 1964, he advised then-director C. Rodney Smith that his daughter and son-in-law were soon leaving San Jose, California, for a trip to Europe. "They expect to fly from Copenhagen to Munich on SAS Flight No. 635, July 26, and from Munich to Paris on Air France Flight No. 737, July 31," the letter stated.

After my father described our educational and professional backgrounds, plus my husband's status as a Czechoslovakian-born U.S. citizen (whom I met when we both worked for Church World Service), Dad concluded the letter with these words: "I am sure they would enjoy a visit to Radio Free Europe. If you or a member of your staff would be so kind as to receive them, I am sure that they would be delighted, and I would consider it a great favor." The visit went through as planned.

Upon our arrival at the headquarters of RFE, a trim, slender gentleman wearing horn-rimmed glasses warmly greeted us. He introduced himself as the RFE director. Like my father, C. Rodney Smith was a retired two-star general, and he had served as head of RFE since 1960. With him were two well-dressed men assigned to take us on a tour. "They will show you as much as possible," General Smith said after introducing us to them. During the tour, our escorts were polite, but straight-laced and as quiet as mice while they guided us down the wide corridors.

"They were probably CIA agents and are used to being reserved," my husband said later, adding, "I heard a rumor that a few Agency employees are placed at RFE headquarters."

It was rewarding to visit facilities we had heard so much about, and we were amazed to see that the complex occupied about half a dozen two-story buildings, connected to each other by long corridors. Inside these buildings were a master control room, libraries, conference rooms, recording studios, and various other rooms.

We were shown more than we had expected, and promptly upon our return to California I wrote a letter to General Smith thanking him for arranging our tour.

Evelyn and my father also did their share of traveling. In the spring of 1966, they visited England, where they toured the historic cathedrals. One of the highlights was a tour of Canterbury Cathedral, seat of the Archbishops of Canterbury and home of the Anglican Communion. In addition to being shown the crypt of thirteenth-century Archbishop John Peckham, they were told interesting facts about several of the Archbishops of Canterbury who preceded and followed him. The first man on that long list was Saint Augustine. The last Roman Catholic Archbishop of Canterbury on the list was Reginald Pole, who died in the sixteenth century. Ever since then, the Archbishops of Canterbury have been Anglicans.

Another highlight of the trip to England was their stop at the American Cemetery at Cambridge, which my father hadn't seen in many years. The superintendent who had worked for him at the AGRC was still there, and he showed them around. Dad wrote these words about the cemetery in a letter to me:

> Although the weather was dismal when we visited the cemetery, in fact a light snow was falling, we were delighted with the beauty and orderliness of the cemetery, and it gives you a thrill always to see the Stars and Stripes flying over a piece of property in a foreign land.

What struck me the most about those words was the way they revealed my father's love for the United States of America and its flag. I have no doubt that it gave him a tremendous thrill to see the Stars and Stripes flying, as he said, "over a piece of property in a foreign land."

Besides traveling and enjoying a busy social life, he became involved in his last major retirement job—executive secretary of the Committee on Purchases of Blind-Made Products. He also busied himself with military-related projects.

For example, in August 1966, at the twelfth annual reunion of the 2nd Armored Division Association, he was elected president of the association for the coming year. During that year he helped to ensure that the division received the recognition he felt it deserved. My father was quite enthusiastic about a special 2nd Armored Division project he was working on, which he described in a letter to my husband and me:

> For about a year, I have been working on a project of having a plaque made—bronze on a walnut base—with the shoulder patch of the Division, in colors, superimposed, to be presented by the Association to the Unknown American of World War II, buried at Arlington. Many such trophies and plaques are displayed in the Trophy Room at the Tomb of the Unknown Soldier in Arlington. The plaque has now been fabricated and approved by the Department of the Army, and we expect to have a presentation ceremony following the reunion in Pennsylvania.

After the ceremony, my father wrote us about it: "The gathering in Pennsylvania was a success, and it was attended by Ambassador Henry Cabot Lodge Jr. and a number of generals who have served at some time or other with the Division." The plaque was approved and is displayed in the Trophy Room at the Amphitheater and Tomb, just as Dad had hoped it would be. I saw it for the first time while on a visit to Arlington in 2001. It made me realize how conscientiously Howard Peckham continued to serve his old division, even in retirement. He worked as president of the 2nd Armored Division Association until sometime in August 1967, which marked the end of a tiring summer for both him and Evelyn.

They had enjoyed a number of social events that season, but sometimes heated discussions about the Vietnam War began to dominate their conversations. Uncertainties about how, or if, the war would proceed caused the atmosphere in their social circle to become subdued. Of course no one wanted Communist North Vietnam to overtake South Vietnam. Like my father, a few of his friends had sons serving in the military about whom they were concerned. When American casualties began to mount, however, some of my father's friends strongly criticized President Lyndon Johnson for failing to secure peace through diplomatic means. This was particularly true when more and more Americans were sent to fight in the escalating war.

Our family didn't know when or if Howie would be sent to Vietnam, but several of his friends were already serving there. In the fall, he came to my house in California bringing with him one of those friends, who had recently returned from Vietnam. The day had started early with an unexpected phone call. "I'll be flying out to the Bay Area for just one night, to get in some flying time," Howie said.

After I invited him for dinner, he asked if he could bring a West Point classmate of his, an air force pilot who had just come home from Vietnam. Both were stationed in Washington, and they would be flying together to California. "That's fine with us," I said brightly. It had been a while since we had seen each other, so my husband and I looked forward to having a reunion with Howie and meeting his classmate.

Sandy Vandenberg's unusual nickname was derived from his middle name, Sanford. His father, who was deceased at the time of his son's visit to our house, was dashing Hoyt S. Vandenberg, who had commanded the United States Ninth Air Force in France during World War II—only one of the many responsible assignments he held during a distinguished military career. The big air force base near Lompoc, California, is named for him.

During dinner in our candlelit dining room that evening, Sandy talked sympathetically about the war's effects on the wives and children of American pilots—the stress they have to endure—while modestly downplaying the bravery he had shown on numerous flying missions over what my brother described as "treacherous terrain." A couple of years later, I learned that Sandy had completed more than ninety missions over North Vietnam.

After dinner, my husband drove Howie, Sandy, and me from our house in San Jose and up Highway 101 to San Francisco. There we went across the Golden Gate Bridge to Hamilton Air Force Base in Marin County, where the two men were billeted for the night. The base was closed down several years later for economic reasons, but in 1967 it was still an important and strategic base. During World War II, planes flew from there to the battle-weary skies of Asia.

At the time that Bob and I bade Howie and Sandy farewell, I didn't know that my brother would be engaged in his own hazardous duty in Vietnam just a few months later. In the middle of his one-year tour of duty, he and his wife Jane enjoyed a short reunion in Hawaii, a welcome rest and recuperation (R & R) break that the U.S. Air Force provided for its pilots. The rest of the time Jane, who lived in a two-story, red-brick house in Arlington, took care of their two sons, Larry and Terry.

On the days when she felt especially lonely and worried about Howie, she would visit my father and Evelyn, who were also concerned about him. "Jane's obviously feeling the strain," my father wrote me. His words made me think about what Sandy Vandenberg had told me during dinner at my house the previous year—how stressful the war was for pilots' wives. Then my father added, "Jane smokes too much. After she leaves our apartment, the ashtrays are filled to the brim."

Dad's friends were also feeling the pressure. For Willis and Josephine Crittenberger, the war was especially devastating. As I mentioned earlier, their son Townsend had died while serving in the European Theater in World War II. Now another tragedy struck them.

In September 1969 their son Dale, a colonel and a graduate of West Point, was killed in a helicopter crash in Vietnam—the second of their three sons to die in combat. My father was extremely saddened by the news. Colonel Dale Crittenberger, like his brother Townsend, was laid to rest in Arlington National Cemetery. He left behind his wife Mildred and eight children. My father knew what a blow the news was for Willis and Josephine, both of whom had always been so hospitable towards him and my mother.

Like Sandy Vandenberg, my brother served as a fighter pilot in Vietnam. "I flew over territory that was a lot less dangerous than Sandy's, but I was under fire a couple of times when the Viet Cong attacked Saigon, where my office was located," he wrote me after his return to the United States in 1969. His safe return brought relief and joy to his family. Larry and Terry were especially proud that their dad was awarded a Bronze Star. His medal was for "good work" he had performed in Vietnam rather than for valor, he explained to the boys. Studies he performed had enhanced some 7th Air Force deployments.

Nevertheless, our family's happiness and relief were short lived. One muggy day in July 1972, his voice cracking, my father called to give me the heartbreaking news that Jane had died of lung cancer in Washington, where she and Howie now lived. She had been sick for only a few months. Dad's beautiful daughter-in-law was in her early forties then, and his two grandsons were only twelve and fifteen. Jane, a graduate of Hollins College and a former teacher, was ironically the daughter of a Virginia tobacco executive. She grew up in the small town of Petersburg, near Fort Lee. My brother was introduced to Jane at a party in 1953, while he was on a visit home. At that time, my father was Fort Lee's commanding general.

It all seemed so terribly ironic, as if the Vietnam War had indirectly led to my sister-in-law's stressful days and nights and incessant smoking, the way World War II had undoubtedly contributed to my mother's drinking problem.

Too soon after Jane's funeral, our family received another devastating shock. In the middle of August, my father wrote Bob and me about the frightening results of his recent physical exam at Walter Reed Army Hospital. "I have been diagnosed with leukemia," he said, but then he added, "I can't believe it's a very serious form of the disease. Actually, I feel reasonably well." It *was* a serious form, however. Only four months after he wrote that letter, and despite weeks of grueling treatment, he died at

Walter Reed Army Hospital in October 1972 at the age of seventy-five.

Father John Harper, Dad's friend and the pastor of St. John's Church, led Howie, Evelyn, and me in prayer at Dad's bedside before his death. A few days later, I heard Father Harper's clear voice again while he recited the West Point Cadet Prayer. I was then sitting in a pew at Fort Myer Chapel, surrounded by many other mourners attending my father's funeral. The prayer asks for help in various areas of a cadet's life. It petitions for assistance in maintaining the honor of the Corps, for example, and for help in living the ideals of West Point in regard to duty and country. The following words struck me as particularly relevant when Father Harper read them:

> Kindle our hearts in fellowship with those of a cheerful countenance, and soften our hearts with sympathy for those who sorrow and suffer.

I recalled how Dad had a "cheerful countenance," a hopeful outlook on life, even when he inwardly grieved. (During a couple of sad movies, however, I saw him take out his handkerchief and wipe away tears that had coursed down his cheeks.)

Then I started thinking about World War II and its aftermath. The prayer's words "soften our hearts with sympathy for those who suffer" brought Dad's work to mind. As head of the Fuels and Lubricants Division, he sympathized with battle commanders whenever critical deliveries of gasoline to the front line were delayed by unavoidable events. When he headed the AGRC in postwar Paris, his gift for showing sympathy for those who suffer served him well when he met with the next of kin, although he left the task of grief counseling to capable army chaplains.

The graveside ceremony for my father, which included an elaborate display of military honors and flourishes, attracted a small group of curious tourists. They watched in fascination as the riderless horse clomped by, a pair of empty boots dangling from the leather saddle on its back. They also observed Howie and me sympathetically, especially when the horse-drawn, flag-draped caisson came into view.

Father Harper then asked us to pray, which eased my emotional pain. This was followed by volleys of muskets fired into the air and by the mournful notes of *Taps* played by a bugler. Another touching moment arrived when Evelyn was presented with the neatly folded American flag that had covered my father's casket.

I recall with appreciation the consoling words Father Harper spoke to Howie and me after the ceremony. Among other observations, he told us that he noticed intense camaraderie among alumni of West Point, particularly those of my father's generation. We thanked him. Then, while I was walking slowly to my brother's car, I received condolences from a couple of Dad's surviving West Point classmates.

One of them wrote a memorial to him. It was signed simply "A Classmate." This is part of it:

> As we sat in the chapel at Ft. Myer hearing the Rector of St. John's Episcopal Church on Lafayette Square, Washington, where Howard had been an active member of the vestry, recite the Cadet Prayer over the flag-draped casket, we realized how closely Howard had lived his life in conformance with the many ideals of West Point. That prayer was answered in Howard Peckham's entire character. . . . Howard was the personification of West Point. As his class's first captain he was its leader. . . . Howard's boundless energy with interests in many fields put him in the group who accomplish much in life. His inherent concern for others coupled with an everlasting optimism made his presence a joy. He was gifted with a fine voice and was always willing to lead the singing, cheering up any occasion. . . . At work he demanded perfection in everything. His graciousness and consideration of others made it a joy to adjust to his dynamic efforts and high standards. Through the passing of his entire life one could always discern in him the virtues of West Point. . . . Without such men, alas America.

It was a fine tribute to a well-liked man. Dad was definitely a "people person" almost until the end of his life, and his letters had always been filled with news about people he had seen. "We had tea with Father Harper at his home," he wrote once. "I visited Bill at the hospital," he wrote at another time. "We stopped by to deliver a present to Carl's grandson." These are typical of the news items he wrote in his letters or recorded in his diaries.

As the mourners began going their separate ways, I stepped into the car and rode with Howie and his two sons to their house, in which I had been staying for a few days. They were still recovering from the loss of Jane, so I helped out as much as I could. The lasagna dinner I made one night was welcome, they assured me. "The boys are tired of the Hamburger Helper meals I've been making night after night," Howie said. The day after Dad's funeral, he drove me to National Airport for my flight to the San Francisco Bay Area, which had been my home for fifteen years. At that time, Howie was an air force colonel stationed at Andrews Field, the large base in Maryland near Washington.

Evelyn joined us on the drive to the airport. When the time came for me to depart, I thanked her for the fond devotion she had shown to Dad and for the diligent care she had given him. Then I embraced her and Howie and boarded the plane. When it roared off the runway and began its ascent, I sat forward slightly in my seat and gazed down on the Potomac River, which wound peacefully between Virginia and Maryland.

My thoughts then centered on the forthright path that had led my father to Washington, where he spent his final years. His military career had taken him to many diverse locations, and my mother, my brother, and I had been fortunate to join him on that often-absorbing journey.

In the early 1970s, not long after my father's funeral, the covert relationship between the CIA and the radios (both RFE and RL) was publicly acknowledged, first in Congress and then in various media. It seems ironic that Howard Peckham had guarded the secret of CIA funding for so many years that was now as open as they sky above Washington's Mall. In 1972, CIA funding for the

FEC ended. Fortunately, the radios continued to receive funds from the United States Government, which recognized their value, influence, and success. In 1976, RFE and RL were united under one corporation, called RFE/RL, Inc.

After my father died, Evelyn started failing rapidly, becoming virtually senile within no time at all. She had no children, but her niece helped her get settled in a nursing home. Howie stopped by to see her a couple of times on visits to Washington from his new home in Florida, but he became discouraged when she failed to recognize him. She probably didn't even remember the anguish she had felt during Dad's final illness, a memory lapse that would have been a blessing in disguise. Soon after Howie's last visit to her, he notified me that she had passed away.

In the 1980s, dramatic political and social events were about to occur in Europe, for which RFE had been hoping over the years. Arch Puddington describes the scene in *Broadcasting Freedom*:

> For Radio Free Europe, 1989 represented the culmination of nearly forty years of service in the cause of East European liberty. To say that it was a year of astonishing developments is an understatement. No one, and certainly not RFE, believed that by the end of the year, communism would no longer survive as a governing system in its target countries.

The author's epilogue continues with these words:

> For in fact the radios proved one of the most successful institutions of America's Cold War effort, and made an important contribution to the peaceful nature of communism's demise.

The end of the Cold War did not end the radio stations or their purpose, however. In the 1990s, they were relocated to Prague, in the Czech Republic, where they continue to broadcast messages of hope to emerging democracies.

Dad wasn't the only member of my family to keep a decades-long secret related to national security. Howie also kept one. In the late 1990s the media revealed that months before the negotiated peace agreement was signed in July 1953, ending the Korean War, several U.S. Air Force pilots flew out of South Korea on dangerous top-secret missions over enemy territory. These overflights, as they were called, were so secret that the air force didn't declassify them until 1996. Howie was one of those pilots. In a letter written to Bob and me dated September 26, 2002, he wrote about the preparations that had been made for the flights and the reasons for them. Here is part of what he wrote:

> All Korean War era F-86 pilots went through training at Nellis Air Force Base [near Las Vegas]. The F-86 was the premier air force fighter jet during the war. . . . In mid-May of 1953, I flew to Kimpo Air Force Base in South Korea, where I reported for duty with the 15th Tactical Squadron. . . .Our lack of information on what the Chinese were doing resulted in their surprise attack on our ground forces that had reached the Yalu River, on the border of North Korea and China. Our existing reconnaissance could not survive [up there], so our country's response was to secretly convert a few F-86 fighter planes [they were small and swift] into RF-86s. We did that by removing all armament and replacing it with a couple of cameras.

Howie explained the important reason for secrecy on the part of the United States:

> The policy of the United Nations at that time was that aircraft of U.N. countries would not cross the Yalu River. Our missions were authorized, of course, but for political reasons they were designated highly classified. During the two or so years remaining in the war, there was a total of perhaps thirty to forty pilots who flew the overflights, but there were never more than four to six [of us] in place at any one time. . . .

My brother ended his explanation with these words:

We were prohibited from mentioning our overflights to anyone. I shared a tent with five other squadron pilots [non-RF-86 pilots] and they never knew, officially anyway, what my "strange" missions were doing.

Obviously, Howie inherited Dad's sense of duty, country, and patriotism. After retiring from the air force and moving back to Florida, he had the good fortune to meet Mollie Billingslea, the charming widow of a navy pilot. Their marriage in the mid-1970s brought together two sets of attractive teenagers: her children Karen and Art and his sons Larry and Terry.

Bob and I had the privilege over the years of making several trips with Howie and Mollie. The most memorable one was a 1983 Royal Viking cruise in the Eastern Mediterranean. On our shore excursions, we marveled at the Acropolis in Greece, the pyramids in Egypt, the religious sites in the Holy Land, and the exotic mosques in Turkey. It was unforgettable. Later, on a Caribbean cruise, Bunny Shaw was able to join the four of us.

Sadly, dear Mollie succumbed to the effects of Parkinson's disease in 2001 at the age of seventy. After attending her solemn graveside service in Arlington Cemetery, I again walked around those hallowed grounds, the resting places of my parents, my grandparents (Fred and Bell), and my uncle (Robert Shaw), as well as so many of their friends. When I looked up at the Stars and Stripes waving proudly above the cemetery, I thought about the first verse of a poem by Edgar Guest, one of Dad's favorite poets:

The Flag on the Farm

> We've raised a flagpole on the farm
> And flung Old Glory in the sky,
> And it's another touch of charm
> That seems to cheer the passerby,
> But more than that, no matter where
> We're laboring in wood and field,
> We turn and see it in the air,

Our promise of a greater yield.
It whispers to us all day long.
From dawn to dusk: "Be true, be strong;
Who falters now with plow or hoe
Gives comfort to his country's foe."

I also thought about the American flag that fluttered above
another farm, the one in Norwich, Connecticut, on which my
father grew up. To a great extent, it had an effect on his eventual
choice of a career. Throughout his life, he chose to serve both his
flag and the great country it represents. I'm quite sure he never
regretted that choice.

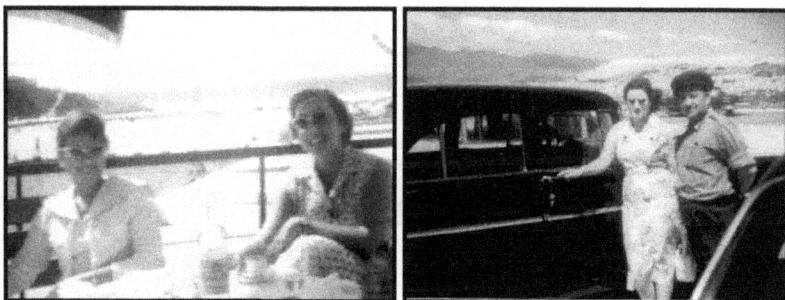

(LEFT) SUE OF RFE AND JEAN AT LUNCH
(RIGHT) BETTY AND THE RFE DRIVER JUAN: PORTUGAL, 1958

MY FATHER'S DIARY ENTRY ABOUT A JOB OFFER FROM GEN. OMAR BRADLEY, 1958

(LEFT) JANE PECKHAM AT HER HOME WITH THE FAMILY PUPPY
(RIGHT) 2ND ARMORED DIVISION PLAQUE FOR WHICH DAD MADE ARRANGEMENTS:
ARLINGTON MUSEUM

FAMILY REUNION: *(L TO R)* JANE, TERRY, HOWIE, DAD, LARRY, MOTHER, JEAN, AND BOB:
FLORIDA, 1962

Tuesday, July 10, 1962

A messenger brought to the Greenbriar, from Mrs. Maxwell D. Taylor, the pen with which Pres. Kennedy signed the bill relieving ASF from paying D.C. Real Estate Tax, and a picture of him signing it.

RADIO FREE EUROPE

Division of the

FREE EUROPE COMMITTEE INC.

One English Garden · 8000 Munich 22 · Germany

Tel. 229921

13 July 1964

Mr. and Mrs. Robert Kavale
c/o American Express
Ameriplatz 1
Munich, Germany

Dear Mr. and Mrs. Kavale:

As you will see from the enclosed letter to General Peckham, we expect to hear from you and to show you something of our facilities and operations at Radio Free Europe.

We should be very glad if you would telephone us so we know that you are in town and so we can arrange a time for you to visit us. You can telephone me or Mr. David Grozier, our Director of Public Affairs, who will be glad to set up a time for your visit.

We look forward to seeing you.

Yours sincerely,

Chester W. Ott
Executive Assistant
to the Director

(TOP) MY FATHER'S DIARY ENTRY ABOUT PRESIDENT KENNEDY, 1962
(BELOW) LETTER TO BOB AND JEAN FROM RFE ABOUT OUR VISIT, 1964

Receives Bronze Star Medal

LOS ANGELES – U.S. Air Force Lieutenant Colonel Howard L. Peckham Jr. (right), son of Major General H. L. Peckham of 4301 Massachusetts Ave. N.W., Washington, D.C., receives the Bronze Star Medal from Brigadier General W.G. King Jr., deputy commander for satellite programs, Space and Missile Systems Organization, Los Angeles Air Force Station.

(U.S. AIR FORCE PHOTO)

(LEFT) DAD'S NEPHEW KENT LAWRENCE: CIRCA 1968
(RIGHT) HOWIE RECEIVING A BRONZE STAR MEDAL: LOS ANGELES, 1969

(LEFT) MY FATHER AND EVELYN NEXT TO THEIR APARTMENT BUILDING
(RIGHT) DAD IN FRONT OF ST. JOHN'S EPISCOPAL CHURCH: WASHINGTON, 1969

EPILOGUE

Duty is the most sublime word in our language. Do your duty in all things.
You cannot do more. You should never wish to do less.

--ROBERT E. LEE

A visit to Europe in 1994 brought my husband and me back to the Czech Republic, where we visited his older brother Joseph, his wife Libuse, and their son, Josef Jr. It was wonderful to see how freely Czech citizens are living now that the Iron Curtain has been lifted. On a previous visit to Prague, in 1975, we saw gloomy people walking on half-empty, drab streets. We had planned to make a side trip there in 1983, in connection with our Eastern Mediterranean cruise, but time didn't allow it.

When we returned to Prague in 1994, we were delighted to see that those formerly drab streets had been beautified and were now filled with fun-loving tourists from many different countries.

After saying goodbye to Joseph and his family, we stayed a few days in Gothenburg, a seaport city on the west coast of Sweden, where my husband's younger brother Karel lives with his Swedish wife Kerstin. From their modern home in Gothenburg, we made a side trip by car one day to Malmö, on Sweden's southern coast. As I have already mentioned, thirty-eight American pilots lost their lives in Sweden's waters and on its land during World War II and were buried at a cemetery here. It was a site I had visited with my parents after the war, and I wanted to see it again.

At a Malmö tourist office, I approached the pale, slender young woman who worked behind the counter and asked her, "Can you tell me where the American fliers are buried? They lost their lives here during World War II." She looked a bit perplexed, which I supposed was forgivable in view of her youth. After hesitating for a moment, she said, "Please wait. I will ask someone about it." When she returned, she gave us a map and a few directions to the large city cemetery, where she said the men had been reinterred.

A city bus took Bob and me there. With map in hand, we walked in the direction of the area the young tourist-office woman had clearly marked on our map. Then, from a distance, I saw a large stone sculpture of a propeller. "There it is, Bob," I called to him while I pointed to it.

I knew we were approaching the site where the airmen were laid to rest whose next of kin decided to have them stay in Sweden. As we came close to it, I saw beneath the propeller the following engraved inscription:

U.S.A.A.F.
DUTY CALLED THEM
TO GOD AND COUNTRY.
THEY REST IN PEACE, WHILE
MEMORY OF THEIR SACRIFICE
IS WRITTEN IN ETERNAL GLORY.

The sentiments expressed in these well-chosen words in a Swedish cemetery could easily also apply to the American military cemeteries overseas. The brave patriots lying at rest in those sites were called by duty to God and country. Although the American cemeteries were closed to future burials, except for victims still found from time to time in battle areas, they will always stand as reminders of the supreme sacrifice made by so many Americans during World War II.

Often I think back to the years my family spent on various army posts, starting in Puerto Rico and ending in Virginia. I also think of the great cities in which we lived—Cleveland, New York, Washington, and Paris—as part of Dad's military work. He yearned to follow his dream of serving his country to the best of his ability, for as long as he was able. He accomplished that goal. After retiring from the army, he continued to serve his country and, in addition, to help various groups of people in need.

(LEFT) JEAN AND BOB ON A MEDITERRANEAN CRUISE, 1983
(RIGHT) MEMORIAL SERVICE FOR UNCLE BOB SHAW, 1990

While serving as a consultant with the FEC and then as representative of the FEC's president, he aided the cause of national security and indirectly assisted European citizens who were desperately trapped behind the Iron Curtain. In his job as executive secretary of the Blind-Made Products Committee, Howard gave encouragement to disabled workers in the sale and distribution of their products. Through his work with the 2nd Armored Division Association, he helped to ensure that the division received the recognition he felt it deserved. His work on the board of the ADF helped to assist those persons who needed reasonably priced, secure retirement housing. By way of his membership on the Board of Trustees of West Point and as president of his alumni class, he continued to foster the ideals of the United States Military Academy.

His lifetime achievements comprise a long and impressive list. The service he performed for his country, for other people, for the U.S. Army, and for West Point will not be forgotten.

JEAN WITH BOB AND HIS BROTHERS JOSEF (WITH WIFE LIBUSE) AND KAREL (WITH WIFE KERSTIN): CZECH REPUBLIC, 1994

MOLLIE, HOWIE, AND AUNT BUNNY SHAW: CARIBBEAN CRUISE, 1995

ACKNOWLEDGEMENTS

Although my own personal recollections and resources, such as my diaries and scrapbooks, helped me in the writing of this book, I also owe a debt of gratitude to several people. I would like to start by acknowledging the family members who are no longer with me but who left valuable resources behind them:

To my parents, Howard and Marion Peckham, I am grateful for the many letters they sent me over the years. I'm so glad I kept those letters. Additionally, I express my gratitude to my father for the diaries in which he wrote each day after retiring from the U.S. Army. They contain important information about his FEC work and were useful to me in doing the research for this book.

To my uncle, Robert Shaw, whose genealogy was most helpful because it includes pertinent facts about the military service of his father, Frederick B. Shaw. The genealogy, which he titled *Clan Shaw and Many Others*, also describes his own valiant service during World War II.

To my aunt, Mary Peckham Lawrence, I owe a debt of gratitude for the childhood recollections she shared with me. I am especially grateful for her written account entitled *My Dad – A Connecticut Yankee*. It helped me to recreate a vivid picture of my father's New England childhood.

Next, I extend thanks to the editors of *A Salute to Patriotism*, whose suggestions were very helpful, and to the conscientious librarians who located government documents and books relating to my father's World War II work. Last, but certainly not least, I express my gratitude to my husband, Robert Kavale, for his patient encouragement of me during all phases of this project.

ABOUT THE AUTHOR

Jean Peckham Kavale, MA, had more than fifteen years of experience as an editor in Silicon Valley, including Senior Editor with PDR Information Services and Contract Editor for Fortune 500 companies, including ROLM, IBM, and GE. She holds a bachelor's degree in English from the University of Maryland at College Park, a teaching credential from San Jose State University, and a master's degree in pastoral theology from the University of San Francisco. She and her husband Bob are enjoying retirement life in California's Central Valley.

BIBLIOGRAPHY

1. *AGRC-EA, Engineer Historical Record of the Design and Development of the U.S. World War II Cemetery at Draguignan, France.* Office of the Quartermaster General. Washington, DC: Historical Section, 1952.

2. Ancell, R. Manning, *The Biographical Dictionary of World War II Generals and Flag Officers: The U.S. Armed Forces.* Westport, CT: Greenwood Press, 1996.

3. Anderson, Jack. *Confessions of a Muckracker: The Inside Story of Life in Washington During the Truman, Eisenhower, Kennedy, and Johnson Years.* New York: Random House, 1979.

4. Badger, Anthony J. *The New Deal: The Depression Years, 1933-1940.* New York: The Noonday Press, 1989.

5. Baldwin, Hanson W., ed. *Command Decisions.* New York: Harcourt, Brace and Company, New York, 1959.

6. Black, Robert W. *Rangers in World War II.* New York: Ivy Books, 1992.

7. Bradley, Omar N., and Blair, Clay. *A General's Life.* New York: Simon & Schuster, 1983.

8. Bradley, Omar N. *A Soldier's Story.* New York: Henry Holt & Company, 1951.

9. Britton, Jack. *United States Military Medals and Decorations.* Tulsa, Oklahoma: M.C.N. Press, 1979.

10. Burns, James MacGregor. *Roosevelt: The Soldier of Freedom, 1940-1945.* New York: Harcourt, Inc., 1970.

11. Buxton, Frank, and Owen, Bill. *Radio's Golden Age.* New York: Easton Valley Press, 1966.

12. Carrion, Arturo Morales. *Puerto Rico: A Political and Cultural History.* New York: W. W. Norton & Company, Inc., 1983.

13. Clay, Lucius D. *Decision in Germany.* Garden City, NY: Doubleday & Company, Inc., 1950.

14. Cohen, Stan. *V for Victory: America's Home Front During World War II.* Missoula: Pictorial Historials Publication Co., Inc, 1991.

15. Cray, Ed. *General of the Army.* New York: W. W. Norton & Company, Inc., 1990.

16. Crittenberger, Willis D. *President's Report for the Year 1957.* New York: Free Europe Committee, Inc., 1957.

17. Current, Richard N. *Secretary Stimson: A Study in Statecraft.* New Brunswick, NJ: Rutgers University Press, 1954.

18. Davis, Franklin M., Jr. *Come as a Conqueror: The United States Army's Occupation of Germany 1945-1949.* New York: The MacMillan Company, 1967.

19. Donovan, Robert J. *Conflict and Crisis: The Presidency of Harry S. Truman 1945-1948.* New York: W. W. Norton & Company, Inc., 1977.

20. Dunning, John. *Tune In to Yesterday.* Englewood Cliffs, N.J.: Prentice-Hall, Inc., 1976.

21. Editorial Board, *The American Pageant.* D.C. Heath & Co., 1987.

22. Editorial Board, *Who's Who in America.* Chicago, ILL: A. N. Marquis Company, Vol. 28, 1954 (first copyrighted in 1899). *Who Was Who* contains an index of all entries.

23. Eisenhower, Dwight D. *Crusade in Europe.* New York: Doubleday and Company, 1948.

24. Encyclopedia Britannica Almanac, Encyclopedia Britannica, Inc., 2004, Chicago.

25. Essame, H. *Patton: A Study in Command.* New York: Charles Scribner's Sons, 1974.

26. Farago, Ladislas. *The Last Days of Patton,* New York: McGraw-Hill Book Company, 1981.

27. Ferrell, Robert H. *Harry S. Truman: A Life.* Columbia, Missouri: University of Missouri Press, 1994.

28. Gallagher, Hugh Gregory. *FDR's Splendid Deception.* New York: Dodd, Mead & Company, 1985.

29. Gardner, Helen, ed. *The New Oxford Book of English Verse: 1250-1950.* New York and Oxford: Oxford University Press, 1972.

30. Harmon, E. N. *Autobiography of a Soldier.* Englewood Cliffs, NJ: Prentice-Hall, Inc., 1970.

31. Hart, Scott. *Washington at War: 1941-1945.* Englewood Cliffs, Prentice-Hall, Inc., 1970.

32. Heavey, William F. *Down Ramp:US Army Amphibian Engineers in World War II*, published in Infantry Journal Press, 1947.

33. Hunt, Frazier, *The Untold Story of Douglas MacArthur.* New York: The Devin-Adair Company, 1954.

34. Leach, Charles R. *In Tornado's Wake,* 8th Armored Division Association and The Argus Press, Chicago, 1956.

35. Littlejohn, Robert M. *Passing in Review*, Harwood, MD: S. N. 1955.

36. Lodge Jr., Henry Cabot. *The Storm Has Many Eyes: A Personal Narrative.* New York: W. W. Norton & Company, Inc., 1973.

37. McLaughlin Green, Constance. *Washington: Capital City, 1879-1950.* Princeton, NJ: Princeton University Press, 1963.

38. MacDonald, Charles B. *A Time for Trumpets: The Untold Story of the Battle of the Bulge.* New York: Quill, 1985.

39. Mardikian, George. *Song of America.* New York: McGraw-Hill, 1956.

40. Marshall, Catherine. *A Man Called Peter.* New York: McGraw Hill Book Co., Inc., 1954.

41. Meyer, Cord. *Facing Reality: From World Federalism to the CIA.* New York: Harper, 1980.

42. Michie, Allan A. *Voices Through the Iron Curtain: The Radio Free Europe Story.* New York: Dodd, Mead & Co., 1963.

43. Murphy, Edward F. *Heroes of World War II,* Novato, CA: Presidio Press, 1990.

44. *Occupation Forces in Europe Series: The Third Year, 1947-1948,* U. S. Army Historical Division, 1949.

45. Patterson, Richard S., the compiler. *The Secretaries of State:Portraits and Biographical Sketches.* Washington, DC: Historical Division, Department of State, 1956.

46. Peckham, Stephen F., *Peckham Genealogy: The English Ancestors and American Descendants of John Peckham* (Reprint), Boonville, NY: Boonville Graphics, 1987.

47. Pogue, Forrest C. *George C. Marshall: Organizer of Victory, 1943-1945.* New York: Viking Press, 1973.

48. Puddington, Arch. *Broadcasting Freedom: The Cold War Triumph of Radio Free Europe and Radio Liberty.* Lexington: University Press of Kentucky, 2000.

49. Randall, Stephen J. *United States Foreign Oil Policy Since World War I.* Canada: McGill-Queen's Press, 2005

50. Risch, Erna. *Fuels for Global Conflict.* Washington, DC: Historical Section, Office of the Quartermaster General, 1952.

51. Risch, Erna. *The Quartermaster Corps: Organization, Supply, and Services, Volume 1, THE UNITED STATES ARMY IN WORLD WAR II: THE TECHNICAL SERVICES* (Washington, DC: Government Printing Office, 1953).

52. Risch, Erna, and Kieffer, Chester, *The Quartermaster Corps: Organization, Supply, and Services, Volume II, THE UNITED STATES ARMY IN WORLD WAR II: THE TECHNICAL SERVICES* (Washington, DC: Government Printing Office, 1955).

53. Ross, William F., and Romanus, Charles F. *The Quartermaster Corps: Operations in the War Against Germany, THE UNITED STATES ARMY IN WORLD WAR II: THE TECHNICAL SERVICES* (Washington, DC: Government Printing Office, 1965).

54. Ruppenthal, Roland G. *Logistical Support of the Armies, Volume I.THE UNITED STATES ARMY IN WORLD WAR II: THE EUROPEAN THEATER* (Washington, DC: Government Printing Office, 1953).

55. Ruppenthal, Roland G. *Logistical Support of the Armies, Volume II, THE UNITED STATES ARMY IN WORLD WAR II: THE EUROPEAN THEATER* (Washington, DC: Government Printing Office, 1958).

56. Stauffer, Alvin P. *The Quartermaster Corps: Operations in the War Against Japan, THE UNITED STATES ARMY IN WORLD WAR*

II: THE TECHNICAL SERVICES (Washington, DC: Government Printing Office, 1956).

57. Steere, Edward, and Boardman, Thayer M. *Final Disposition of World War II Dead: 1945-51.* Washington, DC: Historical Branch, Department of the Army, 1957.

58. Talbot, L. R.*The Story of American Graves Registration Command in Europe and Africa*, 1955.

59. *The Biographical Dictionary of World War II Generals and Flag Officers,* R. Manning Ancell and Christine Marie Miller, Greenwood Press, 1996

60. Thornton, Willis. *The Liberation of Paris.* New York: Harcourt, Brace & World, Inc., 1962.

61. Toland, John. *Infamy: Pearl Harbor and Its Aftermath.* New York: Berkeley Books, 1982.

62. Truman, Harry S. *Memoirs.* New York: Doubleday and Company, Inc., 1955.

63. Watkins, T. H. *Righteous Pilgrim: The Life and Times of Harold L. Ickes, 1874-1952.* New York: Henry Holt and Company, Inc., 1990.

64. Wedemeyer, Albert C. *Wedemeyer Reports!* New York: The Devin-Adair Company, 1958.

65. *Who Was Who in America, Volume 5, 1969-1973.* Chicago: Marquis Who's Who, 1973.

Periodicals

The Stars and Stripes (European Edition), *The LA Times,The New York Times, Daily News Record, The Washington Post, Exchange Post, International Herald Tribune*

Extracts

Extract of Public Law 383 of the 79th Congress (Chapter 261, 2nd Session) approved by President Harry S. Truman and signed by him on May 16, 1946: *An Act to provide for the evacuation and return of the remains of certain persons who died and are buried outside the continental limits of the United States.*

Extract of Public Law 368 of the 80th Congress (Chapter 497, 1st Session), approved by President Harry S. Truman and signed by him on August 5, 1947. *An Act to amend the Act entitled. . . in order to provide for the shipment of the remains of World War II dead to the homeland of the deceased or of next of kin, . . .*

Extract of Executive Order 10057 signed by Harry S. Truman and approved by him on May 14, 1949. *Transferring to the American Battle Monuments Commission Functions Pertaining to Certain United States Military Cemeteries.* Federal Register, The National Archives of the United States, Volume 14, Number 94.

Congressional Hearings

Hearings before the Special Committee Investigating the National Defense Program (The Canol Project), The United States Senate, Seventy-Eighth Congress, First Session, Washington, DC, U.S. Government Printing Office, 1944.

Hearings before the Special Committee Investigating Petroleum Resources. The United States Senate, Seventy-Ninth Congress, Washington, DC, U. S. Government Printing Office, 1945.

Hearings before the Subcommittee of the Committee on Appropriations. The United States Senate, Eighty-Second Congress, Second Session, Washington, DC, U. S. Government Printing Office, 1952.

Patriotism is not short, frenzied, outbursts of emotion, but the tranquil and steady dedication of a lifetime.

-ADLAI STEVENSON

www.ingramcontent.com/pod-product-compliance
Lightning Source LLC
Chambersburg PA
CBHW051747040426
42446CB00007B/248